EuR
EUROPARECHT

Beiheft 1 | 2018

Armin Hatje/Luboš Tichý [Ed.]

Liability of Member States for the Violation of Fundamental Values of the European Union

Nomos

Die Deutsche Bibliothek verzeichnet diese Publikation in der Deutschen Nationalbibliografie; detaillierte bibliografische Daten sind im Internet über http://dnb.ddb.de abrufbar.

ISBN 978-3-8487-5176-1 (Print)
ISBN 978-3-8452-9372-1 (ePDF)

ISSN 1435-5078

1. Auflage 2018

Foreword

Article 7 TEU protects the European Union against political development in one or more Member States that undermines values on which the common association stands. We may identify three particular reasons for such provision. First, the level of cooperation achieved within the European Union requires consensus on fundamental values among public officials of the Member States who participate in the EU decision-making. Second, since the European Union is not merely an association of states, but a polity of constitutional quality, diversion from the common values would undermine realization of rights of private persons of other Member States in their cross-border activities. Finally, Article 7 TEU protects citizens and resident legal persons of the violating state against political changes that do not respect liberal values, even if achieved through a democratic process. The last issue, which, as the Polish and Hungarian cases revealed, has been the most controversial, forms in fact the very core of the European integration project.

Article 7 TEU does not state a mere political sanction, but creates a special liability regime. The legal scholarship, however, has not yet undertaken a serious analysis of its particular components. A comprehensive analysis requires bringing together legal experts on European law, constitutional law, law of delict and torts, and experts that can bring comparative perspective about solutions in other jurisdictions. The contributions to this book have been discussed during a conference at the Charles-University Prague 2016.

This book is bringing together legal experts on European law, constitutional law, law of delict and torts, and experts that can bring comparative perspective about solutions in other jurisdictions. We are glad to present the results of a conference, held in November 2016 at the Charles University in Prague, to a broader public.

We would especially like to thank Ludmilla Novackova for supporting the organization of the conference and Lili-Marie Iwen for preparing the printed version of the contributions.

Armin Hatje, Hamburg | Luboš Tichý, Prague

Table of Contents

Foreword ... 3

Part I: Protected Values

Prof. Dr. Rudolf Streinz, Munich
Principles and values in the European Union ... 9

Prof. Dr. Gavin Barrett, Dublin
Reflections on What the Rule of Law Means and its Significance at EU Level ... 23

Dr. Emmanuel Sur, Bordeaux
From the uncertain to the implicit (passing by the problematic). Reflections on the reference to the rule of law and on its protection in the Treaty on European Union ... 39

Prof. Dr. Aalt Willem Heringa, Maastricht
Fundamental rights, EU membership and Art. 7 TEU ... 59

Prof. Dr. Andreas Haratsch, Hagen
Democracy – A Value common to the Member States of the European Union .. 73

Part II: Liability of Member States

Prof. Dr. Luboš Tichý, Prague
The nature and requirements for liability of a Member State under Article 7 TEU ... 87

Prof. Dr. Laurent Sermet, Aix-en-Provence
Comparative study on enforcing common values against subnational units, member states in federations and other international organizations. De societatis et de civitatis ... 109

Prof. Dr. Ewa Bagińska/Prof. Dr. Sylwia Majkowska-Szulc, Gdańsk
Causation as a requirement for the Member State liability under Art. 7 TEU in conjunction with Art. 2 TEU ... 125

Prof. Dr. Ulrich Magnus, Hamburg
Wrongfulness and Fault as Requirements of the „European Delict“ under Art. 7 TEU? ... 145

Prof. Dr. Michael Potacs, Vienna
Balancing Values and Interests in the Art. 7 TEU Procedure 159

Prof. Dr. Mirosław Wyrzykowski, Warsaw
Rule of Law: European Commission v. Poland 169

Part III: Enforcement

Dr. Tomas Dumbrovsky, Prague
Beyond Voting Rights Suspension. Tailored Sanctions as Democracy Catalyst under Article 7 TEU 203

Prof. Dr. Jiří Zemánek, Prague
Constitutional remedies of persons facing consequences of the Council decision on suspension of certain Member State´s rights 229

Prof. Dr. Matthias Niedobitek, Chemnitz
Right and duty to pursue the “wrongdoer” and a possible abuse of Art. 7 TEU 233

Part I:
Protected Values

Principles and values in the European Union

*By Rudolf Streinz, Munich**

One element of the EU's "poly-crisis" (Jean Claude Juncker) is the lacking respect for the principles and values which are the basis of the EU and should be common to all Member States. The "values" named in Art. 2 TEU are legal principles, especially the rule of law. The rule of law does not require the existence of a constitutional court at all, but at least the separation of powers and the independence and impartiality of a judiciary, whose decisions must be respected by the political organs. Out of respect for their national identity the Member States are competent to organize their political system. However, the respective political systems must be in accordance with the requirements of Union law, and not only to become a member of the EU but permanently. The EU must respect its principles and values and must enforce them against its Member States also. This requires effective enforcement procedures and the development of concrete standards striking the right balance between the scope of organizational freedom of the Member States regarding their political system and the principles and values, which must be real, common and inalienable for a community based on law.

I. Introduction

"True is that we have seen better days".[1] It is evident after the recent development that the current state of the European Union reflects its most serious crisis since the foundation of the European Communities. Challenges like the financial crisis or the reception and distribution of refugees are unsolved because of disparate interests of Member States.[2] In the United Kingdom the majority of the participating electorate voted to "leave" the EU.[3] The acceptance of the European Union as a supranational organization by the citizens and the acceptance of European Union law, of its primacy ("supremacy") and of its determining effect concerning national, especially constitutional law are shrinking. Moreover, Member States only reluctantly accept the limitation of their own power to shape domestic policies by the rules of European Union law, at least concerning matters which they regard to be part of their national identity. Conversely, the European Commission was concerned about the development in some Member States (Hungary, Poland) regarding the implementation of the "values" of the European Union which should be "common to the Member States" according to the "homogeneity

* Professor of European Union and Public Law at the Ludwig-Maximilians-University Munich.

1 D. Senior, in: *Shakespeare*, As You Like It, Act II, Scene 7.

2 See e.g. Editorial Comments, From eurocrisis to asylum and migration crisis: Some legal and institutional considerations about the EU's current struggles, CMLRev 51, 2014, p. 1437 ff.

3 See e.g. *P. Craig*, Brexit: A Drama in Six Acts, European Law Review 41, 2016, p. 447 ff.; Editorial Comments, Withdrawing from the "ever closer union"?, CMLRev 53, 2016, p. 1491 ff.

clause"[4] of Art. 2 sentence 2 of the Treaty on European Union (TEU). As such these values are binding on the European Union and its institutions as well as on the Member States and their institutions. The EU Commission set out a new Framework for the Rule of Law. It describes the "rule of law" as "the backbone of any modern constitutional democracy", "one of the founding principles stemming from the common constitutional traditions of all Member States of the EU and, as such, one of the main values upon which the Union is based".[5] The EU Commission called the rule of law both a "principle" and a "value". This leads to a reflection on the terms "principle" and value" and on their relationship to each other.

II. The terms principle and value and their relationship to each other

The terms "principle" and "value" have different meanings in different contexts (e.g., philosophy, mathematics, ethics, economics).[6] Generally, "principle" means "basic truth", "general law of cause and effect". Therefore in law the term "principle" means a basic, fundamental rule, which is – albeit broad – binding.[7] The "values" enumerated in Art. 2 TEU characterize the self-conception of the Union and its Member States representing the mentalities and the mindsets of their societies. The use of the term "value" which alludes to a meta-legal content was criticized as misleading, because what is meant by "values" in this context is actually "principles", i.e. fundamental principles of EU law.[8] The Preamble of the EU Charter on Fundamental Rights on the one hand repeats that "the peoples of Europe, in creating an ever closer union among them, are resolved to share a peaceful future based on common values" and that "the Union is founded on the indivisible, universal values of human dignity, freedom, equality and solidarity". On the other hand, in part it qualifies some of the same "values" of Art. 2 TEU as "principles", namely "the principles of democracy and the rule of law". That all "values" enumerated in Art. 2 TEU have legal importance, though, follows from Art. 49 TEU, which requires that a European State applying for EU membership must respect "the values referred to in Art. 2 and is committed to promoting them". This is further underpinned by a systematic interpretation in conjunction with Art. 7 TEU.[9] After their accession to the European Union Member States

4 Not official, term by *S. Mangiameli*, in: Blanke/Mangiameli (eds.), The Treaty on European Union (TEU), a Commentary, 2013, Art. 2 TEU.

5 A new EU Framework to strengthen the Rule of Law. Communication from the Commission to the European Parliament and the Council, COM, 2014, 158 final/2, p. 2.

6 See e.g. the headings „principle" and „value" in: Shorter Oxford English Dictionary on Historical Principles, 5th ed. 2002, vol. 2, p. 2347 and p. 3500.

7 Cf. *A. Jakab*, Re-Defining Principles as 'Important Rules' – A Critique of Robert Alexy, in: Borowski (ed.), On the nature of Legal Principles, 2010, p. 145.

8 See *D. Kochenov*, The Acquis and Its Principles: The Enforcement of the 'Law' versus the Enforcement of 'Values' in the European Union, in: Jakab/Kochenov (eds.), The Enforcement of EU Law and Values. Ensuring Member States' Compliance, 2017, p. 2 f.

9 See *A. von Bogdandy/M. Ioannidis*, Systemic deficiency in the Rule of Law: What it is, what has been done, what can be done, CMLRev 51, 2014, p. 59 ff.; European Commission, Communication from the Commission

must continue to respect these values. Otherwise, the procedure of Art. 7 TEU can be initiated, because Art. 7 TEU refers to the "values referred to in Art. 2". The early warning system (Art. 7 para. 1 TEU) starts with a reasoned proposal by one third of the Member States, by the European Parliament or by the European Commission to determine "a clear risk of a serious breach by a Member State of these values", and the procedure for sanctions requires the determination of the existence of a serious and persistent breach by a Member State of these values. Consequently, it is necessary "to turn Art. 2 TEU into a down-to-Earth provision".[10] While a regression from principles to values is not possible,[11] the inclusion of "values" into a legislative or constitutional act transplants them into the realm of law. Hence, once inserted into a legal text, these values, which represent legal terms and not only "aspirational provisions" like "the Most Holy Trinity" in the preamble of the Irish Constitution,[12] become "principles" that can be interpreted and help to create a system.[13]

In the text of the EU Treaties the term "principle" is often used, but – also compared with other authentic languages – with different meaning and different significance.[14] Some principles – laid down in the text or elaborated by the European Court of Justice from "the terms and the spirit of the Treaties"[15] – can be characterized as fundamental principles and "constitutional principles".

III. Constitutional principles of the European Union

1. The need for a European Constitution and for constitutional principles – The Treaty of Lisbon as the "Constitution" of the EU

Constitutional principles based on and representing values are regularly elements of the Constitution of a State. For instance, the Basic Law of the Federal Republic of Germany names the principles of the German Constitution in its Preamble, in Art. 1 (Fundamental Rights) and in Art. 20 (Democracy, Rule of Law, Republic, Federal State, Social State) which cannot even be abolished by an amendment of the Constitution by the pouvoir constitué. Art. 23 Basic Law contains the obligation to be engaged in the construction of a European Union.[16] However, the name

to the Council and the European Parliament on Article 7 of the Treaty on European Union. Respect for and Promotion of the Values on which the Union is based, COM, 2003, 606, p. 5.

10 Cf. *D. Kochenov*, How to turn Article 2 TEU into a down-to-Earth provision?, verfassungsblog.de/how-to-turn-article-2-teu-into-a-down-to-earth-provision/ (8 December 2013); *D. Kochenov* (fn. 8), p. 2.

11 *S. Mangiameli* (fn. 4), Art. 2 TEU, mn. 7.

12 Example referred to by *D. Kochenov* (fn. 8), p. 2. But "aspirational principles" can also have – although only with minor significance – legal importance concerning the interpretation of a constitution. Cf. *R. Streinz*, Gott im Verfassungsrecht – warum nicht im EU-Verfassungsvertrag?, in Gornig/Schöbener/Bausback/Irmscher (eds.), Iustitia et Pax, Gedächtnisschrift für Dieter Blumenwitz, 2008, p. 826-840.

13 *S. Mangiameli* (fn. 4), Art. 2 TEU, mn. 7.

14 See *A. von Bogdandy*, Founding Principles of EU Law: A Theoretical and Doctrinal Sketch, ELJ 16, 2010, 95.

15 See e.g. ECJ, C-6/64 (Costa/ENEL), ECLI:EU:C:1964:66, ECR 1964, 585, 593.

16 See German Federal Constitutional Court, (Lissabon), ECLI:DE:BVerfG:2009:es20090630.2bve000208, BVerfGE 123, 267, 346 ff.: „Der aus Art. 23 Abs. 1 GG und der Präambel folgende Verfassungsauftrag zur

"Constitution" is not necessarily reserved to (traditional) States. Having in mind that a Constitution normatively legitimizes and limits the exercise of public authority and that the European Union exercises a lot of traditional State functions in which it is bound by the principles of fundamental rights and the rule of law (Art. 2 and Art. 6 TEU), the de facto function of the Union's existing primary law must be and is indeed that of a Constitution. Furthermore, the European Union is in its nature a community based on law (Rechtsgemeinschaft)[17] and therefore "a Community based on the rule of law"[18] with all the consequences deriving from this rule, especially that neither its institutions nor – if they are acting within the scope of application of the Treaties – its Member States can avoid judicial review.[19] Although the Member States after the failure of the Rome Treaty on a Constitution for Europe abandoned the term "Constitution" and the idea of a Constitutional Treaty to create a single, coherent document named "Constitution", the Treaty of Lisbon is the de facto "Constitution" of the European Union as the Treaties founding the European Communities have been from the very beginning. Already in 1986 the European Court of Justice in Les Verts named "the Treaty" (then the Treaty establishing the European Economic Community) "the basic constitutional charter".[20] In its opinion on the Agreement on the Accession of the EU to the Convention for the Protection of Human Rights and Fundamental Freedoms the ECJ clarified and referred to the "constitutional framework" of the European Union.[21] Despite the term "Constitution" supposed coverage of all forms of public authority, one must not forget, however, the considerable structural differences between traditional nation states on the one hand and international organizations on the other – even if the latter are "supranational" in character like the European Union. These structural differences can justify different forms to implement principles like democracy.[22]

Verwirklichung eines vereinten Europas […] bedeutet insbesondere für die deutschen Verfassungsorgane, dass es nicht in ihrem politischen Belieben steht, sich an der europäischen Integration zu beteiligen oder nicht." („The constitutional mandate to realise a united Europe, which follows from Art. 23.1 of the Basic Law and its Preamble […] means in particular for the German constitutional bodies that it is not up to their political discretion whether or not they participate in European integration").

17 *W. Hallstein*, Der unvollendete Bundesstaat, 1969, p. 33 ff.

18 ECJ, C-294/83 (Parti Ècologiste „Les Verts"/European Parliament), ECLI:EU:C:1986:166, ECR 1986, I-1339, mn. 23; ECJ, C-50/00 P (Unión de Pequeños Agricultores/Council), ECLI:EU:C:2002:462, ECR 2002, I-6677, mn 38; ECJ, Joined Cases C-402 and 415/05 P (Kadi and Al Barakaat/ Council and Commission), ECLI:EU:C:2008:461, ECR 2008, I-6351, mn. 281. See *T. von Danwitz*, The Rule of Law in the Recent Jurisprudence of the ECJ, Fordham International Law Journal 37, 2014, p. 1311, 1314 ff., 1322 ff., 1335 ff.

19 ECJ, Joined Cases C-402 and 415/05 P (Kadi and Al Barakaat/Council and Commission), ECLI:EU:C:2008:461, ECR 2008, I-6351, mn. 281.

20 ECJ, C-294/83 (Parti Ècologiste „Les Verts"/European Parliament), ECLI:EU:C:1986:166, ECR 1986, 1339, mn. 23.

21 ECJ (Full), Opinion 2/13, ECLI:EU:C:2014:2454, mn 177 referrinto mn 155-176.

22 See German Federal Constitutional Court, (Maastricht), BVerfGE 89, 155 (182 ff.); (Lissabon), ECLI:DE:BVerfG:2009:es20090630.2bve000208, BVerfGE 123, 267 (348): "Das Grundgesetz kann nach Art. 23 Abs. 1 S. 3 GG an die Entwicklung der Europäischen Union angepasst werden; zugleich wird dieser Möglichkeit durch Art. 79 Abs. 3 GG, auf den die Norm verweist, eine absolute Grenze gesetzt". („.Pursuant to Art. 23 para.1 third sentence of the Basic Law, the Basic Law can be adapted to the development of the European Union; at the same time, this possibility is set an ultimate limit by Art. 79 para. 3 of the Basic Law, to which the provision makes reference".).

2. *Fundamental principles as constitutional principles of the European Union*

The fundamental principles as constitutional principles of the European Union can be distinguished by their different functions.

a) Structural principles of the European Union

Structural principles characterize the "nature" of the European Union as a Federation of States ("Staatenverbund") on which the Union is based and as a Union of States and citizens. This is illustrated by Art. 48 TEU and Art. 50 TEU. According to the ordinary revision procedure in Art. 48 TEU an amendment of the Treaties needs to be ratified by all Member States in accordance with their respective constitutional requirements (Art. 48 para. 1, para. 4 subpara. 2 TEU). As a result any increase of the competences conferred on the Union requires the consent of all 28 Member States as the "masters of the Treaties" and within the Member States at least the consent of their parliaments. The European Union has not the competence to create further competences by itself, i.e. by its insitutions (European Council, Council, European Parliament). The "Kompetenz-Kompetenz"[23] remains with the Member States.[24] Additionally, Art. 50 TEU permits every Member State to withdraw from the European Union, according to a regulated procedure, but at last unilaterally. A Member State cannot be forced to stay in the Union.[25] Thus, the European Union is not a Federal State but a Federation of States. The German Federal Constitutional Court characterized it in its Maastricht Decision as a "Staatenverbund". The Court explained this concept in its Lisbon Decision: "The concept of *Verbund* covers a close long-term association of states which remain sovereign, an association which exercises public authority on the basis of a treaty, whose fundamental order, however, is subject to the disposal of the Member States alone and in which the peoples of their Member States, i.e. the citizens of the states, remain the subjects of democratic legitimation."[26] The term "Staatenverbund" as well as the concept of the Federal Constitutional Court have been criticized.[27] Yet, if understood correctly, it meets the unique structure of the European Union, by taking into consideration that it is also a Union of citizens.[28] To justify its concept of the direct effect of EU-law (then EEC-law), the ECJ already in 1963 in van Gend en Loos asserted that the Tretay has created a Commu-

23 Concerning the terminus see *P. Lerche*, "Kompetenz-Kompetenz" und das Maastricht-Urteil des Bundesverfassungsgerichts, in: Ipsen/Rengeling/Mössner/Weber (eds.), Verfassungsrecht im Wandel. Zum 180 jährigen Bestehen der Carl Heymanns Verlag KG, 1995, p. 409, 415 ff.

24 See German Federal Constitutional Court, (Lissabon), ECLI:DE:BVerfG:2009:es20090630.2bve000208, BVerfGE 123, 267 (348 ff.).

25 The headline of Art. I-60 of the Treaty on a Constitution was: "Voluntary withdrawal from the Union".

26 German Federal Constitutional Court, (Lissabon), ECLI:DE:BVerfG:2009:es20090630.2bve000208, BVerfGE 123, 267, (Headnote 1).

27 See e.g. *H.-P. Ipsen*, Zehn Glossen zum Maastricht-Urteil, EuR 29, 1994, p. 1, 8; „der neue Versuch einer Gestaltbenennung, der alsbald vergessen sein sollte". But the term has been widely accepted.

28 So the Foreign Office of Germany, Auswärtiges Amt, Denkschrift zum Vertrag von Lissabon vom 13. Dezember 2007, p. 5: „Doppelnatur der Europäischen Union als Bürger und Staatenunion".

nity not only of States but also of peoples and persons and therefore not only Member States but also individuals must be visualised as being subjects of Community law.[29] An approach that corresponds squarely with the concept of the German Federal Constitutional Court emphasizing that democratic legitimization of the European Union must be based on two pillars: The pillar of the Union, i.e. the directly elected European Parliament, and the pillar of the Member States whose representatives in the Council need the legitimization by their national Parliaments which are elected by the citizens of each Member State. This concept has been confirmed by the Treaty of Lisbon. The provisions on democratic principles on the one hand include the role of the European Parliament,[30] but on the other hand also the role of national parliaments which "contribute actively to the good functioning of the Union".[31] Art. 12 TEU underlines the role of national parliaments by illustrating their active contribution to the functioning of the EU, i.e. taking part in the Treaty revision procedures in accordance with Art. 48 TEU,[32] as well as the role of national parliaments concerning the law making process of the European Union.[33] There may be and there are problems to realize this concept effectively. And this is mainly the task of the Member States. Regardless of efficiency issues, this concept does, however, meet the structure of the European Union. Therefore the discussion on a democratic deficit predominantly derives from a comparison of the European Union with a nation state which disregards its special and different structure.[34]

The fact that the European Union is a not only a Union of States but also a Union of citizens has been demonstrated expressively by the inclusion of a "Citizenship of the Union" by the Treaty of Maastricht. But this was only a further step – how the jurisprudence of the European Court of Justice has demonstrated a mostly underestimated step[35] – in developing Union citizenship. In Grezelcyk the ECJ proclaimed that "the Union citizenship is destined to be the fundamental status of nationals of the Member States".[36] And in Ruiz Zambrano the Court requested that the protection of a "substance" of Union citizen rights must be respected even if

29 ECJ, C-26/62 (van Gend en Loos), ECLI:EU:C:1963:1, ECR 1963, 1, 12: „The objective of the EEC Treaty [...] implies that this Treaty is more than an agreement which merely creates mutual obligations between the contracting states. This view is confirmed by the preambule to the Treaty which refers not only to governments but to peoples. [...] Community law therefore not only imposes obligations on individuals but is also intended to confer upon them rights which become part of their legal heritage".

30 Art. 10 TEU.

31 Art. 12 TEU.

32 Art. 12 lit. d TEU.

33 Art. 12 lit. a-c TEU.

34 Cf. *R. Streinz*, Die Verfassung Europas: Unvollendeter Bundesstaat, Staatenverbund oder unvergleichliches Phänomen?, in: Hermann/Gutmann/Rückert/Schmoeckel/Siems (eds.), Von den Leges Barbarorum bis zum ius barbarum des Nationalsozialismus, Festschrift für Hermann Nehlsen, 2008, p. 758-766. See also *F. Cheve-nal/S. Lavenex/F. Schimmelfennig*, Demoi-cracy in the European Union: principles, institutions, policies, Journal of European Public Policy 22, 2015, p. 1.

35 Cf. *R. Streinz*, Vom Marktbürger zum Unionsbürger, in: Breuer/Epiney/Haratsch/Schmahl/Weiß (eds.), Im Dienste des Menschen: Recht, Staat und Staatengemeinschaft. Forschungskolloquium anlässlich der Verabschiedung von Eckart Klein, 2009, p. 69-71.

36 ECJ, C-184/99 (Grzelczyk), ECLI:EU:C:2001:458, ECR 2001, I-6193, mn. 31.

there is no cross-border element.[37] This led von Bogdandy and others to construct a "Reverse-Solange Doctrine" based on fundamental rights of the EU citizens which should be applicable if there is a violation of the "essence of fundamental rights" in the sense of Art. 52 para. 1 sentence 1 of EU Charter of Fundamental Rights.[38] According to this construct the ECJ was entitled to review acts of the Member States even in purely domestic cases if the matter was brought before it by a preliminary ruling (Art. 267 TFEU) of the courts or tribunals of the Member States asking on the interpretation of the relevant provisions of the EU Charter on Fundamental Rights. The aim was not merely to bring in the ECJ, but to strengthen national liberal checks and balances in times of political crisis.[39] But even before the recent developments there was at least doubt whether this proposal would be workable in practice,[40] due to its "heavy reliance on national courts, whereas the judiciary is normally the first institution which illiberal forces would seek to capture".[41] A hypothesis that has since been proven true by the laws the Polish Parliament adopted to infringe upon the independence of the judiciary putting it under political control. The EU Commisssion is concerned, because the independence of the judiciary is a "key component of the rule of law" and the current reforms would increase the systemic threat to rule of law significantly, as identified in the Recommendations the Commission had sent to Poland in 2016.[42] But it is improbable that a pro-authoritarian government will be much impressed by rulings from Luxembourg.[43] And some of the challenges to liberal democracy cannot be captured – let alone countered – by focusing just on human rights violations.[44] Finally an extensive reading of Art. 51 EUChHR would not only run counter to the article's wording and meaning but would be considered as an unjustified "intervention" and lead to an enhanced institutional controversy not only between the ECJ and national constitutional courts,[45] but generally between the EU and its Member States.

37 ECJ, C-34/09 (Ruiz Zambrano), ECLI:EU:C:2011:124, ECR 2011, I-1177, mn. 41 ff.

38 *A. von Bogdandy/M. Kottmann/C. Antpöhler/J. Dickschen/S. Hentrei/M. Smrkolij,* "Reverse Solange – Protecting the Essence of Fundamental Rights against EU Member States, CMLRev 49, 2012, 489-520; *A. von Bogdandy/C. Antpöhler/M. Ioannidis,* Protecting EU Values Reverse Solange and a Systemic Deficiency Committee, in: Jakab/Kochenov (fn. 8).

39 *J.-W. Müller*, Should the EU Protect Democracy and the Rule of Law inside Member States?, ELJ 21, 2015, 141.

40 *D. Kochenov* (fn. 8): „most probably unworkable in theory and practice".

41 *D. Kochenov* (fn. 8), p. 16/25.

42 The Polish President Duda vetoed two of the four judicial reforms after protests, but signed the other two. See Remarks of Frans Timmermans (First Vice-President of the EU Commission) on European Commission action to preserve the rule of law in Poland (http://europa.eu/rapid/press-release_SPEECH-17-2170_en.htm). The EU Commission launched legel action (first step of of the Art. 258 TFEU procedure) against Poland.

43 This is underlined by the (lacking) results of the so called "dialogue" between the EU Commission and Poland and recently by the reaction of Hungary on the decision of the ECJ in the Refugees Case, ECJ (Grand Chamber), Joined Cases C-643/15 and C.647/15 (Slovak Republic and Hungary/Council), ECLI:EU:C:2017:631, concerning Council Decision (EU) 2015/1601 (OJ 2015 L 248/80). The Slovak Republic and Hungary were supported by Poland, the Council was supported by Belgium, Germany, Greece, France, Italy, Luxembourg, Sweden and the European Commission.

44 *J.-W. Müller* (fn. 39); see also *D. Kochenov* (fn. 8).

45 *T. von Danwitz* (fn. 18), p. 1338 f.

b) Principles concerning the relations between the European Union and its Member States

Principles concerning the relations between the European Union and its Member States are the principle of conferral of limited competences (Art. 4 para. 1, Art. 5 paras. 1 und 2 TEU),[46] the principles of subsidiarity (Art. 5 para. 3 TEU) and proportionality (Art. 5 para. 4 TEU),[47] the principle of sincere cooperation (Art. 4 para. 3 TEU) and the principle of mutual respect of the Union and the Member States (Art. 4 para. 2 TEU). Based on Art. 4 para 3 TEU (formerly based on Art. 10 TEC) the ECJ derived from the principle of sincere cooperation further concrete priciples concerning the application of EU law by the Member States, e.g. the principles of "equivalence" and of "effectiveness" which are limitations of the principle of national procedural autonomy.[48] The principle of mutual respect includes that the Union shall respect the national identities of the Member States. The interpretation of this term of Union law is the task of the ECJ. But the Court must have in mind that Art. 4 para. 2 TEU acknowledges different "identities" of the Member States, which are laid down in their constitutions and which are stated more precisely by their (constitutional) courts. Therefore, the ECJ concedes to the Member States a margin of appreciation concerning basic principles like "human dignity", even if these rights are common to all Member States. Because while they are also elements of Union law (Art. 1 EUChHR) the interpretation of these principles in terms of legal consequences differs among Member States (e.g. "human dignity" according to Art. 1 German Basic Law compared with the law of UK).[49] Since the national identities which the Union shall respect "are inherent in the fundamental structures, political and constitutional," of the Member States, these are competent to organize their own political systems accordingly. Nevertheless, these systems must be consistent with the requirements of Union law, in particular with the requirements of Art. 2 TEU at least, and not only to become a member of the EU (Art. 49 TEU) but permanently. Moreover, the Member States must also respect the other requirements that come along with the membership in the European Union as a supranational organization. To this extent the political creative power of the Member States is necessarily limited which must be accepted by them and politically explained to their people within them.

46 See *T.C. Hartley*, The Foundation of European Union Law, 7th ed. 2010, § 2.

47 To establish the conditions of the application of these principles and to establish a system for monitoring their application Protocol (No 2) on the application of the principles of subsidiarity and proportionality (OJ 2016 C 202) was added to the Treaty of Lisbon.

48 See *P. Craig/G. de Búrca*, EU Law. Text, Cases and Materials, 6th ed. 2016.

49 ECJ, C-35/02 (Omega Spielhallen und Automatenaufstellungs GmbH/Oberbürgermeisterin der Bundesstadt Bonn), ECLI:EU:C:2004:614, ECR 2004, I-9619 („Laserdrome"). Concerning Art. 4 para. 2 TEU see e.g. ECJ, C-208/09 (Ilonka Sayn-Wittgenstein/Landeshauptmann von Wien), ECLI:EU:C:2010:806, ECR 2010, I-13693, mn 81 ff. See *R. Streinz,* Die Verfassungsidentität der Mitgliedstaaten und das Recht der Europäischen Union, in: Stumpf/Kainer/Baldus (eds.), Privatrecht, Wirtschaftsrecht, Verfassungsrecht. Privatinitiative und Gemeinwohlhorizonte in der europäischen Integration. Festschrift für Peter-Christian Müller-Graff zum 70. Geburtstag, 2015, p. 1193, 1201 ff. with further references.

c) Principles ensuring the functioning of the European Union as a supranational organization

The principles ensuring the functioning of the European Union as a supranational organization were developed by the European Court of Justice from "the terms and the spirit of the Treaties". These are the principle of primacy (supremacy) of the law of the Union,[50] the "autonomy of EU law",[51] the principle of direct effect, firstly the direct effect of primary law, especially of the fundamental freedoms,[52] and secondly the direct effect of directives,[53] this being the first step to ensure the "effet utile" of directives if they are not correctly implemented by the Member States (followed by the principle of state liability for breach of EU law).[54]

d) The principle of mutual trust

The ECJ emphasizes that the essential characteristics of EU law (autonomy, primacy, direct effect) "have given rise to a structured network of principles, rules and mutually interdependent legal relations linking the EU and its Member States, and its Member States with each other, which are now engaged, as is recalled in the second paragraph of Article 1 TEU, in a "process of creating an ever closer union among the peoples of Europe" and that "this legal structure is based on the fundamental premise that each Member State shares with all the other Member States, and recognises that they share with it, a set of common values on which the EU is founded, as stated in Article 2 TEU. That premise implies and justifies the existence of mutual trust between the Member States that those values will be recognised and, therefore, that the law of the EU that implements them will be respected."[55] Actually, the principle of mutual trust is essential for a supranational organization, which is based on the conferral of national competences and the principle of mutual recognition, both being essential for the European Union as "an area without internal frontiers" concerning the fundamental freedoms (Art. 26 para. 2 TFEU) and an "area of freedom, security and justice" (Title V, Arts. 67-89 TFEU). But the ECJ was forced to see and to accept the limits of this principle of mutual trust if the standard that is necessary for the EU as a community based on law is not met in some Member States, firstly in asylum cases[56] and recently in cases concerning the European arrest warrant and the surrender procedures be-

50 Based on ECJ, C-6/64 (Costa/ENEL), ECLI:EU:C:1964:66, ECR 1964, 585,593. See Declaration (No 17) concerning primacy (OJ 2016 C 202). See also ECJ (Full Court), Opinion 2/13, ECLI:EU:C:2014:2454, mn. 166.

51 ECJ (Full Court), Opinion 2/13, ECLI:EU:C:2014:2454, mn 166, 183. Nevertheless, the Treaties are based on the (permanent) consent of the Member States which are free to leave the Union (Art. 50 TEU).

52 See *P. Craig/G. de Búrca* (fn. 48), p. 268 ff., 272 ff.

53 See e.g. ECJ, C-41/74 (van Duyn/Home Office), ECLI:EU:C:1974:133, ECR 1974, 1337. See *P. Craig/G. de Búrca* (fn. 49), p. 279 ff.

54 See ECJ, Joined Cases C-6 and C-9/90 (Francovich and Bonifaci), ECLI:EU:C: 1991:428, ECR 1991, I-5357.

55 ECJ (Full Court), Opinion 2/13, ECLI:EU:C:2014:2454, mn. 166-167.

56 See ECJ (Grand Chamber), Joined Cases C-411/10 and C-493/10 (N.S. and Others), ECLI:EU:C:2011:865, ECR 2011, I-13905; ECJ, C-4/11 (Puid), ECLI:EU:C:2013:740. The ECJ followed the decision of the ECtHR (Great Chamber) of 21 January 2011, No 30696/09 (M.S.S./Belgium and Greece).

tween Member States.[57] Therefore, it is evident that a minimum standard of homogeneity concerning the values of the EU is necessary within all Member States not only at the date of accession to the EU (Art. 49 TEU) but permanently and that the adherence to this standard must be controlled by the competent organs of the EU.

e) The principle of solidarity

The principle of solidarity is mentioned in Art. 2 TEU and some other provisions of the TEU and the Treaty on the Functioning of the European Union (TFEU),[58] but typically in areas where there is no "solidarity" in practice, e.g. concerning the asylum policy which should be "governed by the principle of solidarity and fair sharing of responsibility" (Art. 80 TFEU).[59]

3. Values of the European Union as constitutional principles

As shown above, the "values" enumerated in Art. 2 sentence 1 TEU are actually fundamental, i.e. constitutional principles. This is at least the case concerning the principles of democracy, i.e. democracy in a state where freedom prevails,[60] as democracy is defined by the Strasbourg European Court on Human Rights[61] and the respect for human dignity as the basis for respect for human rights and the rule of law.

IV. Values of the European Union

1. The values named in Article 2 TEU: Binding the European Union and its Member States

The values referred to in Art. 2 TEU are binding on the European Union and its institutions as well as the Member States and their institutions. Nevertheless, there may be differences concerning the concrete requirements, having in mind

57 ECJ, Joined Cases C-404/15 and C-659/15 PPU (Aranyosi and Căldăraru), ECLI:EU:C:2016:198.

58 Art. 2 sentence 2 TEU; Art. 80 (policies on border checks, asylum and immigration), Art. 122 para. 1 (appropriate measures in cases of severe difficulties; para 2: including financial aid), Art. 194 para. 1 (energy), Title VII ("solidarity clause"), Art. 222 para. 1 sentence 1 (terrorist attacks or natural or man-made desasters) TFEU. See *E. Kücük*, Solidarity in EU Law. An Elusive Political Statement or a Legal Principle with Substance?, Maastricht Journal of European and Comparative Law 2016.

59 See *E. Kücük*, The Principle of Solidarity and Fairness: Sharing Responsibility: More than a Window Dressing?, ELJ 22, 2016, p. 448-469.

60 Cf. German Federal Constitutional Court, (SRP-Verbot), BVerfGE 2, 1, 12 – prohibition of the Sozialistische Reichspartei (SRP): "freiheitlich-demokratische Grundordnung" (free democratic basic order). Reiterated in German Federal Constitutional Court, (unconstitutionality of the Nationaldemokratische Partei Deutschlands (NPD)), ECLI:DE:BVerfG:2017:bs20170117.2bvb000113, Judgement of 17 January 2017, mn. 418 ff.

61 See e.g. ECt5HR, Application no. 23885/94 (ÖZDEP/Turkey), Judgement of 8 December 1999, mn. 43 ff. – „necessary in a democratic society".

the differences in structure between the EU as a federation of states and the Member States, and differences concerning the intensity of the binding force.

2. Values on which the Union is founded: Rule of law, Democracy, Human Rights

The "values" which are enumerated in Art. 2 TEU are "values on which the Union is founded" and are declared to be values common to all Member States. Actually being principles, these "values", namely the rule of law, respect for human dignity and for human rights, including the rights of persons belonging to minorities, freedom and democracy and equality must be translated into concrete legal requirements. With regard to the sphere of the European Union, the Treaty on European Union includes further provisions which are binding on the Union itself and its institutions, e.g. provisions on democratic principles (Title II, Art. 9-12 TEU), especially the principle of democracy with the two pillars of the democratic legitimacy of the European Union, the European Parliament where the citizens are directly – although degressively proportional (Art. 14 para. 2 sentence 2 TEU) – represented at Union level, and the European Council and the Council, where the Member States are reprensented by their governments, which are (or should be) themselves democratically accountable either to their national Parliaments, or to their citizens (Art. 10 para. 2 TEU). Human rights are now guaranteed by the European Charter on Fundamental Rights, which is binding on the institutions and bodies of the Union, but also on Member States, however only when they are implementing Union law (Art. 51 para. 1 EUChHR). Thus Art. 6 para. 3 TEU has only a supplementary function. The accession of the Union to the European Convention on Human Rights and Fundamental Freedoms (ECHR) is blocked by Opinion 2/13 of the European Court of Justice[62] who opposed the idea of being subject to another court above it.[63] The rule of law is essential for the European Union as a community based on law ("Rechtsgemeinschaft"). Consequently, among the "values" enumerated in Art. 2 TEU, the rule of law plays a key role. It aims to prevent arbitrary use of public power by a number of organizational and procedural principles such as the distribution of powers, protection of individual rights by independent courts and the principles of legality, legal security, protection of legitimate expectations and proportionality. The underlying substantive goal of the rule of law is the protection of human dignity, of individual freedom, and the guarantee of equal treatment.[64]

62 ECJ (Full Court), Opinion 2/13, ECLI:EU:C:2014:2454, mn. 258.

63 See *W. Michl*, Still a flawed decision, http://verfassungsblog.de/still-a-flawed-decision-2/ (13 March 2015); *T. Streinz,* The Autonomy Paradox, http://verfassungsblog.de/still-a-flawed-decision-2/ (15 March 2015).

64 *K.-P. Sommermann* (fn. 4), Art. 3 TEU, mn. 23.

3. Common values of the Member States and their societies: How "common" are they and how common must they be?

Recent developments have shown that the extent of real common values among Member States and their societies may be limited. The question is: How "common" are the common values and how common must they be? The motto of the EU according to the Constitutional Treaty was "United in diversity". The diversity is characteristic for the European Union.[65] Nonetheless, a "Union" which shall be to a certain extent a "Political Union" must be based to a certain extent on common values and principles. Therefore: Do "pluralism" and "tolerance" also allow for different concepts of implementing the "values" by the Member States and, if so, to what extent? In Omega the European Court of Justice accepted different national approaches to the meaning of "human dignity".[66] Does the Luxembourg Court generally concede a "margin of appreciation" as the Strasbourg European Court on Human Rights (ECtHR) does? It seems to be so in special cases, having in mind that the Union shall respect the "national identities" of the Member States, "inherent in their fundamental structure, political and constitutional" (Art. 4 para. 2 sentence 1 TEU).[67]

4. In particular: Does EU-law require a constitutional court?

Concerning Poland: Does EU-law require a constitutional court at all? Or isn't the problem rather the encroachment on the independence of the judiciary?[68] In its recommendation of 27 July 2016 regarding the rule of law in Poland the Commission mentions "including constitutional justice, where it exists". Thus a Constitutional Court is not a necessary element to fulfill the requirements of the rule of law. But: Where constitutional justice exists in a Member State, the rule of law requires it to be exercised in accordance with the Constitution of this Member State so long as this Constitution has not been amended according to its rules of amendment. The rule of law requires at least the separation of powers, the independence and the impartiality of the judiciary and that decisions of the Courts are respected. The existence of a Constitutional Court is not common to all Member States. Moreover, in the Netherlands the Courts explicitly have no jurisdiction to review the constitutionality of laws which are adopted by the Parliament.[69] So: To abolish the Constitutional Court, if necessary with the majority requested by the

65 Cf. *W. Kaegi*, Discordia concors. Vom Mythus Basels und von der Europa-Idee Jacob Burckhardts, in: Discordia concors: Festgabe für Edgar Bonjour zu seinem siebzigsten Geburtstag am 21. August 1968.

66 ECJ, C-36/02 (Omega), ECLI:EU:C:2004:614, ECR 2004, I-9609, mn. 38.

67 See *R. Streinz*, Die Rolle des EuGH im Prozess der Europäisachen Integration. Anmerkungen zu gegenläufigen Tendenzen in der neueren Rechtsprechung, AöR 135, 2010, p. 2, 19 f.

68 See *A. Seibert-Fohr*, European Standards for the Rule of Law and Independent Courts, JRP 20, 2012, 161, 163.

69 Art. 120 of the Constitution: „The constitutionality of Acts of Parliament and treaties shall not be reviewed by courts". Concerning other Member States (e.g. the "parliamentary sovereignty" in UK) and different forms of constitutional review (concentrated or difussed system) see *M. de Visser*, Constitutional Review in Europe. A Comparative Analysis, 2014.

Constitution, and all problems are solved? It is questionable whether the rule of law can be really effective, if there is no judicial control over all measures of the authorities of a Member State which can limit the rights of the citizens. This is the case also in the Netherlands: The Courts have jurisdiction to review all acts of the Dutch authorities, including legislation, as to whether they are in accordance with EU law – this is a consequence of the primacy of EU law – but also as to whether they are in accordance with public international treaties, especially the European Convention on Human Rights.[70]

5. Promotion of the values of the European Union

To be credible, "values", or actually the legally binding principles of the European Union, must be promoted both on the EU level, e.g. in the framework of the external relations of the European Union or the accession procedure,[71] and within the Member States. To ensure that said principles and values are not only law in the books but law in action, their enforcement is paramount, if necessary also by the institutions of the European Union against its Member States. This requires not only effective enforcement procedures[72] but also concrete standards concerning the real common and inalienable "values" or rather principles.[73]

V. Conclusion

The "values" named in Art. 2 TEU are principles, especially the rule of law, democracy and the human dignity as the basis of all fundamental rights. They shall have legal consequences as requirements for the admission to the European Union (Art. 49 TEU) and as a cause for countermeasures, if there is a clear risk of a serious breach of these values by a Member State (Art. 7 TEU). However, to be applicable, these "values", being the background for legal principles, must be turned into down-to-earth provisions. Therefore, concrete tests are needed to qualify the specific requirements on the European Union on the one side, and concerning the "common" requirements on the Member States on the other side.

70 See *J. C. A. de Poorter*, Constitutional Review in the Netherlands: A Jointly Responsibility, Utrecht Law Review 9, 2013, p. 89, 95 ff.

71 Because of an evident breach of the values referred to in Art. 2 TEU the European Parliament in a (non-binding) resolution called on the European Commission and the Council to formally suspend the accession negotiations with Turkey. But there is no unanimity among the Member States and therefore within the Council about this particular issue

72 Concerning alternative instruments (Art. 258 and Art. 260 TFEU) against democratic backsliding, having in mind the deficits of Art. 7 TEU, see *U. Sedelmeier*, Anchoring Democracy from Above? The European Union and Democratic Backsliding in Hungary and Romania after Accession, JCMS 52, 2014, 105, 113 f.

73 Concerning the Council of Europe see *A. S. Fohr*, JRP 2012, 168 f.: "a careful balance should be drawn between independence, accountability and efficiency of the judiciary which are all necessary for the right to access to justice […]. The decisive factor to measure compliance with the European Convention is the result, not the means adopted".

Reflections on What the Rule of Law Means and its Significance at EU Level

*By Gavin Barrett, Dublin**

The rule of law is simultaneously of great political, legal and economic importance. Paradoxically, however, this protean and elusive concept is also plagued by definitional problems. At EU level, it has attributes that both link it to national concepts and distinguish it from them, and its profile at this level has risen steadily since the entry into force of the Maastricht Treaty. Numerous Treaty provisions now make explicit or implicit reference to the rule of law. Yet here too it lacks an explicit definition. With its elaboration having been left for long to the judicial branch, however, the understanding of the rule of law at EU level has evolved gradually from a thin concept to a thick one. The Court of Justice has nonetheless never sought to take it beyond the status of a primary constitutional principle. The importance of the concept of the rule of law for the purposes of the Article 7 TEU procedures and under the Commission's 2014 Communication 'A New EU Framework to strengthen the Rule of Law' now make it imperative for the EU to guard itself against the opposing dangers of overreach on the one hand and excessive lightness of touch on the other.

One of the Most Exalted Concepts in Modern Legal Orders

For several reasons, the rule of law is one of the most exalted concepts in modern political and legal orders. It is in the first place one of the most important and widely shared *political* ideals of our time.[1] Fukuyama has described respect for the rule of law and the maintenance of reasonably effective institutions and practices to protect it as central attributes of modern functioning legitimate political order.[2] Waldron has described it as 'one of a cluster of ideals constitutive of modern political morality; the others are human rights, democracy and perhaps also the principles of free market economy.'[3]

Beyond its political significance, it is accurately also regarded as a key concept in contemporary *legal* orders (sharing this position with respect for fundamental rights and democracy),[4] even if its ascent to this status in Europe can be described

* Professor of Law, Sutherland School of Law, University College Dublin.

1 *J. Waldron*, The Concept and the Rule of Law, (2008), 43 Georgia Law Review, p. 1, 3.

2 *F. Fukuyama*, Why is Democracy Performing so Poorly?, (2015), 26 Journal of Democracy, 11, cited in: *A. Magen*, Cracks in the Foundation: Understanding the Great Rule of Law Debate in the EU, (2016), 54 JCMS, p. 1050, 1055.

3 *Loc. cit.*, 1.

4 *M. Claes/M. Bonelli*, The Rule of Law and the Constitutionalisation of the European Union, Chapter 16 of *W. Schroeder*, Strengthening the Rule of Law in Europe, 2016, p. 265, 266.

as a phenomenon of relatively recent vintage,[5] and even if, as Lord Bingham has accurately pointed out, this does not mean that it can be universally applied without exception.[6] It is a principle of constitutional value[7] – and not just any principle, at that, but a defining one, "commonly recognized as one of the foundational principles undergirding and legitimating all European constitutional systems."[8]
Observance of the rule of law is also of *economic* significance. It is a precondition for optimal economic development: a fact not lost on scholars and leaders in rapidly developing economies, such as that of China.[9] A corollary of this point is that the rule of law is correctly viewed as the bedrock of the Single European Market (and also, for that matter, the European Union's Area of Freedom, Security and Justice).[10]
The rule of law has other significances beyond these. As Waldron has pointed out, it is also a valuable means of *evaluation and assessment* of legislation, "a critical and demanding standard for evaluating the form of positive law" and a valuable "basis for criticizing, rather than [...] a basis for admiring, the legal culture with which we are familiar."[11]

Plagued by Definitional Problems

In spite of all the praise heaped on the rule of law, and the value attributed to it, it is an idea plagued by definitional problems. It may however, be more accurate to say that confusion as to the meaning of the rule of law *derives from* the value attributed to it rather than being *'in spite of'* it. In other words, a certain *dissensus* on the actual *meaning* of the rule of law has probably been the price to be paid for

5 Schroeder has pointed out that notwithstanding the ancient provenance of the rule of law in English history at least, the concepts of rule of law in the UK, of *Rechtsstaatlichkeit* in Germany and the *État de droit* in France really acquired special meaning and impact only after the nineteenth century and that the constitutions of most EU member states became familiar with the concept of the rule of law only from the 1970s onwards. (See *W. Schroeder*, The European Union and the Rule of Law – State of Affairs and Ways of Strengthening, Chapter 1 of *W. Schroeder*, Strengthening the Rule of Law in Europe, 2016, p. 3, 20-21).

6 Bingham offers as an example the fact that certain proceedings cannot be held in public *e.g.*, those involving trade secrets. (*T. Bingham*, The Rule of Law, 2010, p. 8) Family proceedings are of course also held *in camera* in many states. Waldron gives the further example that in many individual areas of the law, the state of the law may be so uncertain as to make the outcome of a case unpredictable even to professionally trained lawyers (See *J. Waldron*, The Law, 1990, p. 48).

7 *L. Pech*, 'A Union Founded on the Rule of Law': Meaning and Reality of the Rule of Law as a Constitutional Principle of EU Law, 2010, 6 European Constitutional Law Review, p. 359, 362.

8 *L. Pech*, 'A Union Founded on the Rule of Law': Meaning and Reality of the Rule of Law as a Constitutional Principle of EU Law, 2010, 6 European Constitutional Law Review 359, 362; *L. Pech* (fn. 7).

9 In consequence, the World Bank has a rule of law indicator. See *M. Claes/M. Bonelli*, The Rule of Law and the Constitutionalisation of the European Union, Chapter 16 of *W. Schroeder*, Strengthening the Rule of Law in Europe, 2016, p. 265, 267.

10 *D. Kochenov*, EU Law Without the Rule of Law: Is the Veneration of Autonomy Worth It?, 2015, 34 Yearbook of European Law, p. 74, 86 and *S. Wolff*, The Rule of Law in the Area of Freedom, Security and Justice: Monitoring at Home What the European Union Preaches Abroad, 2013, 5 Hague Journal on the Rule of Law, p. 119 both cited in: *A. Magen*, Cracks in the Foundation: Understanding the Great Rule of Law Debate in the EU, 2016, 54 JCMS, p. 1050, 1056.

11 *J. Waldron*, The Law, 1990, p. 36, 48.

obtaining widespread *consensus* on its *value*.[12] It has gained esteem, in certain measure, by becoming all things to all people.
Like equality, it is a protean and rather elusive concept,[13] easier at times to explain in terms of what it stands against rather than what it stands for.[14] It also a 'moving target' (*i.e.*, an evolving concept) which changes and becomes more refined as the society which gives rise to it changes.[15] It seems impossible to define exhaustively:[16] as Steiner tells us we are left with "an omnipresent notion, but when it comes to defining it, no single definition can be given, nor a single universally accepted model of it identified."[17] So much doubt exists as to what the rule of law involves that some very eminent jurisprudes have gone so far as to doubt whether the 'rule of law' is useful as a concept at all. Thus

> "Professor Raz has commented on the tendency to use the rule of law as a shorthand description of the positive aspects of any given political system. Professor Finnis has described the rule of law as '[t]he name commonly given to the state of affairs in which a legal system is legally in good shape.' Professor Judith Shklar has suggested that the expression may have become meaningless thanks to ideological abuse and general overuse: 'It may well have become just another one of those self-congratulatory rhetorical devices that grace the public utterances of Anglo-American politicians. No intellectual effort need therefore be wasted on this bit of ruling class chatter.' [...] Professor Jeremy Waldron, commenting on the decision of the US Supreme Court in *Bush v. Gore* [...] in which the rule of law had been invoked by both sides – recognized a widespread impression that utterance of those magic words meant little more than 'Hooray for our side'. Professor Brian Tamanaha has described the rule of law as [...] analogous to the notion of the Good in the sense that 'everyone is for it, but has contrasting convictions about what it is'."[18]

So great is the degree of uncertainty surrounding it that, ironically, it can be argued that attempts to enforce the rule of law *per se themselves* run the risk of violating the rule of law – in that they involve attempts to enforce a norm that lacks

12 To paraphrase *S. Chesterman*, An International Rule of Law?, 2008, 56 American Journal of Comparative Law, p. 331, 332 quoted by *L. Pech*, 'A Union Founded on the Rule of Law': Meaning and Reality of the Rule of Law as a Constitutional Principle of EU Law, 2010, 6 European Constitutional Law Review, p. 359, 360.

13 By which is meant that it is able to change into many different forms or able to do many different things.

14 *M. Rosenfeld*, The Rule of Law and the Legitimacy of Constitutional Democracy, 2001, 74 California Law Review, p. 1307, cited in: *M. Claes/M. Bonelli*, The Rule of Law and the Constitutionalisation of the European Union, Chapter 16 of *W. Schroeder*, Strengthening the Rule of Law in Europe, 2016, p. 265, 267.

15 See *M. Claes/M. Bonelli*, The Rule of Law and the Constitutionalisation of the European Union, Chapter 16 of *W. Schroeder*, Strengthening the Rule of Law in Europe, 2016, p. 265, 267; and *G. O'Donnell*, Why the Rule of Law Matters, 2004, 4 Journal of Democracy, p. 15.

16 *M. Claes/M. Bonelli*, The Rule of Law and the Constitutionalisation of the European Union, Chapter 16 of *W. Schroeder*, Strengthening the Rule of Law in Europe, 2016, p. 265.

17 *E. Steiner*, The Rule of Law in the Jurisprudence of the European Court of Human Rights, Chapter 8 of *W. Schroeder*, Strengthening the Rule of Law in Europe, 2016, p. 135, 136.

18 *T. Bingham*, The Rule of Law, 2010, p. 5.

the legal certainty normally seen as required by the rule of law.[19] In this sense, the rule of law is, as Groucho Marx would put it, a club that would never have itself as a member.[20]

Such uncertainty is a serious problem in particular when there are provisions in the EU Treaty which seek to operationalise the rule of law *vis-à-vis* the member states.[21] As Polakiewicz and Sandvig put the matter, "attaching legal consequences and especially negative ones to a term, the meaning of which is unclear, runs counter to several if not most interpretations of the rule of law".[22]

Although many have perceived the very real difficulty in framing the rule of law as an operational concept – one which tells us what to do in concrete cases – this has not prevented its operational implications occasionally having been drawn out in very great detail – at Council of Europe level[23] or in the framework of the World Justice Project Rule of Law Index,[24] for example. But however worthy, these attempts undoubtedly are, they also alert us to Magen's criticism that the rule of law is 'uniquely vulnerable to conceptual overstretching' as well as being malleable in the face of shifting political agendas.[25]

19 Hence Schroder's observation in the EU law context that a concretisation of the rule of law beyond the mere reference in Article 2 TEU is needed from the point of view of the rule of law itself. (*W. Schroeder*, The European Union and the Rule of Law – State of Affairs and Ways of Strengthening, Chapter 1 of *W. Schroeder*, Strengthening the Rule of Law in Europe, 2016, p. 3, 20).

20 *G. Marx*, Groucho and Me, 1959.

21 As Schroeder points out, it is problematic to operationalise the rule of law *vis-à-vis* the Member states without having clarified its content before. (See *W. Schroeder*, The European Union and the Rule of Law – State of Affairs and Ways of Strengthening, Chapter 1 of *W. Schroeder*, Strengthening the Rule of Law in Europe, 2016, p. 3, 19.

22 *J. Polakiewicz/J. Sandvig*, The Council of Europe and the Rule of Law, Chapter 7 of *W. Schroeder*, Strengthening the Rule of Law in Europe, 2016, p. 115 at, 121, paraphrasing *E. Wennerström*, The Rule of Law and the European Union, 2007, p. 81, 87.

23 Where the Venice Commission's six-headed enumeration of elements of the rule of law – incorporating (i) legality (taken to include a democratic, accountable and transparent process; (ii) legal certainty; (iii) a prohibition of arbitrariness; (iv) access to justice (including judicial review of administrative acts) in impartial independent courts; (v) respect for human rights; and (vi) equality before the law – has been operationalised into a check-list with sub-requirements under each heading. (See European Commission For Democracy Through Law (Venice Commission), Rule Of Law Checklist (Study No. 711 / 2013, CDL-AD(2016)007, Strasbourg, 18 March 2016) available online at the time of writing at http://www.venice.coe.int/webforms/documents/default.aspx?pdffile=CDL-AD(2016)007-e) See more generally *J. Polakiewicz/J. Sandvig*, The Council of Europe and the Rule of Law, Chapter 7 of *W. Schroeder*, Strengthening the Rule of Law in Europe, 2016, p. 115, 120.

24 The *World Justice Project (WJP) Rule of Law Index* describes itself as "the world's leading source for original data on the rule of law", and measures and ranks the performance of 113 states and jurisdictions, using 44 indicators derived from eight primary rule of law factors, namely: (i) constraints on government powers, (ii) absence of corruption, (iii) open government, (iv) fundamental rights, (v) order and security, (vi) regulatory enforcement, (vii) civil justice, and (viii) criminal justice. (see more generally http://worldjusticeproject.org/rule-of-law-index).

25 *A. Magen*, Cracks in the Foundation: Understanding the Great Rule of Law Debate in the EU, 2016, 54 JCMS, p. 1050, 1051, where he comments that "the term is commonly brandished by politicians, diplomats, jurists, economists, soldiers, journalists, bureaucrats and academics to imply at least six meanings that are distinct, but seldom differentiated by those who invoke the term: (1) state authority bound by law, (2) equality before the law, (3) law, order and human security, (4) respect for property rights, (5) predictable, accessible and efficient justice, and (6) public power respectful of fundamental rights. In addition, international lawyers and organizations increasingly call for the building of an 'international rule of law,' meaning a world governed by rules not force".

Moreover, Schroeder strikes the reader as being correct in acknowledging that

> "constitutional law problems are primarily to be solved on the basis of constitutional principles that are closer to the problem and form part of the meta-concept of the rule of law, for example, principles such as legal certainty or separation of powers ; the concept of rule of law should be drawn upon only subsidiarily".[26]

Schroeder denies the rule of law lacks independent normative value - what he calls "normative self-reliance" – arguing that its role is to link various elements in a systematic fashion, thereby giving rise to functional insights. This is perhaps another way of saying this that the rule of law is really best regarded a bundle of concepts, a series of jurisprudential floating charges, one or more of which will need to crystallize depending on the specific context.[27]

Rule of Law at EU Level - Links with National Concepts and Distinctions from Them

The concept of the rule of law at EU level has attributes that both link it to national concepts and distinguish it from them.

The concept of the rule of law originated in the context of democratic state systems, for example in the common law concept of the *rule of law* (first clearly articulated by A. V. Dicey) with its emphasis on formal and procedural rights, the French law concept of the *État de Droit* with its emphasis on the need for compliance with the Constitution and written law and the German law concept of the *Rechtsstaat,* with its emphasis on fundamental rights.

It is not merely the historical origins of the rule of law at EU level which are national. The European Union understanding of what the rule of law means and what its functions are also reflect national understandings.

It can scarcely have come as any surprise that the rule of law would require some redefinition to fit into an EU context. Indeed, in its very adaptability and its ability to be moulded by judges, the EU concept of the rule of law can be said to reflect national constitutional experience. The Court, interestingly, in its ruling in *Les Verts* shied away from using the terminology of the *Rechtsstaat* and the *État de Droit*, preferring the terminology of the *Rechtsgemeinschaft* and the *Communauté de Droit,* but the member states in later amending the Treaties to take account of the principle showed no such tender sensibility. The same basic idea was involved, regardless of the terminology used.

Not just the ability to be moulded by the Courts, but the very fashion in which the rule of law *has* been moulded by the European Court of Justice over the years mirrors national experience as well: in the intensification of judicial review to

26 *W. Schroeder*, The European Union and the Rule of Law – State of Affairs and Ways of Strengthening, Chapter 1 of *W. Schroeder*, Strengthening the Rule of Law in Europe, 2016, p. 3, 21.

27 *Ibid.*

which it has led, in its leading the EU legal system along the path of further protection for the individual, in the non-equation, as Pech would tell us, of *the* rule of law to *a* rule of law.

A further link with national legal systems is to be found in the fact that in populating the contents of the rule of law at European level (*i.e.,* in the form of general legal principles), recourse is had to principles derived from national legal systems.

This is not to say that all of the aspects of the principle at EU level reflect national experiences, however. The Article 7 procedures, the status of observance of the rule of law as a precondition for membership and the assumption of its exportability beyond the European Union's borders are all added value at EU level.

The invocation of the rule of law ceased long ago to be the exclusive preserve of states (and within states, democratic states). International instruments ranging from the 1948 Universal Declaration of Human Rights[28] to the 1950 European Convention on Human Rights[29] to the Treaty on European Union also refer to it, and in doing so, have amplified the importance of the principle. It has thus become "an organizational paradigm of modern constitutional law at the national *and* international levels".[30]

Why the Rule of Law Matters Within the European Union

-Historically

The rule of law has seen a gradual increase in its profile in the time since the Communities were first founded in the 1950s. Although implicit in the very nature of the then Communities as organizations designed to shield Europe from arbitrariness and force, the rule of law first received indisputable express recognition from the Community legal order in the ruling of the European Court of Justice in *Les Verts v. European Parliament* [1986] ECR 1339 that the (then) Community (now Union) was "based on the rule of law". The rise of the rule of law to acceptance by consensus was accelerated by the triumph of western liberalism with the fall of the Berlin Wall and the end of the Cold War – Fukuyama's so-called 'end of history'. This appears to have provided impetus for Treaty reform. In successive steps after this time, the prominence and role of the rule of law at EU level were boosted on each occasion the Treaty was amended at Maastricht in 1992, Amsterdam in 1997, Nice in 2001 and most recently Lisbon in 2007.

28 The preamble of which declared it to be essential "that human rights be protected by the rule of law".
29 The preamble of which referred to the governments of European countries as having a heritage of, *inter alia,* the rule of law.
30 Pech, *loc. cit.,* p. 367. Emphasis added.

-Legally

Judged from a legal perspective, as opposed to an historical one, there are now numerous reasons why the rule of law should feature as part of the EU law firmament. In the first place, advancing the rule of law is part of the *raison d'être* of what is now the European Union, in that from the very beginning the European Communities were meant to shelter their member states from the vagaries of arbitrariness and force.

It was for this reason even before Article 2 (with its reference to foundational values) made its appearance in the Treaties, that Tridimas identified as the most important single provision in the then Treaties the stipulation now found in Article 19(1) which characterized the role of the European Court of Justice as being "to ensure that in the interpretation and application of the Treaties the law is observed"

Secondly, respect for the rule of law is part of an assumed shared legal patrimony on the part of member states who are members of the European Union. This assumption is reflected in several treaty articles which will be seen presently.

Thirdly, the various sources of European law both formal and informal and make extensive reference to the rule of law. The rule of law has long featured in the case-law of the European Court of Justice, beginning with its famous ruling in *Les Verts v. European Parliament.*[31]

The rule of law is also now explicitly mentioned in a string of Treaty articles: Articles 2, 7, 49, and 21 of the TEU. According to Article 2 TEU, in a somewhat curious rewording of earlier Treaty law,[32] the rule of law has the status of a founding *value* of the EU. More exactly, it provides that

> "the Union is founded on the values of respect for human dignity, freedom, democracy, equality, *the rule of law* and respect for human rights [...]" and further asserts that "these values are common to the Member States" [33]

Article 49 TEU effectively makes respect for, a commitment to promote the rule of law a condition for applying for membership of the European Union. Hence according to this article, "any European State which respects the values referred to in Article 2 and is committed to promoting them" – and these of course include the rule of law – "may apply to become a member of the Union."

According to Article 21(1) TEU, "the Union's action on the international scene shall be guided by the *principles which have inspired its own creation, development and enlargement, and which it seeks to advance in the wider world*"[34] These are stipulated to include the rule of law.

31 ECJ, C-284/83 (Les Verts/European Parliament), ECLI:EU:C:1986:166, ECR 1339, 1339.

32 The earlier Article 6(1) TEU referred to principles, not values.

33 More exactly, "in a society in which pluralism, non-discrimination, tolerance, justice, solidarity and equality between women and men prevail.".

34 Emphasis added.

Under Article 21(2) "the Union shall define and pursue common policies and actions, and shall work for a high degree of cooperation in all fields of international relations" in order to achieve eight stipulated objectives. The second of these objectives is to "consolidate and support democracy, *the rule of law*, human rights and the principles of international law".

It is not merely in those articles in which it is explicitly mentioned that the rule of law features – respect for it arguably features implicitly in many other Treaty articles – Articles 263 and 265 TFEU providing for judicial review, Articles 258 to 260, providing for an enforcement method aimed at prevented failures to fulfil obligations under the Treaties, Article 267 with its provision for a preliminary reference procedure for the benefit of national courts and tribunals, Article 218(11) with its provision that for obtaining the binding opinion of the Court of Justice as to whether an international agreement envisaged by the Union is compatible with the Treaties.

Fourthly, the rule of law is of sufficient significance to have garnered mention in the Preamble to the Treaty on European Union, and it is (a) "drawing inspiration" from the cultural, religious and humanist inheritance of Europe, from which have developed universal values – including the rule of law[35]; and in the second place (b) "confirming" the signatory states' attachment to principles which include the rule of law.[36]

Fifthly, the rule of law is also mentioned in the Preamble of the Charter of Fundamental Rights, the second indent of which declares that

> "Conscious of its spiritual and moral heritage, the Union is founded on the indivisible, universal values of human dignity, freedom, equality and solidarity; *it is based on the principles of democracy and the rule of law.*"

Why Has the Rule of Law Become a Question of Concern to the EU in Recent Times?

Concerns regarding the rule of law have been prominent in recent times. It is interesting that although what is now the Article 7(2) mechanism was originally conceived at least in part as a kind of signal to the acceding (and newly democratic) EU member states of 2004 and 2007 that backsliding in respect of fundamental principles would not be allowed in an EU context, in the event, the problems that have arisen have been very far from affecting CEE states alone. At the time of writing, issues that have given rise to rule of law issues or worries have concerned

35 The others mentioned are the inviolable and inalienable rights of the human person, freedom, democracy and equality.

36 As well as liberty, democracy and respect for human rights and fundamental freedoms.

- Austria – where controversy was generated by the entry of a far-right party into government;
- Italy – where control of broadcast and printed media by the executive raised concerns;
- France – which raised fears with the threatened deportation of members of the Roma community;
- Hungary – in which recent rapid and extensive legal changes, including to the Constitution by government using its majority to steamroll constitutional protections have led to concern, as has the threatened creation of an 'illiberal state';
- Romania – where there was a refusal to obey constitutional court rulings court;
- Poland – in which there is an ongoing conflict over the constitutional court, involving defiance of its rulings, non-publication by the executive of unfavourable decisions and executive refusal to appoint validly elected judges; and
- Turkey – a candidate state in which there are media control issues, freedom of assembly issues, judicial independence issues, and last but not least, general fundamental rights issues.[37]

Existing rule of law mechanisms at national, Council of Europe and indeed European Union level do not seem to have measured up to the task of dealing comprehensively with all of these issues. The backsliding which the provisions found in Article 7(2) TEU were intended to indicate was impermissible is now happening. The question is whether the EU is able to make up for the lack of the ability of other levels of governance to cope with this phenomenon, or whether there is what might be called a rule of law deficit at EU level (as well as, of course, at national, and intergovernmental level), to be added to the supposed democratic deficit.

What Does the Rule of Law Mean for the European Union? What Obligations Should it Impose?

Central to any attempt to enforce the rule of law at European Union level must be the giving of a meaning to the concept of the rule of law. It seems scarcely possible to ask ourselves what concrete obligations the rule of law imposes in particu-

37 It has been suggested that at least two other challenges to the rule of law in an EU context other than those of the kind outlined above can be identified. (See generally Anon., *"The Rule of Law in the Union, the Rule of Union Law and the Rule of Law by the Union: Three Interrelated Problems"* (2016) 53 Common Market Law Review 597.) These are, namely (a) the challenges emanating from national systems for respect for EU law – for example, in the case law of the *Bundesverfassungsgericht* or (one might now suggest) the ruling of the Supreme Court of Denmark in the *Ajos* case (analysed in S. Klinge, *Dialogue or disobedience between the European Court of Justice and the Danish Constitutional Court? The Danish Supreme Court challenges the Mangold-principle,* EU Law Analysis, 8 February, 2018 (available at http://eulawanalysis.blogspot.ie/2016/12/dialogue-or-disobedience-between.html); and (b) the need for respect by the EU itself for the law.

lar cases, without defining the rule of law, however imperfectly. Clarity in this regard is scarcely assisted, however, by the failure of the EU law *acquis* to provide any such definition. In this, of course, the EU law system is far from unique. The European Convention on Human Rights, which also refers to the rule of law in its Preamble,[38] provides no definition. Nor has one been given to the rule of law by the European Court of Human Rights (which has preferred to conceive of it as an open concept and as the sum of its many manifestations, which the existence of the rule of law underscores).[39] Nor is any authoritative comprehensive definition of it attempted elsewhere in a Council of Europe context.[40] Nor has any definition been provided for the purposes of German, English or French law: indeed, difficulties in translating the concept of 'rule of law' (and in particular the issue of whether it should be rendered as *respect pour la loi* or *État de Droit*[41]) – in drafting the European Convention on Human Rights reflected deeper philosophical issues.

Various efforts, if not to define the rule of law, then at least to identify some of its core elements, have been attempted. Crabat and Bel, neatly summarize the Council of Europe's Venice Commission in this regard, say that

> "the rule of law ensures in essence that all public powers act within the constraints set out by law, in accordance with the values of democracy and fundamental rights and under the control of independent courts"[42]

Lord Bingham suggests that the core of the principle is that

> "all persons and authorities within the state, whether public or private, should be bound by and entitled to the benefit of the laws publicly made, taking effect (generally) in the future and publicly administered by the courts"[43]

In a more international context, Kofi Annan has advanced the idea of the rule of law comprising

> "a principle of governance in which all persons, institutions and entities, public and private, including the State itself, are accountable to laws that are publicly promulgated, equally enforced and independently adjudicated, and which are consistent with international human rights norms and standards."[44]

38 Which announces the signatory governments to be "resolved, as the governments of European countries which are likeminded and have a common heritage of political traditions, ideals, freedom *and the rule of law*, to take the first steps for the collective enforcement of certain of the rights stated in the Universal Declaration".

39 *W. Schroeder*, *loc. cit.*, p. 25.

40 In 2008, the Committee of Ministers asserted that no 'list of key rule of law requirements accepted by the Council of Europe, let alone a definition' could be devised. (See *W. Schroeder*, *loc. cit.*, p. 24).

41 An ambiguity mirrored in Russian.

42 *E. Crabit/N. Bel*, The EU Rule of Law Framework, Chapter 11 of *W. Schroeder*, Strengthening the Rule of Law in Europe, 2016, p. 197, 198.

43 *T. Bingham*, The Rule of Law, 2011, p. 8.

44 *K. Annan*, The Rule of Law and Transitional Justice in Conflict and Post-Conflict Societies (Report of the Secretary-General to the United Nations Security Council, 23 August 2004, S/2004/616).

Thick and Thin Conceptions of the Rule of Law

Magen has observed that "at the heart of the struggle for conceptualization of the rule of law lies a fundamental choice between what has been variably called 'formal' and 'substantive' [...] or 'rule book' as opposed to 'rights'-based understandings".[45] As the same writer puts the matter, formal conceptions "tend to stress procedural safeguards for Leviathan to obey".[46] Along these lines, Joseph Raz, in giving his (formal) account of the rule of law has thus stressed such features as the need for adequately publicized and clear rules, which should be prospective in nature and stable. Raz has also stressed such features the need for an independent judiciary, the right to a fair trial and the right to review laws for compliance with such standards as those just mentioned.[47]

The advantage of such a thin conception of the rule of law is that there is less danger of conceptual overlap and confusion. However, another consequence of adopting a 'thin' conception of the rule of law is to limit severely its impact. As Raz himself has acknowledged, under such a conception of the rule of law, 'a nondemocratic legal system, based on the denial of human rights, on extensive poverty, on racial segregation, sexual inequalities, and religious persecution may, in principle, conform with the requirements of the rule-of-law better than any of the legal systems of the more enlightened Western democracies".[48]

A 'thick' conception, on the other hand, is seen as involving adherence to substantive, material principles, such as for example, fundamental rights. This idea of the rule of law as combining both formal and material elements has found favour in many states, including for example, Germany.[49]

Whichever view is taken, it is undeniably the case that – as can be seen by the example of the European Union – invocations of the rule of law are often accompanied by simultaneous invocation of ideals such as democracy and fundamental rights. The rule of law thus generally forms one of a cluster of ideas seen as fundamental.

Notwithstanding the fact that Article 2 lists separately the values the Union is said to be founded *viz.*, respect for human dignity, freedom, democracy, equality, *the rule of law* and respect for human rights, which might be contended to argued to be evidence for a 'thin' conception of the rule of law, it is in fact a 'thick' approach to the rule of law which has found favour at European Union level, where

45 *A.* Magen, (fn. 2), p. 1052. See in more detail, *P. Craig*, Formal and Substantive Conceptions of the Rule of Law: anAn Analytical Framework, 1997, Public Law, p. 467. Note also *L. Fuller*, The Morality of Law, 1964 and *J. Raz*, The Rule of Law and its Virtue, Chapter 11, in: *J. Raz*, The Authority of Law: Essays on Law and Morality, 1979, p. 221, and see Witteveen/van der Burg (eds.), Rediscovering Fuller: Essays on Implicit Law and Institutional Design, 1999.

46 *Ibid.*

47 *J. Raz, loc. cit., [2 notes before]* (fn. 45), p. 221, cited in: Pech, p. 379.

48 *Ibid. See also J. Raz,* The Rule of Law and its Virtue in Cunningham (ed.), Liberty and the Rule of Law, 1979, p 4.

49 See *W. Schroeder*, The European Union and the Rule of Law – State of Affairs and Ways of Strengthening, 3 in Schroeder (ed.), Strengthening the Rule of Law in Europe, 2016, p. 3, 23.

the view has been taken that the concept is organically linked with concepts such as fundamental rights.

It is perhaps more accurate to say that there has been an evolution in the concept from a thin approach to a thick one. Because the concept, although frequently invoked in the Treaty, is not defined there (a phenomenon shared with nearly all national constitutional orders in Europe), its elaboration has been, for much of the history of what is now the European Union, left to the judicial branch (a phenomenon which is also common in member states). The Court started from a largely formal understanding in *Les Verts* but has gravitated over time in its case-law to a more material view and to include those material standards relevant to judicial shaping of law-making, such as legal certainty, legitimate expectations and proportionality. As *Pech* has commented, there is still work to be done to make the substantive aspect of the principle more explicit, but cases such as *Kadi* and *Pequeños* have seen the material aspect consolidated and built upon.

What else can be said of the EU concept of the rule of law beyond the foregoing? Its inclusion in so many provisions of the Treaty, and the significance attached to it by the Court of Justice mean that it cannot lightly be dismissed as a mere 'hollow slogan' or 'meaningless verbiage', to paraphrase Pech and Bingham,[50] (although as Pech observes, this is not to deny that there might be a gap between EU rhetoric and the reality of its constitutional framework).[51]

Nor, however, and notwithstanding the ruling in the *Kadi* case,[52] has the Court given it (or any other fundamental principle) the status of a supranational norm which cannot be departed from.[53] Nor does it have the status of (or, it may be added, the clarity required for) a rule of law by reference to which an act of one of the EU institutions can be annulled. Instead, its role is to provide the constitutional *justification* for review proceedings.[54] Pech further argues that as what he calls a primary constitutional principle,[55] the rule of law must always inform the interpretation of other constitutional and infra-constitutional norms.[56]

The Article 7 Procedures and the Commission's 2014 Communication 'A New EU Framework to strengthen the Rule of Law'

The insertion at Amsterdam of what is now the Article 7(2) procedure to determine the existence of a serious and persistent breach by a Member State of Article 2 TEU values, the addition at Nice of what is now the Article 7(1) procedure

50 *L. Pech*, 'A Union Founded on the Rule of Law': Meaning and Reality of the Rule of Law as a Constitutional Principle of EU Law, 2010, 6 European Constitutional Law Review, p. 359, 361, *T. Bingham*, The Rule of Law, 2007, 66 Cambridge Law Journal, p. 67, 69.

51 *Ibid.*, p. 378.

52 In which the principles of liberty, democracy and human rights and fundamental freedoms are referred to as forming part of the foundations of the Community legal order (about which the court observed no challenge would be permitted) but the rule of law is curiously overlooked. (See para. 304 of the Court's ruling.).

53 *L. Pech*, *loc cit.* (fn. 45), p. 365.

54 *Ibid., p.* 376.

55 Holding this status with principles like democracy, liberty and fundamental rights protection.

56 *Ibid.*, p. 377.

for determining that there is a clear risk of a serious breach by a Member State of Article 2 TEU values and most recently the Commission's 2014 Communication *'A New EU Framework to strengthen the Rule of Law'* have each in their turn added to the urgency of arriving at a workable conceptualization the rule of law. (Article 7 is actually about more than merely the rule of law but the 2014 Commission communication focused on this in particular.) Under Article 7, potentially severe consequences are made to attach to breaches of the rule of law. Notable features of the article, however, include its strong deference to member state sovereignty, particularly in the requirement of unanimity of all of the other member states in order to reach a determination of the existence of a serious and persistent breach of Article 2 values on the part of any member state of the EU and its preference for a political rather than a judicial process in order to determine the existence of any such breach. Both requirements seem fatal to the potential of its deployment in the current crisis involving the Polish and Hungarian governments. As for the 2014 Commission Communication, its main importance was not that it recognized for the first time the rule of law. As has already been seen, such recognition has for long been provided in both Treaty law and case-law but rather its recognition that further action is needed beyond that set out in Article 7 in order to safeguard the rule of law. The Communication is really a means of settling a rule of law dispute prior to the political deployment of Article 7 TEU – which, in political terms, was accurately compared to the use of a nuclear weapon by former Commission President Barroso. The 2014 Communication procedure is in itself incapable of achieving results against an uncooperative state. Given this, and given the political and systemic difficulties already noted in relation to Article 7, it seems strongly arguable that the combination of Article 7 and the operation of the Communication will not be an adequate or effective means of protecting the rule of law.

A particular reason why the 2014 Communication is significant for present purposes, however, is that Annex 1 to it summarizes the case law of the Court as finding the rule of law as the source of fully justiciable principles applicable within the EU legal system, of which six are deemed to be noteworthy:

a) *the principle of legality*, which in substantial terms includes a transparent, accountable, democratic and pluralistic process for enacting laws;
b) *legal certainty*, which requires *inter alia* that rules are clear and predictable; and cannot be retrospectively changed;
c) *the prohibition of arbitrariness of executive powers*; whereby any intervention by the public authorities in the sphere of private activities of any person must have a legal basis and be justified on the grounds laid down by law, and protection provided against arbitrary or disproportionate intervention.
d) *independent and effective judicial review, including respect for fundamental rights;*
e) *separation of powers, implying an independent and effective judicial review*
f) *equality before the law.*

Rather than a definition, this is more properly seen as a non-exhaustive list of of legal principles associated with the rule of law. It emulates extraordinarily closely the conceptual model of a 2011 Venice Commission report on the rule of law, which the 2014 Communication expressly cites.[57]

A Concluding Thought

Given the combination of an open and non-exhaustive definition of the rule of law with a mechanism which imposes hugely significant sanctions for breaches of this rule, how can the European Union be saved from overreaching itself in relation to the Article 7 mechanism and associated 2014 Communication procedure? It is suggested that various means exist for preventing such overreach.

One of them is that the Article 7 procedure itself has made such extensive concessions to state sovereignty as to be in its most serious consequences incapable of deployment against offending member states (given the unanimity requirement for Article 7(2) sanctions and the politically extreme nature of Article 7'sdeployment in the first place).

A second is the limitations provided for in Article 7 which limit it to clear risks of serious breaches in the case of Article 7(1) and serious and persistent breaches of Article 2 values in the case of Article 7(2). This would appear to rule out its deployment in anything other than fairly extreme situations (of which, however, there appear to be at least two in the European Union at the time of writing). Such a restriction is necessary in order to preserve the integrity of other rule of law related mechanisms in the Treaties such as Article 258.

A third means of limitation may well be to limit the conceptualization of what constitute the requirements of the rule of law and what therefore constitutes a breach thereof. Although the Commission Communication does not purport to contain a closed definition of the rule of law. It may be that the relatively restrictive nature of what is envisaged in the Annexes to the Commission Communication will nonetheless play a role in keeping Article 7 within workable bounds.

The risk of overreach is not the only cloud on the horizon, however. If the danger of promising more than the European Union is capable of delivering constitutes a Scylla threatening the viability of Treaty and non-Treaty EU procedures aimed at ensuring compliance with the rule of law, then inactivity on the part of the Union in the face of increasing blatant threats to the rule of law by some of its member states constitutes a Charybdis. The challenges facing the Union in this respect should not be under-estimated. The need for the Union to walk a fine line between overreach and inactivity never been greater. Closer analysis of the terrain upon which this line must be traced – in particular, the Article 7 TEU procedures

57 Report of the Venice Commission of 4 April 2011 Study No. 512/2009 (CDL-AD(2011)003rev).

and the procedure set out in the Commission 2014 Communication is consequently provided elsewhere in this journal.

From the uncertain to the implicit (passing by the problematic). Reflections on the reference to the rule of law and on its protection in the Treaty on European Union

*By Emmanuel Sur, Bordeaux**

In referring to the rule of law, Article 7 of the Treaty on European Union seems to invoke an agreed notion, but it is one of which only the negative meaning – the rejection of arbitrariness – occurs to us more or less spontaneously. What is its positive meaning, then? Using the examples of Britain, Germany and France, this study focuses first on the genealogy of the notion of the rule of law in order to show the indivisibility of this concept from the frameworks and traditions of states and in consequence, the semantic ambiguities of its transfer to European level. Beyond words and what we pragmatically call language, this article then investigates the main functionalities of the European reference to the idea of the rule of law.

> « *I fear those big words which make us so unhappy* »
> James Joyce, *Ullyses*

The European legal phraseology derives so much from the semantic universe of the States that the words it uses come often from such a universe. The words of the creature – Europe – logically follow those of the creators – the States – in the same way that the European emblems are part of the centuries-old political imagination already traced by the States. The historical precedence of the States explains this feeling of familiarity we feel when the words they have forged are now expressed by other mouths.

Affirming that "*The Union is founded on the values of [...] the rule of law [...]*", article 2 TEU typically refers to such anteriority as well as when it aims at the respect of human dignity, liberty, democracy or equality. If this anteriority was translated into terms of semantic primacy, then it should be supposed that irrespective of the legal significance given by the political or jurisdictional European institutions, we would have at least a little idea of what it is meant by rule of law, democracy or equality. As article 2 is apparently of recognition nature, since it is limited to refer to values on which the Union "*is based*", it would be enough, to understand it, to point out such an idea, even if the wording would necessarily be imprecise. But this approach would be far from satisfactory.

The first pitfall is that there is not only one State conception of the rule of law, but as many as there are States in the European Union. In that regard, it is quite remarkable that article 2 TEU does not use the same words in the different versions of the text. To take only three of them into consideration, the words *État de droit*

* *Dr. Emmanuel Sur*, Maître de conférences en droit public, habilité à diriger des recherches, membre du Centre de Recherche et de Documentation Européennes et Internationales (CRDEI), Faculté de droit et science politique, Université de Bordeaux.

appear in the French version, when the word *Rechtsstaatlichkeit* appears in the German version and those of *Rule of law* in the English one. Except to ignore that these different words do not have the same meaning, it is clear that article 2 does not refer to a univocal and official concept of rule of law, precisely because the EU is based on several States and not on only one. The only theoretical possibility of semantic connection between the rule of law under article 2 TEU and the Member States would consist in finding common characters to the different States' traditions using the method of overlapping, if however, this was possible and made sense.

What is more, a roughly constant principle of EU law indicates that the reference to the rule of law has to be understood in the TEU with regard to its execution matters. By hypothesis, even if these matters had nothing to do with those under the States' conceptions of the rule of law, they should necessary profit at least from a beginning of definition and thus from a minimum of semantic autonomy. At first glance, there is still a legal blur surrounding this notion, even if the formal reference to the rule of law is explicit in the TEU and the Charter of Fundamental Rights[1], and if the ECJ has already used it.[2]

But the TEU is not limited to refer to the rule of law. Its article 7 provides a coercive mechanism on two floors according to the degree of "*serious breach*" of article 2: in case of "*clear risk of a serious breach*", the Council, acting by a majority of four fifths of its members after approval by the European Parliament and on a reasoned proposal by one third of the Member States, the European Parliament or the European Commission, can see such a risk and address some recommendations to the Member State; in case of "*serious and persistent breach by a Member State*", the Council, acting unanimously this time on a proposal of one third of the Member States or of the European Commission and after approval by the European Parliament, may decide to suspend certain rights arising from the application of the treaties to the Member State in question.

In this study, we wish to approach the main difficulties that not fail to raise such provisions. The first question is quite naturally to define the concepts and to know what has to be understood by rule of law. Wishing to find some certainty, we finally meet only uncertainties. Whether it is assessed at the level of the States or of the EU, the notion of rule of law does not seem to provide the conceptual and semantic stability which would be appropriate for a legal concept on which are based some political consequences of the greatest importance. Then, the second question is to evaluate the meaning and the scope of the protection of the rule of law in the particular system of the EU. Naturally, there would be no interrogation if one considered by hypothesis that the answer was already in the question. But it

1 CFR, Preamble par. 2: "*Conscious of its spiritual and moral heritage, the Union is founded on the indivisible, universal values of human dignity, freedom, equality and solidarity; it is based on the principles of democracy and the rule of law. It places the individual at the heart of its activities, by establishing the citizenship of the Union and by creating an area of freedom, security and justice*".

2 See *L. Pech*, The Rule of Law as a Constitutional Principle of the European Union, Jean Monnet Working Paper, No. 04/09.

is well known that the legal techniques are one thing, their effects quite another. Except confusing the technique and its effects, the question of the reference to the rule of law and its protection in the TEU cannot be tackled without considering the not-written project hiding behind the words. We thus explicitly enter the implicit while giving up any certainty from the start.

The essence of the words is not in the words themselves, but in what the language conveys. Once the language acquired, grammar will be built and developed as it will progressively evolve. The rules resulting from this will be taught. But who knows grammar can remain foreign to the language. It thus seems that beyond an exegetic analysis or of a purely polemical criticism, it is necessary to ask the most general questions in order to weigh up what we regard as the European language, in this case the rule of law.

From this point of view, the uncertain meaning of the concept of rule of law according to the States must be noted (I), as well as the implicit character of the meaning and of the scope of the reference to the rule of law in the TEU (II).

I. The uncertain: the meaning of the concept of rule of law according to the States

The starting point of our analysis is the observation of a very strong contrast between, on the one hand, the polysemy of the notion of rule of law and, on the other hand, its apparently unequivocal wording in article 7 TEU. This article works *as if* this polysemy was intended to be reduced, or even to disappear, because of its integration into the TEU.[3]

For an overview, it is interesting to focus on the meaning of the rule of law in three States having exerted an influence in Europe on the legal structuring of the other States and continuing in a certain manner to do so: the United Kingdom, Germany and France.[4] Naturally, these three States do not have the monopoly of the rule of law, but their different meanings of the same concept are so far from each other that they give at least a significant idea of its polysemy.

As each State and each national dimension of the rule of law refers to a plurality of conceptions, it is essential to use sufficiently operational criteria of classification to give an idea of the substance and to avoid all peripheral considerations: the historical construction, the theoretical foundations and the political implications.

3 It is true that some of doctrinal direction to consider that the meaning of the words is given by a competent authority justifies the lack of interest in the issue of the *a priori* semantic value of words. It is unfairly it relates itself to the so-called school of realistic interpretation of the law, as the proponents of this school, starting with Hart, have never theorized this new form of arbitrariness. Indeed, we cannot confuse the act of will *of* the judge on a semantic value that is already established and the constitution of any semantic value *by* the judge.

4 For a comparative law study, see *L. Heuschling*, État de droit, Rechtsstaat, Rule of Law, 2012.

1. The historical construction of the rule of law in the United Kingdom, Germany and France

Two types of historical formation process can be distinguished: "from bottom to top", which means firstly by the courts or by the local authorities and then by the State's rules; "from top to bottom", which means with the proclamation of principles and rules by the central power.

- The United Kingdom is the archetype of a "from bottom to top" construction process. As Dicey observes in 1889:

> *« We may say that the constitution is pervaded by the rule of law on the ground that the general principles of the constitution [...] are with us the result of judicial decisions determining the rights of private persons, in particular cases before the courts; whereas under many foreign constitutions the security [...] given to the rights of individuals results, or appears to result, from the general principal of the constitution. »*[5]

In the same way, it is appropriate to approach the well-known written texts of the British Constitution (Magna Carta, 1215; the Petition of the Rights, 1628; Sir Matthew Hale's resolutions in the 1660s; the Habeas corpus, 1679; the Charter of the Rights, 1689; and the Law of Establishment, 1701) as genuine compilations of rules already built and accepted by the social body, and recognized as producing beneficial effects for the unit of the community. Of course, this does not mean that such a process has never been imposed without difficulties or resistance. Far from it, but although it may sound a bit pompous, the British genius has always shown its ability to maintain and deepen the cohesion of basic principles despite of the turmoil of the centuries.

On the opposite, the rule of law appears "from top to bottom" in Germany and France.

- In Germany, more precisely in Prussia in the first half of the 19th century, the concept of *Rechtsstaat* is theorized by the famous jurists Mohl, Stahl and Geist in opposition to the *Polizeistaat.*[6] First significant advance of individual freedom, the *Rechtsstaat* concerns the relationships between the Government and the citizens regarding their individual status. Its principles are summarized quite simply: 1. a formal law is required to avoid any arbitrary executive power; 2. the approval of Parliament (*Landtag*) is required when the State intends to intervene in the freedom and property of the person; 3. the administration should intervene *secundum legem* in the areas of the individual status of the citizens. For its part, the *Polizeistaat* is not considered as a lawless situation: it

5 Introduction to the Study of the Law of the Constitution, 3rd ed. 1889, p. 96.
6 See *B. B.-Kriegel*, L'État de droit, Dictionnaire constitutionnel, 1992, pp. 416-418.

means more the principle whereby the applicable law is that of the Government in the strict sense, as it is laid down through individual and collective rules.[7]

A new step is taken at the end of the 19th century with the first great positivist jurists. The famous theory of self-limitation defended by Jellinek now seems to express a point of tension between the dualistic and the monistic conceptions of law. It is not really dualistic, since the State, not being above law, is necessarily limited by it, but it is not either really monistic since Jellinek, by distinguishing between the legal and the social purposes of the State, subjects the knowledge of the State law to the achievement of the social State once a community is unified by a certain goal.[8]

The precarious balance of the first German positivists between dualism and monism may explain the later direction of a part of the doctrine towards a radical monism or a dualism of strict obedience. Against any form of monism, *Constitutional Theory* by Carl Schmitt, published in 1928, offers a purely voluntary approach according to which the constitution is based on the will of an immanent and substantial being: the people. For the future jurist of the Third Reich, the rule of law looks like a bourgeois screen to silence the will of the people. Against any form of dualism, the first edition of Hans Kelsen's *Pure Theory of Law*, published in 1934, regards the expression of *Rechtsstaat* as a pleonasm, since the concept of sovereignty cannot have any legal content and since the power of the State is thus summarized with the effectiveness of the legal order.[9]

The Basic Law adopted in 1949 has powerfully contributed to reorient the German thought of the *Rechtsstaat* towards the idea of complete subjection of all public authorities to the respect of the Constitution. The political ambition to guarantee the liberal character of the State and to prevent any return of Nazism results in a particularly constraining constitution which proclaims the legal intangibility of certain principles: those of the first 19 articles relating to the individual and collective basic rights; the democratic source of all powers and the federal form of the German State. This new conception of the rule of law was an indisputable success. The philosopher Jürgen Habermas even suggested the idea of constitutional patriotism to indicate the dissociation of the citizenship and the national identity, according to which patriotism would be understood like respect towards the constitutional values.[10] In other words, the reference to the nation, like

7 The distinction between the *Polizeistaat* as principle of lawlessness and as principle of subjection of the Government to its own rules is in particular established by *C. Émeri*, L'État de droit dans les systèmes polyarchiques européens, R.F.D.C., 1992, p. 112.

8 See *É. Maulin*, La théorie de l'État de Carré de Malberg, 2003, Section 6.

9 Kelsen's judgment on the theory of self-limitation is not subject to appeal. In Allgemeine Staatslehre (1925), he writes: "*The radical vice that resides in this conception dominating all the modern State theory, consists of the law is not a special content, but the form of the State, more exactly this ordering State itself with all its contents. The State cannot pursue a goal any otherwise than in the form of law; and, with regard to the report of the means for the purpose, the law and the State are always a way and never a goal. What in a bad terminology we call a goal of law is only one mean to achieve a goal, which is not the law, [...] but can be indicated as goal of culture or goal of power*", (translation by the author), p. 42.

10 See Sur l'Europe, 2006; *J. Lacroix*, Patriotisme constitutionnel et identité postnationale chez Jürgen Habermas, 2002.

the one celebrated by de Gaulle in his famous speech about "*La France éternelle*",[11] would be absent from such patriotism.

- But it is in France that the historical construction of the *État de droit* is the most complex. To summarize, four main stages deserve to be underscored.

The first is "the State of justice" and corresponds to the pre-revolutionary period.[12] Contrary to a generally accepted idea, the monarchy at the end of the XVIII° century is by no means despotic, but on the contrary collapses under the complexity of the rights and the privileges. The 18th century creates almost no new rights, instead it is confined to regulate already existing rights.[13] Before the French Revolution in 1789, the courts are taken over by a true frenzy of legal disputes, so much so that at the end of the *Ancien régime*, France is readily compared to a people of litigants. Then there is only one possibility to overcome the cumbersome procedures before the courts: the "*lit de justice"*. It was a special session of Parliament, according to the name which was then given to the jurisdictions, which allowed the King, considered as the ultimate guarantor of any justice, to overcome the decisions of the sovereign courts: *adveniente principe, cessat magistratus*.

The second stage corresponds to the period named by the jurist Raymond Carré de Malberg "the legal State".[14] It essentially acts as the new architecture of power born from the French Revolution as it is practiced under the 3rd and 4th Republics. The first concern of the Revolution is to reverse the State of justice by proclaiming from now on the primacy of the supreme political power on the law. Its basic principle is contained in article 6 of the *Declaration of the Rights of Man and of the Citizen* in August 26th, 1789: "*The law is the expression of the general will*". If such is the case, two consequences must be drawn about it: the law can not only do everything without causing any prejudice but, what is more, the judge, being "*the mouth of the law*",[15] must be subjected to it.

At the beginning of the 20th century, the legal State does not completely match the French reality of law: it is gradually diffused by posing successive brakes to the principle of the *Politzeistaat*. The French administrative law knows this principle quite well and, in a certain manner, the French venerate it since Napoleon. The criticisms come from all sides against a system which puts the Parliament in the center of the political game and which ensures limitation of power only by limiting itself. And still, the judgment is severe against the German theory of self-limitation: for Marcel de la Bigne de Villeneuve, it is a "*pure nonsense*"[16].

In its vast majority, the French doctrine is then favorable to a dualistic thought of law and State, but on very different terms which only the main will be recalled.

11 Speech at City Hall of Paris, August 25th, 1944.

12 See *J. Krynen*, L'État de justice: France XII°-XIX°siècles, 2009; *M. Fioravanti*, Stato e Costituzione: Materiali per una storia delle dottrine costituzionali, 1993.

13 See *J.-L. Mestre*, Introduction historique au droit administratif français, coll. Droit fondamental, 1985.

14 See La Loi, expression de la volonté générale, 1984.

15 *C. Montesquieu*, De l'esprit des lois, Livre XI Chapitre VI : De la Constitution d'Angleterre, 1979, p. 301.

16 In Traité général de l'État, 1929, p. 221.

On behalf of a sociological positivism, the lawyer from Bordeaux Léon Duguit estimates that the "*objective law*" (*droit objectif*) is the law formed in the entrails of the society by the feeling of solidarity binding the men while "*the State law*" (*droit de l'État*) is only the recognition of this "*objective law*". The French natural law has not abdicated to positivism, while voluntarist doctrines flatter the idea of sovereignty of the people at the very same time when the Parliament is considered to be primarily responsible for the ills of the country.

The third stage starts in 1958, when the new constitution wanted by general de Gaulle to decrease the powers of the Parliament and to increase those of the president of the Republic creates a new public body in charge to sanction any inclination of the Parliament to intervene in the area of the executive: the *Conseil constitutionnel*, precisely nick-named "*the watchdog of the executive"* in the beginning of the 5th Republic. But in a fundamental decision of July 16th, 1971, whose real motivations remain still fuzzy in spite of the official versions,[17] the *Conseil constitutionnel* extends its competence to review the constitutionality of the laws to the whole preamble of the Constitution, which means mainly the 1789 Declaration. In 1971, the legal State, already strongly weakened in 1958, becomes a constitutional State including a substantial control of the laws with respect to the fundamental rights.

2. *The main theoretical foundations and political implications of the rule of law in the United Kingdom, Germany and France*

In its basic sense, the rule of law means the subjection of the State to the law. Three questions deserve to be asked: the status of such a subjection, its content and its limits.

- The first observation is that, especially in Germany and France, the very status of this principle of subjection is unclear because it can be the subject of – at least – two radically different approaches.

According to the first approach, which meets Kelsen's normative, the principle of subjection is nothing else than a sham since the "law in itself" (*la juridicité*) can only be imagined within the "State in itself" (*l'étaticité*) and vice versa. The identification of a State cannot proceed from a deductive approach starting from prescriptive external criteria, but is based on the existence of a binding legal order. The rule of law is thus a pleonasm, since any binding legal order reveals a State. The direct consequence is logical: the *étaticité* is not based on any intrinsic political quality, since it can give birth to the best and to the worst without it changes its nature.

Rather curiously, this approach is regularly denounced by some German and French jurists as being hostile to the liberal requirements of modern States. This

17 For a non-academic but realistic point of view, see the journalist *É. Zemmour*, Le suicide français, 2014, p. 32 : La trahison des pairs.

criticism is very disconcerting, as it blithely mixes certain political requirements and the conditions of the *juridicité*. Not only Kelsen is by no means hostile to the liberal requirements of modern States, since he is one of the first jurists to have highlighted them, but all his thought of the constitutional architecture only aims at protecting freedoms. So to say that what we understand today by rule of law corresponds for Kelsen to the State, *plus* certain political requirements which do not imply *in themselves* any subjection since the power of State and the effectiveness of a legal order are one and the same thing.
According to the second approach, the rule of law is on the contrary a particular quality of some States, whose power is indeed subject to the respect of an external rule.[18] The assumptions of this approach are clear: law may be some object of knowledge, regardless of the area – moral or metaphysical – to which it relates; the power of the State is distinct from law and acquires some dignity only on condition that it serves such law. So there are at least two distinct types of States: the *États de droit* and those which are not.[19]
Even when it is based on the goodwill of the world, this approach leads logically to three worrying consequences. The first is that there is often only one step between the dualistic thought and the dogmatic thought, if we mean by that a thought being contingent on a structure of certainty.[20] In practice, we all know that the logic of knowledge can easily oppose the political freedom it is supposed to defend. All the tyrannies come from a structure of certainty excluding any doubt. The second is that by focusing on law, the dualistic logic leaves untouched the question of the power of the State, which then resembles the Hobby is marine monster swimming in open waters. Thus, the dualistic logic creates its weakness where it believes to find its force: the power of the State only requires to be reinvested by any theory of sovereignty, which always ends by sweeping any legal requirement. More largely, the third is that on the international level, the concrete translation of the distinction between the *États de droit* and the others doesn't even have to be described.[21]
However, the connection between the British notion of rule of law and the principle of subjection seems easier to define. If the two meanings (and not the two conditions) of the rule of law set out by Dicey in 1889 are taken into considera-

18 The genealogy of such an approach would be tiresome to establish, but it is necessary to point out the "accidental" role played in France by the Marxist ideology. Official ideology of almost all of the French intelligentsia from the *Libération* until the 1980s, Marxism ridicules the rule of law as the triumphant form of the bourgeois State. Progressively facing the reality of the Communist regimes, the Marxists' speeches begin to change from the 1970s. Former Marxists become unconditional supporters of the rule of law as a substantially distinct State while others, such as Alain Badiou calling in an unbelievable paper published in *Le Monde* in 1979 to protect the Khmer Rouge from "*an act of barbarism*", remain loyal to their political beliefs. See *A. Badiou*, Kampuchea vaincra!, Le Monde, January 17th, 1979.

19 For a particularly significant illustration of this approach, see *B. B.-Kriegel*, L'État et les esclaves, 1989.

20 Structure of certainty opposed by Kelsen to the "*relative truth*" in La démocratie: sa nature – sa valeur, 2004, p. 84.

21 See *J. Derrida* and *J. Habermas*, Le "concept" du 11 septembre, 2003. The authors analyse the "*autoimmune disease*" of the occidental democracies resulting from the need to deploy non-democratic means to defend themselves against the terrorist threat and criticize the American doctrine of the rogue States as being necessarily aggressive.

tion,[22] one quickly realizes that they do not refer to a theoretical model, but on the contrary to an already existing practice. In other words, the subjection here refers to the spontaneous, and not forced, recognition of principles and legal rules deserving to be respected. If a more recent interpretation of the rule of law is now taken into consideration, such as for example that of Tom Bingham in 2011,[23] one realizes that it is about the same, even if some criteria have been revised because of the political evolution of the United Kingdom.

- While the question of the status of the subjection is problematic, the content of such subjection seems apparently more simple.

Here again, the British conception of the rule of law seems quite unique. Even if the extensive reading of article 2 § 1 of the *European Communities Act* 1972[24] by the British courts could accredit the idea of importation of external criteria to the rule of law, the British constitutional practice shows, on the contrary, that no "fundamental right" cannot be considered as such unless the Parliament has allowed it explicitly, even if for granting a superior legal value, as is the case in the *European Communities Act*.

Directly or indirectly, the rule *of* law still refers to the rule *by* law, which means to contents that cannot be determined in advance but which implementation provides some minimum rules. In our opinion, it is wrongly that we usually consider the rule *by* law as a subset of the rule *of* law, which means as a procedural condition to which substantial criteria should be added. Reality reveals exactly the opposite: the rule *of* law is only a doctrinal *a priori* which receives its solemn consecration by the national law. So it seems also erroneous of considering the attribution of a discretionary competence by the law as an exception to the rule of law.[25]

In Germany or in France, the choice between a dualistic and a monist approach weakly affects the content of the rule of law. The monist approach explicitly supposes the *étaticité* and regards the additional criteria as political ones, whereas the

22 *1. "No man is punishable or can lawfully be made to suffer in body or goods except for a distinct breach of law established in the ordinary courts of the land [...]"; 2. "Here every man, whatever be his rank or condition is subject to the ordinary law of the realm and amenable to the jurisdiction of the ordinary tribunals"*, op. cit.

23 See The Rule of law, 2011: "*the accessibility of the law*"; "*application of the law and not exercise of discretion for questions of legal rights and liability*"; "*ministers and public officers at all levels must exercise the powers conferred on them in good faith, fairly, for the purpose for which the powers were conferred*"; "*adequate protection of fundamental Human Rights*"; "*means must be provided for resolving bona fide civil disputes*"; "*a fair trial*"; "*compliance by the State with its obligations in international law*"; "*protection of the people against terrorism*".

24 "*All such rights, powers, liabilities, obligations and restrictions from time to time created or arising by or under the Treaties, and all such remedies and procedures from time to time provided for by or under the Treaties, as in accordance with the Treaties are without further enactment to be given legal effect or used in the United Kingdom shall be recognised and available in law, and be enforced, allowed and followed accordingly; and the expression and similar expressions shall be read as referring to one to which this subsection applies*".

25 Contra: *M.-F. Toinet*, Le pouvoir politique en Grande-Bretagne, 1990, pp. 71-72. In our opinion, the most striking example is the Patriot Act voted in 2001 by the Congress of the United States of America. Most English and American jurists saw there a perhaps debatable law, but in conformity with the rule *by* law, while many continental jurists saw an unbearable attack against the rule *of* law.

dualistic approach implicitly supposes the *étaticité* and regards the criteria of the rule of law as intrinsically legal.

The definition of the criteria of the *étaticité* is generally addressed in reference to two main criteria. The first criterion, *sine qua non*, is always the separation of powers because it is well known, since Montesquieu and Kant that the *res publica* could not exist if the authority to enforce the law was the same as that in charge to make it. The other correlative criterion is also known: a set of legal rules objectively defined as legal by the shape they borrow and sanctioned by the public authorities, which already assumes the existence of a central power. On the other hand, the question of the definition of the additional criteria, political for some and legal for others, is much more problematic although two series of criteria are generally proposed: those concerning the consecration and the protection of the fundamental rights and those concerning the political participation.[26]

In other words, the tension between two very different logics of the rule of law cannot be ignored: the liberal logic, according to which the protection of rights is sufficient, the void left by politics being now occupied by the regulatory judge and the economy; the democratic logic, which presupposes a permanent process of legitimization of the rights and, consequently, of the judge's activity. However, as rightly noted Slobodan Milacic, "*The history proved us empirically and the analysis confirmed: there is no lasting freedom without stable democracy*".[27] This tension has found a point of balance, certainly precarious and unstable, in the "constitutional democracy" or in the "liberal democracy", but it seems today largely outdated for the benefit of all-liberal ideology, that is to say at the expense of democracy.

- The limits of the subjection to law offer contrasting answers in the three States we are interested in. If the British rule *by* law only allows in principle the national legislature to determine the subjection to the principles and rules it lays down directly or indirectly, there is also a broad political consensus on the need to respect the constitution. Whether the constitution is fully respected is another matter. In Germany, there does not exist one single category of law which may not be subjected to the respect of the Constitution, including the amendments of the constitution subjected to the respect of the Basic Rights and the federal structure of the State. In the matter of constitutional order, Germany is thus with Austria the most protective European State.

The French conception of subjection to law is much more limited, since the constitutional review of laws relates to the laws voted by the Parliament on an optional basis only and to the organic laws, in charge with supplementing the constitution, on an obligatory basis. Other laws, i.e. the referendum laws[28] and the

26 About the interpretation of the Republican principle as a principle of participation and not only of protection, see *Q. Skinner*, La liberté avant le libéralisme, 2000.

27 See L'État de droit pour quoi faire?, Mélanges Jean Gicquel: Constitutions et Pouvoirs, 2008, p. 174.

28 Decision n° 62-20 DC, November 6th, 1962; Decision DC n° 92-313, September 23rd, 1992.

amendments to the constitution[29], can by no means be submitted to the *Conseil constitutionnel*.

In France, the constitutional review of the laws voted by the Parliament is still often seen as politically illegitimate, including by the governments, even if it is accepted for a long time as a legal technique. In 1993, Mr. Édouard Balladur, then Prime Minister, was publicly indignant about censorship of a law on the control of immigration by the *Conseil constitutionnel*. Finally, the Congress of Parliament amended the Constitution and then voted again the initial law. If the reactions are now quieter, they still sometimes refer to the remark made by a former Minister: "*you are legally wrong because you are politically minority*".

But the French fascination for a supreme political power released from any legal coercion expresses itself mainly through the justification for the absence of jurisdictional control on the amendments of the constitution, while the Germans estimate perfectly normal that it may be subjected to the respect of the Constitution. The issue, appeared on July 10th 1940 about giving full powers to Maréchal Pétain by the left-wing Assembly elected in 1936, curiously did not had a single wrinkle since. At the price of an obvious confusion between the (sovereign) constituent power and the power of constitutional amendment (legally formed, so subject to the constitution), Georges Vedel justified the dominant conception of the political supremacy this way:

> *"There beyond this network of distributed skills, there's a legal place where democratic sovereignty is exercised without sharing. This place is the constituent power. Derived constituent power is not a power of a different nature than the original constituent power."*[30]

Regarding the question of the limits of the *État de droit*, the French response is clear: the supreme political power will always have the last word. The conclusion is therefore that if there are common directions between the United Kingdom, Germany and France on the conceptualization of the rule of law, there is no consensus on its status, its content and its range.

II. The implicit: the meaning and the scope of the reference to the rule of law in the TEU

Neither the nominal reference to the rule of law nor the reference to the rule of law as a possible motive for a sanction against a Member State are a novelty of the TEU.[31] But for justifying sanctions, the rule of law must acquire some seman-

29 Decision n° 2003-469 DC, March 26th, 2003.

30 Schengen et Maastricht, R.F.D.A., 1992, pp. 173-174. The argument is almost word for word the same than in the first edition of his Manuel de droit constitutionnel published in 1949.

31 Since the Treaty of Amsterdam, the EU Council had competence to sanction a Member State because of "*serious and persistent breach*" of the values of the EU. The treaty of Nice then set up a preventive procedure in the event of "*clear and serious risk of violation*" of the basic rights by a Member State.

tic value, even if such a value is partly granted by the authorities in charge to interpret it. So it is clear that the determination of such a value is before all an intellectual operation induced by the requirement to justify the use of a procedure by a political institution: the EU Council. In other words, the very notion of rule of law becomes a quasi-criminal concept whose meaning depends of the understanding of the legal architecture in which it fits.
This intellectual approach is certainly necessary to understand a main dimension of articles 2 and 7 TEU, but it is insufficient to understand all their dimensions. It could be relevant to adopt another logic of analysis, on the basis of the simple idea that the interest of these articles does not only lie in what they are supposed to protect – and to sanction –, but also in the effects which they are likely to produce. On this question also, it seems that there is a gap between the apparent claim of such provisions and their functional interest in the current political context.
The implicit character of the meaning and the scope of the reference to the rule of law in the TEU is obviously not without raising theoretical questions and opening political prospects.

1. The main theoretical questions raised by the rule of law in the TEU

- The first question that arises is obviously that of the legitimacy of a legal architecture which apparently uses the rule of law *against* the States. The response corresponds to the common base of European legitimacy in a general way: the TEU, like all the European treaties, is based on the will of the States such as it has been expressed by all of them at the time of the ratification process. But as convincing this answer in legal terms may seem, it is not entirely devoid of ambiguities.

Chief among them is the use of a formal notion of legitimacy certainly finding its basis in democracy, but only in representative democracy. The extreme devaluation from which this classical form suffers in the name of the eternal opposition between the people and their representatives finds one of its causes in their chronic confrontation regarding the EU. The parliamentary ratifications are only a mere formality when the rare referendums are generally balanced by unfavorable votes. In this manner, article 7 TEU may be perceived as a weapon invented by the elites to extend at the European level the domination they already enjoy at the State level through the mechanisms of representative democracy. Unfortunately, no one can prevent it could be perceived this way. Even less so – it is here the second ambiguity – that this idea is echoed in some minority but significant theories of law, whose conclusions would certainly consider the impossibility for an international organization to assess whether a State respects rule of law or not.[32]

32 We think primarily about Schmitt's voluntarism according to whom what concerns the constituent act (sovereignty of the State and fundamental political rules) can only be decided by the people. Such voluntarism, very fashionable in the French doctrine in the 1990s, may be subject to various interpretations. Olivier

If one must consider that the legitimacy of the EU is based above all upon the representative democracy within the States, then it is coherent to regard as legitimate the system of sanction set up by the EU. But at the same time, such legitimacy exists only because the EU is not a State. Indeed, two States cannot sanction each other on the basis of what each expects from the other, but two States can establish a common mechanism to sanction them on the basis of the mutual obligations defined by such common will. The point is that the EU is not a State, because it does not hold *Kompetenz-Kompetenz* but on the contrary enforces its jurisdiction on the basis of the competences delegated by the States. Consequently, the EU's legitimacy does not pose any particular legal problem, even when it relates to the power of sanction against States. All States have wanted such power of sanction; each one, in the name of its sovereignty, can no longer take it and leave the Union.

- A second question which is not explicitly resolved by the TEU is the extent of the Council's competence in accordance with article 7. If one sticks strictly to what constitutes the basis of the European legitimacy, i.e. the will of States expressed in the forms of representative democracy, one should normally understand that the Council's competence is strictly limited to the field of application of the TEU.

However, it was noted that in the recent period, several proposals have been made to extend the jurisdiction of the ECJ to the compatibility check of any national measure with the fundamental rights of the UE, or even to make the CFR enforceable against Member States in every situation.[33] Even if it seems that such proposals would assume an unlikely revision of the treaties, they would, if they were adopted, purely and simply remove any ability for States to define what they mean by rule of law, that is to say to govern themselves freely notwithstanding the respect for the EU law.

To say the least, we would come in such case to a very paradoxical conception of political freedom, since the capacity of action would not be guided by an informed choice between an infinity of possibilities, but by conformity of the action to a unique rule considered as good. To return to a well-known distinction made by Kant in *Towards Perpetual Peace* between republicanism and dogmatism, the EU would evolve towards dogmatism, since it would choose a principle of subjection to a truth closed on itself.[34]

- But the main question lies in the content of the rule of law protected by article 2 TEU as well as in in the articulation between its various elements. The diffi-

Beaud proposed one, meant to liberalize Schmitt, see La souveraineté de l'État, le pouvoir constituant et le traité de Maastricht, 1993, p. 1046.

33 *D. Kochenov/L. Pech/S. Platon*, Ni panacée ni gadget: le nouveau cadre de l'Union européenne pour renforcer l'État de droit, RTD Eur., 2015, p. 689. This is respectively the proposal made by the advocate general Mr Poiares Maduro in his conclusions on the case of *Centro Europa*, and that of the Commissioner for the Justice Mrs Viviane Reding in 2013.

34 Vers la paix perpétuelle, 1991.

culty is that no one of them makes it possible to give a legal consistency to such a concept.

Important indications are however in a document presented by the Commission on 11th March 2014 concerning "*A new EU framework to strengthen the rule of law*".[35] José Manuel Barroso summarized thus the general philosophy of it: "*The rule of law is one of the founding pillars of the European Union. This is what our Union is built upon* […]", while Viviane Reding was more emphatic: "*Respect for the rule of law is a prerequisite for the protection of all other fundamental values upon which our Union is founded.*"[36]

Based on a report of the Venice Commission[37], the text presents some principles meant to be common to the constitutional traditions of the Member States.[38] Those principles include legality, which implies a transparent, accountable, democratic and pluralistic process for enacting laws; legal certainty; prohibition of arbitrariness of the executive powers; independent and impartial courts; effective judicial review including respect for fundamental rights; and equality before the law.

While the vast majority seems to be satisfied with such principles, it seems at first glance that there is at least one notable absentee: the separation of powers. Yet, we know since Montesquieu that there can be no political freedom without separation of powers[39] and since Kant that it is a prerequisite of the distinction between the public and the private will.[40] But this "oversight" is easily explained: the EU is not a State, and thus is not subjected to the fundamental condition to which all the States are subjected because of the rule of law: the separation of powers. Moreover, the notion has no special legal status within the EU, since the ECJ has only had reference to the typically liberal notion of balance of powers designating the acceptable point of "*functional cooperation*"[41]. However, the po-

35 COM (2014) 158 final. On 19th March, a new document cancels the English version and replaces it with a new on account of a translation error concerning "*The fundamental importance of the rule of law for the EU*": COM (2014) final/2.

36 IP-14-237_EN.

37 Venice Commission, 4th April 2011, Study n° 512/2009 (CDL - AD (2011) 003rev).

38 On the idea of a European model of rule of law, see *É. Carpano*, État de droit et droits européens, 2005.

39 Op. cit., p. 294: "*When the legislative and executive powers are united in the same person, or in the same body of magistrates, there can be no liberty; because apprehensions may arise, lest the same monarch or senate should enact tyrannical laws, to execute them in a tyrannical manner*" (translation by the author).

40 "*Republicanism is the political principle of the separation of executive power (Government) and the legislature; despotism is the principle whereby the State makes implementation of its own laws, as a result it is the public will wielded by the head of State as if it were his private will*"(translation by the author), in Vers la paix perpétuelle, 1991, pp. 86-87.

41 In the words of Mr. Jean-Marc Sauvé, Vice President of the French *Conseil d'État*, in 130ème anniversaire du Conseil supérieur de la magistrature "Séparation des pouvoirs et droit de l'Union européenne": Le rôle du "comité 255" dans la séparation des pouvoirs au sein de l'Union européenne, Document Conseil d'État, Paris, jeudi 24 octobre 2013. See also CJE, 23 avril 1986, Les Verts c. Parlement européen, aff. 294/83. One can consider that the Court behaves as "*real constitutional court responsible for ensuring the constitutional within the Community system balance*", in *M. Karpenschif/C. Nourissat*, Les grands arrêts de la jurisprudence de l'Union européenne, 2010, p. 123. But more generally "*distribution of assignments, characteristic of the Community institutional system, is not in fact a modality of the separation of powers and cannot be for this reason that institutions do not proceed from one and same legitimacy*" (translation by the author), in *J. Boulouis*, Droit institutionnel de l'Union européenne, 1997, p. 159.

litical contradiction is obvious: the legal nature of the EU does not justify that it can be unaware of the fundamental condition of the rule of law when it claims at the same time to impose the model of it. In general, who cannot do the less can even less do the more.

But the principles identified by the Commission reveal once more a systemic imbalance of the EU between the liberal and the democratic principles.

First, this imbalance is formal, since article 2 TEU regards "*rule of law*" and "*democracy*" as two "*values*" of the EU without including them one in the other. At a pinch, one could understand such a semantic distinction but according to the States' constitutional traditions, it would be expected that the two terms were related to the functional exercise of political power. From this point of view, it is very disappointing that regarding the rule of law, the only reference of the Commission to democracy relates to the law-making process and thus merely to a technical aspect.

Second, this imbalance is also statutory, since in the EU's system, democracy is certainly a fundamental political value, but it has only a *secundum legem* legal value. If the EU's legitimacy relies on the will of States, its purpose is to define a common framework of government. That is to say that it cannot, by nature, accept all the democratic requirements from the Member States. Thus, democracy cannot constitute a basis for the EU, but an operative mode within the protection of fundamental and non-negotiable values.[42]

Third, this imbalance is also functional, since the EU's system has a very low potential for democratic negotiation of rights due to the omnipotence of the jurisdictional power. The legitimacy of the judge is by no means in question, but it is obvious that the more the definition of the rights depends on the jurisdictional power, the more it acquires with time a not easily negotiable rigid form.

For the Member States, the European primacy of the liberal principle can lead to situations of direct confrontation with the expression of democracy. As we know, it is what happened when Hungary democratically adopted a new constitution in 2011, which seemed to question some of the values protected by the UE. Legally, such a confrontation is inevitable, insofar as such values enter the field of application of the TEU. But politically, it is obvious that it illustrates the voluntary inversion of the primacy of the liberal principle to the profit of the democratic principle. Now, in this area, any imbalance is alarming, wherever it's coming from and whatever may be the cause. As superbly says Slobodan Milacic in the name of a certain idea of liberal democracy which we can deplore the evanescence: "*The rule of law ensures the conditions of freedom and its use. Democracy gives it content, if not a soul. And then, finally, how unfair would be freedom without equality and how sad would be equality without freedom.*"[43]

42 What is more, article 7 can lead the Council to deprive a State of its democratic participation to this institution.

43 Op. cit. (translation by the author).

2. *The main political prospects opened up by the rule of law in the TEU*

Once understood the general architecture of the rule of law in the TEU, it is not forbidden to evaluate its principal political prospects.

- First, it can reasonably be thought that the two levels of reaction envisaged in article 7 TEU correspond to a police logic of the rule of law, not very compatible with the climate of trust and respect which must characterize the relations between the EU and the Member States. Actually, it is quite impossible to imagine for a moment that a State, whatever it has done, could be devoid of voting rights within the Council. Not only such a situation would be fraught with consequences for the democratic principle, but it would be also catastrophic in symbolic terms. What would be said of a Europe of fraternity that would ban one of its own?

This is particularly true, given that under article 354 TFEU[44] defining the voting methods applicable to article 7 TEU, it is almost certain that the "big" States will never be affected, even if there could be serious reasons. It has even been suggested that the Member States had voluntarily instituted a procedure which implementation would be nearly impossible to protect themselves.[45]
Using its initiative under article 7, the Commission seems to have understood such disadvantages by proposing on March 11th, 2014, a preliminary procedure within "*A new EU framework to strengthen the rule of law*"[46]. This new frame-

44 (ex article 309 TEC): "*For the purposes of Article 7 of the Treaty on European Union on the suspension of certain rights resulting from Union membership, the member of the European Council or of the Council representing the Member State in question shall not take part in the vote and the Member State in question shall not be counted in the calculation of the one third or four fifths of Member States referred to in paragraphs 1 and 2 of that Article. Abstentions by members present in person or represented shall not prevent the adoption of decisions referred to in paragraph 2 of that Article.*
For the adoption of the decisions referred to in paragraphs 3 and 4 of Article 7 of the Treaty on European Union, a qualified majority shall be defined in accordance with Article 238(3)(b) of this Treaty.
Where, following a decision to suspend voting rights adopted pursuant to paragraph 3 of Article 7 of the Treaty on European Union, the Council acts by a qualified majority on the basis of a provision of the Treaties, that qualified majority shall be defined in accordance with Article 238(3)(b) of this Treaty, or, where the Council acts on a proposal from the Commission or from the High Representative of the Union for Foreign Affairs and Security Policy, in accordance with Article 238(3)(a).
For the purposes of Article 7 of the Treaty on European Union, the European Parliament shall act by a two-thirds majority of the votes cast, representing the majority of its component Members".

45 See *P. Verluise*, EU: suspend a Member State, *www.diploweb.com*.

46 Op. cit. In 2006, the Commission also set up a "*Mechanism for cooperation and verification*" with Romania and Bulgaria, leading to an exchange of reports between the States and the Commission.

work includes three main stages: 1. Commission assessment;[47] 2. Commission recommendation;[48] 3. Follow-up to the Commission recommendation.[49]
At first, this procedure is innovative enough to arouse interest, since it is both much more flexible than article 7 and more respectful of the States. It has been initiated on January 13th, 2016, with Poland, about the dispute over the composition of the Constitutional Court, the absence of publication of its judgments, as well as on the effectiveness of the constitutional review of the new laws, including a law on the media. Following a first notice on the rule of law in Poland on June 1St, 2016,[50] the Commission, considering the response of the Polish Government as insufficient, sent 21 recommendations in December, including a recommendation to fully execute the decisions of the Constitutional Court[51]. On October 25th, 2016, the EU Parliament also voted recommendations to the Commission on the establishment of a new EU mechanism for democracy, rule of law and fundamental rights.[52]

If it is clear that the Parliament wishes to strengthen the control on the rule of law, it is much more difficult to understand to difference between the procedure instituted by the Commission and the first stage under article 7, i.e. the capacity of the Council to make recommendations to the State in question. In both cases, the effects are actually strictly the same, in such a way that the interest in this procedure is considerably attenuated. The Commission, aware of the consequences of the rules laid down by article 354 TFEU, maybe tried to bypass them for its own benefit, the only difference being that it cannot suspend the voting rights of the State in question within the Council.

- Second, such methods for the protection of the rule of law are fraught with consequences for the political nature of European integration, and thus for the perception of the Union by the people.

47 The Commission will collect and examine all the relevant information and assess whether there are clear indications of a systemic threat to the rule of law. If, as a result, the Commission is of the opinion that there is indeed a situation of systemic threat to the rule of law, it will initiate a dialogue with the Member State concerned, by sending its "rule of law opinion", which will be a warning to the Member State – and substantiating its concerns. It will give the Member State concerned the possibility to respond.

48 Unless the matter has already been satisfactorily resolved, the Commission will issue a "rule of law recommendation" addressed to the Member State. It will recommend that the Member State solves the problems identified within a fixed time limit and informs the Commission of the steps taken to that effect. The Commission will make public its recommendation.

49 The Commission will monitor the follow-up given by the Member State to the recommendation. If there is no satisfactory follow-up within the time limit set, the Commission can resort to one of the mechanisms set out in Article 7 TEU.

50 MEMO/16/2017.

51 IP-16-4476.

52 2015/2254 (INL). The "European Pact" proposed by the Parliament would work in the following manner: objective criteria would help to assess the situation of democracy, the rule of law and human rights; a panel of independent experts would propose a report on the situation in the Member States and would make draft recommendations by country; the report and the recommendations would be adopted by the Commission; inspired by the "European semester" budget, a European semester on human rights would take place, as a result of the adoption of this report.

Originally based on the pragmatic logic of the Schuman declaration, European integration gradually relied on human rights to create a political identity around liberal values. As much as a process of identity construction is always a condition of sustainability of a political organization,[53] such sustainability is ensured only if it relies, at least partly, on reality.[54] This reality is always infinitely complex, since it mixes the transcendent, the material, the politics and the symbolic, but the true genius of Europe used to take support on reality to propose active solidarities in the name of principles. But from now on, it seems to take support on primarily moral principles to impose the constitution of a moral order regardless of reality. Such an inversion is not without producing perverse effects.

From this point of view, the situation in many Central and Eastern European States admitted in the EU at the last enlargements is particularly alarming. For those among them which are the object of a procedure before the Commission, one cannot prevent the risk for the EU to be perceived like a "liberal club" against which "*illiberal*"[55] impulses are burgeoning. The construction of a State identity *against* European identity is not even a risk any more: it's an ongoing process that no one knows the outcome yet. However, three possibilities can be imagined: a regularization of the legal situation at the cost of inevitable internal confrontations; the exit from the EU; the reconstruction of the EU around a core group of States.[56]

But the primarily moral dimension of the European identity is also an ongoing issue in the States which are not the object of a procedure before the Commission. Indeed, no one ignores two simultaneous phenomena: the recurring criticism of the liberal ideology; the spectacular development of political parties at the two extremes of the political chessboard. If the example of France is taken, the rise to power of the *Front National*, the maintenance on a high electoral level of the *France insoumise* and the significant number of small anti-system formations make it possible to relativize the credit which are supposed to enjoy the liberal values. And of course for living, even values need the people to make them live.

- Finally, it should be noted that all the methods of integration of a political space, starting with European integration, should necessarily be accompanied by a common defense. Indeed, the European protections of the rule of law would probably be more effective if they were diffused within a Europe united

53 See the excellent realistic analysis of the integrating force of fundamental rights in the context of the "Good Friday Agreement" between the United Kingdom and the Republic of Ireland: *I. Bacik/S. Livingstone*, Towards a Culture of Human Rights in Ireland, 2001.

54 De Gaulle said in 1953: "*To be able to lead to valid solutions, it is necessary to take account of reality. Policy is anything else than the art of realities. However, reality, it is that Europe is currently composed of nations. It is starting from these nations that it is necessary to organize Europe and, if it is necessary, to defend it*", in De Gaulle a déclaré, Espoir n°26, 1979 (translation by the author).

55 In the words of the Hungarian Prime Minister Mr. Viktor Orbán in his speech on July 26th, 2014: http://budapestbeacon.com/public-policy/full-text-of-viktor-orbans-speech-at-baile-tusnad-tusnadfurdo-of-26-july-2014/10592.

56 Maybe a new Machiavelli would teach that the return to Carolingian Europe is the goal sought by the advocates of the rule of law.

by a true common defense. Paradoxically, the EU protection of the rule of law could be a brake on its evolution, since, as things stand, it is a source of discord while a common defense would be a source of unity with the rule of law as a goal.

So far, NATO has been the safe haven of a Europe which wouldn't and anyway couldn't develop a common defense. For three decades at least, the American administration complained to the European States of their weak financial participation in the NATO budget, the participation percentage having never varied since the creation of the organization in 1949. The new American president Mr. Donald Trump took his account of such criticisms, while stating that he intended to draw concrete conclusions on the level of the American engagement in Europe. At the same time, the Russian Government has not hesitated to intervene twice on its western border: in 2008 in Georgia; in 2014 in Ukraine.

In view of all that, it is clear that Europe might enter into a phase of history where it has never been more vulnerable. But we could make this weakness a force, if we considered that before the protection of rule of law, we should first protect the States on behalf of an unwavering European fraternity, without conditions of any kind.

The reference of the TEU to the rule of law only apparently borrows from the semantic register of the States, since the few elements on which it is based create the idea of a common concept when there are actually only basic divergences. Its protection mechanisms are certainly comprehensible according to a functional logic, but the analysis reveals obvious tensions, even contradictions, between the sought-after goal and the produced effects. Moreover, the geopolitical challenges that Europe will be facing in the coming years should more encourage it to search a convergence of the fundamental interests instead of focusing on a moral assessment of the States.

But in a general way, the European ground is by nature evolutionary, even if it proclaims “closed” values. For this reason, it finally seems to us that the question of rule of law depends only on the goal that the States will give to the EU. Should remain this organization so singular that no words can describe it, should it disappear in favour of existing States or should it instead replace them? Nobody knows yet, even if there are serious indices about the goal that the EU gives to itself. All that is known is that anyway the State will ultimately prevail, since no State has never said “*I am not an État de droit*” and when it says “*I am an État de droit*”, it is already something else.

Fundamental rights, EU membership and Art. 7 TEU

*By Aalt Willem Heringa, Maastricht**

When to apply art. 7 TEU in the context of human rights violations by EU member states? How does art. 7 relate to art. 258 TFEU, art 259 TFEU, the Charter, the European Convention on Human Rights and the Court in Strasbourg? And does, and if so how, the 2014 Framework, which according to the wording, predominantly focuses on the Rule of Law, incorporate human rights violations. What violations of human rights would trigger the application of the 2014 Framework and of art. 7 TFEU; and would application of the Framework be a necessary first step for any application of art. 7 TEU, or does the Framework apply to the Rule of Law only and may serious human rights violations only be taken into account as long as and when they can be considered as violations of the Rule of Law? Do human rights equal rule of law and vice versa in the context of the Framework and art. 7 TEU? These are the issues that will be dealt with in this article. And my analysis will lead to a variety of conclusions, with quite a few open ends, since we will have to wait and see how these instruments will develop in practice. However, some conclusions may be drawn such as:

1. *first of all we can conclude that the 2014 Framework and art. 7 TEU do not fully match concerning the applicability of all art. 2 TEU values*
2. *primordial in the guarantees as applied so far in practice (Poland, Hungary, Romania) is the presence of an effective, independent and sufficiently powerful national judiciary which will have to secure the constitutional balance but must and may also provide protection against human rights violations and is therefore crucial in preventing and punishing systemic violations. The absence of effective courts may be considered a rule of law violation but also as a violation of fair trial as such, specifically the reduction of powers and /or independence of a constitutional court*
3. *the Framework mechanism specifically with regard to human rights focuses on structural deficiencies which may be difficult to handle by the individual petitioning system of the ECHR: for instance, the curtailing of a constitutional court may, when other courts with effective powers do exist, be difficult to question by the ECtHR. In that respect the Framework sits in an area (integrity, stability or the proper functioning of the institutions and safeguard mechanisms) which falls largely outside the scope of the ECtHR and may not always be fit for an individual challenge*
4. *for human rights violations the Framework and art. 7 TEU may be considered as last option: national remedies, access to the EctHR, art. 258 TFEU, inter-state petitions under the EU and the ECHR, application of the Charter*

* Professor of comparative constitutional law, Maastricht University. Author of Constitutions Compared, Intersentia 2016, 4th edition and of Legal Education, Intersentia, 2013.

and collaboration between national courts and the ECJ, discussion between the EP and national parliaments and the Commission and states, reports by the FRA, collaboration with the Venice Commission and the Council of Europe, can be seen as a variety of tools that are available to tackle or prevent systemic human rights violations. A Rule of Law Scoreboard, as an addendum to the Justice Scoreboard within an European semester like framework may be an interesting suggestion in that respect

5. *and furthermore proposals are being forwarded to work with the ECtHR when defining systemic violations and to seek further tools and mechanisms and collaborations and benchmarks to enable monitoring human rights observance closely*

I. Introduction

Let's forget the Brexit for a while and assume that the UK would repeal the Human Rights Act and replace it with another document which sits below the standards protected by the ECHR and the EU Charter? Must, or would this trigger art. 7 TEU?

Assume as another example that another EU member state would change its constitutional situation from monism into dualism and would not allow for the courts to assess the compatibility of national legislation with treaties, and would also stick to disallowing the courts to test the constitutionality of legislation? Must, or would this trigger art. 7 TEU?

Or, assume the legitimacy crisis of representative democracies in quite a few EU member states would lead quite a few states to settle many issues by referendum, and that by referendum these states would want to restrict immigration, enable life-term punishment without possibility of parole, and maybe even the death penalty for quite a few terrorist offences, and the repeal of citizenship (even with the consequence of statelessness) for perpetrators of terrorist crimes, or the establishment of a Guantanamo-like facility for people associated with international terrorist organisations.

These issues evidently do touch upon fundamental rights. They would probably also be an issue under accession negotiations. But would and do they also qualify under the terms of art. 7 TEU and the 2014 Framework established by the Commission to pro-actively present art. 7 TEU issues, and specifically rule of law aspects?

And what about the phenomenon that the Dutch courts do not have the power to test the constitutionality of legislation, so how can we then claim that if constitutional review does exist, it may not be restricted, or narrowed, or limited? How does the UK Human Rights Act relate to art. 7 TEU since it specifically allows parliament to ignore, even if in practice this possibility may never or only rarely been used, declarations of incompatibility issued by the courts?

Furthermore, with respect to Bulgaria and Romania, the EU is monitoring corruption and organized crime as part of the follow up after the accession, on the basis of art. 38 of the Act of Accession; and also a Cooperation and Verification Mechanism (CMV) was created to cooperate and verify progress with respect to the reform of the judiciary and concerning the fight against corruption and organized crime.[1]
This contribution will be about fundamental rights in the context of the art. 7 TEU mechanism, the framework, and these two viewed broader in the context of art. 2 TEU and the guarantees it contains to monitor and enforce member states' compliance such as the infringement procedure and inter-state complaints. I will also relate the issue of fundamental rights and the art. 7 TEU mechanism to the European Convention on Human Rights (ECHR) and the ECtHR, since through art. 6 TEU and the Copenhagen- accession requirements this treaty and court do play an eminent role.

II. The different procedures

Adherence to the Copenhagen criteria is an essential condition for accession of a new member-state of the EU. Without meeting these criteria accession is impossible. However, they are not just accession criteria but remain binding under art. 2 TEU upon all member-states. One of the basic values referred to in art. 2 TEU is the respect for human rights, which have to be permanently abided by as a continuous obligation of EU membership; this commitment is made more specific and concrete through article 6 TEU and through the EU Charter. The obligation of compliance with fundamental rights does not only relate to the application of the Charter, however for the Charter only within the scope of application of EU law, but it is relevant indeed over-all since art. 2 TEU nor art. 6 TEU make a similar distinction or impose a similar restriction as the Charter does, limiting its validity to the scope of EU law. Compliance with the art. 2 TEU values is a binding EU obligation for all domestic law and for all legal and other relations in a member-state, within or outside the scope of EU law. Is it an obligation? I believe it is, since it is part of the treaty and referred to in art. 7 TEU as well as made part, and of an increasingly important nature and status, of the accessions process for new member states. The obligation as laid down in art. 2 binds the national states and their legislature, executive, courts, and sub-federal and decentralised or devolved authorities and covers negative and positive obligations. If it covers all human rights and all situations and all public authorities, the important question is: when can a member-state be considered to meet or to violate the member-state obligation of abiding by the duty to fully respect human rights (and a similar question

1 COM (2006) 6570; COM (2006) 6569.

arises for the other values of democracy and rule of law). And furthermore when, in the context of a violation, may and does art. 7 TEU apply?

1. Art. 258/259 TFEU

First of all we have to remark that all infractions of EU obligations may give rise to an application of art. 258 TFEU. Non-compliance with EU obligations or the Charter (the latter however within the scope of EU law) may lead the Commission to ask the ECJ for a ruling against a state. An example here is ECJ 6 November 2012[2], in which the ECJ judged that Hungary had violated the Directive 2000/78/EC, specifically the rules about age discrimination. The issue was the forced early retirement of judges (lowering their sudden retirement from 70 to 62).

Dawson and Muir have also pointed in this direction[3] referring to the letters sent by the then Euro Commissioner Kroes to the Hungarian government in 2011 signalling that Hungarian reforms may create an "unjustified restriction of the fundamental right of expression and information". Dawson and Muir indicated that the arguments used by Kroes were based on the internal market to address restrictions on media freedom, and concerned a contravention of the 2010 Audiovisual Media Services Directive.

They however are cautious about this approach of what they call an indirect strategy, which could be seen as interfering in policies beyond the remit as established by the EU treaties. However, one may argue that art. 2 to 7 TEU allow the EU to intervene and that evidently art. 258 TFEU would only permit interventions when these are clearly within the ambit of a specific primary or secondary law obligation, such as the two directives I have referred to supra. When secondary EU law contains specific human rights (related) obligations, I believe it is pertinent and relevant to also address lack of compliances thereof as such, without at the same time invoking the Charter. In such a way human rights are mainstreamed and integrated in other EU obligations and policies, which ensures their guarantee more effectively and widely.

But we may take the issue even further and ask the question whether art. 2 TEU may not even give rise to procedures under art. 258 or 259 TFEU? And since art. 2 TEU contains legal obligations, it does appear totally reasonable and plausible, specifically in the domain of fundamental rights, considering that these right have been given specific content and substance and specificity through art. 6 TEU and the Charter. This assumption indeed has potentially far reaching implications, since the art. 2 TEU guarantees are not limited to the member states only when operating within the scope of EU law, but in general! Great advantage of the application of art. 258 by the Commission or of art. 259 by another member state is

2 ECJ, C-286/12 (Commission v. Hungary), ECLI:EU:C:2012:687.

3 *M. Dawson/E. Muir*, Enforcing Fundamental values: EU Law and Governace in Hungary and Romania, Maastricht Journal of European and Comparative Law, 2012, 19, p. 469-477.

the circumstance that it is a Court that gives a final ruling about the infringement or violation. That alleviates the political implications that always may lie behind the utilization of art. 7 TEU.

2. *The ECHR*

Secondly, the ECHR, which is part of the human rights package and of EU membership, can and must also play a role in enforcing compliance with human rights. This reliance upon the ECHR is a consequence of art. 6 TEU and may even considered to be wise as division of work, the more so since one of the accession criteria is being a contracting party to the ECHR. The system of individual petitions, and possibly also of inter-state complaints, and in the future the Protocol 16 possibility for national highest courts to seek the EctHR's advice will assist as well as in enforcing human rights for all state parties, including the member states of the EU. A future accession of the EU to the ECHR may also allow the ECJ to ask the opinion of the EctHR, thus not only leading to harmonized interpretations but also to the assessment of (systemic) compliance of member states of the ECHR.
Similarly, this reliance upon other treaties and other supervisory mechanisms may and does also apply to other Council of Europe Treaties, such as the Social Charter. The Council of Europe can also vote to subject a state to a monitoring procedure. Furthermore, in the recent Polish context with regard to the role and position of the Polish constitutional court, the Commission leans on and cooperates with the Council of Europe Venice Commission[4], which issued an opinion on the Polish issue on 11 March 2016.[5] Such collaboration, specifically for monitoring, but also to build objective consensus about compliance and systemic deficiencies, would be effective and efficient.

3. *Art. 7 TEU and the 2014 Framework*

Thirdly, art. 7 TEU specifically indicates that fundamental rights may be a cause for the application of this article and any exchange of opinion in that context. Here however we do encounter a problem of interpretation with regard to the 2014 Framework, which I will deal with in paragraph 4. Art. 7 TEU speaks in section 1 of a clear **risk** of a serious breach by a Member State of the values referred to in Article 2. This assessment may lead to a discussion with the relevant member-state and to possible recommendations.
A next step is section 2 in case of the existence of a **serious and persistent breach** by a Member State of the values referred to in Article 2. And such a finding may lead ultimately to the sanctions referred to in the same article.

4 This Venice Commission was also active in the Hungarian context with its Opinion on three legal questions arising the drafting the New Constitution of Hungary, (CDL-AD(2011)001, 25-26 March 2011).
5 Opinion no. 833/2015, CDL-AD(2016)001.

It is important to note that section 1 and 2 mention different indicators: a clear risk of a serious breach in section 1; and a serious AND persistent breach in section 2. In the first section there has to be an obvious risk of a serious breach; in the second the serious breach must have materialized and be persistent!
The new 2014 Framework (to strengthen the Rule of Law) sits in, or better before, section 1: its purpose is "to prevent the emerging of a systemic threat to the rule of law in (a) Member State that could develop into a clear risk of a serious breach"[6]. The mechanism even sits therefore before a systemic threat (words that are absent in section 1 by the way).
The inclusion of that word 'systemic' seems to answer part of the question as to **when** art. 7 TEU may be applied and utilized: not really in incidental or isolated cases, but in the context of a system or structure: a structural flaw. And this flaw must not only be **systemic** but also (in the end) be considered to be a **serious** (and for section 2: **persistent**) breach. Note here that the idea of persistent breach is only present in section 2 and not in section 1, but may have found its way into the Framework, for the pre-article 7 phase, also for section 1, through the word 'systemic'.
Section 1 indicates a risk, for instance the repeal of a statute guaranteeing the independence of courts; section 2 is at stake if and when this law is applied systematically and in time (persistent) and courts and judges are subjected to infringements of their freedom to decide cases.

4. National courts

A fourth possibility has been suggested by Von Bogdanyi et al[7] as they have suggested to rely upon national courts and the ECJ to supervise potential violations of fundamental rights in the Member States. National courts and the ECJ should presume and verify that national public law structures comply with EU fundamental rights guarantees. This proposal fits evidently with the subsidiary nature of the ECHR and of EU supervision: allowing and facilitating the domestic courts to remedy non-compliance. And it also fits with the focus of the ECJ upon EU citizens as watchdogs to bring violations of EU law to the light and expose such violations by taking a member-state to court.

III. Systemic violations

Before I will go into the issue whether the Framework may be considered to apply to fundamental rights, and even to all fundamental rights which can be considered

6 COM (2014) 158 final/2.

7 *A. Von Bogdanyi* et al, Reverse Solange – Protecting the Essence of Fundamental Rights against EU Member States, 49 Common Market Law Review 2, 2012, p. 489.

to be covered by art. 2 TEU, I will first say a few words about the notion of systemic, or persistent as opposed to incidental violations.

Is an occasional election fraud or a mistake in electing a president a reason to assume a violation of fundamental membership values and obligations? Or the introduction of the death penalty, even if only for a limited number of crimes? And how about the existence of a life sentence without a possibility of parole? Or a persistent situation of maltreatment in prisons or of neglect in the care of children or the elderly? Or the absence of legal aid? Or the absence of judicial review? Or is it the absence of an internal correction mechanism? Or is it a systematic nature of violations? Or specifically the violation of some specific rights or elements of rights? Or is it the added nature of human rights violations? Art. 7 does, that at least seems obvious, not aim at individual and isolated cases of human rights violations.

We may safely assume that incidental violations of human rights will not trigger the application of the framework nor will it lead to findings of violations of art. 2 TEU. At least as long as there exist sufficient and relevant and adequate remedies (in national courts specifically and assisted through international mechanisms). The presence of effective, fair and adequate legal remedies and access to court are in that respect relevant as a basic right in itself and as a yardstick to measure overall human rights compliance. This explains the conversation with Hungary at the time and with Poland, since both countries were/are considered to have impacted the independence, impartiality and power of their respective constitutional courts. And doing so is, says the Framework, likely to systematically and adversely affect the integrity, stability or the proper functioning of the institutions and the safeguard mechanism established at national level to secure the rule of law. So for France undoing the review by the Council, and for the UK to repeal the possibility for the courts under the HRA may indeed be questionable, and probably as well the repealing of the power of courts to invoke human rights treaties. In this respect in Dutch parliament a proposal is pending to restrict the powers of the courts to rely upon treaty human rights provisions: would that invoke the application of the Framework and art. 7 TEU? Or, does the notion of systemic also relate to an overall assessment of a constitutional situation, and if so how?

IV. Framework v. art. 7 TEU

Here we may have to distinguish between art. 7 TEU and the Framework. Art. 7 refers to all values mentioned in art. 2 TEU, that is also fundamental rights. The Framework aims to strengthen the rule of law. What does that mean or imply for a human rights violation? Is the intention to limit the framework AND art. 7 TEU to the criteria in the framework? That does seem to me to be against the text and spirit of art. 7 TEU. Or can we consider all other values as mentioned in art. 2 TEU to also be a part of the Framework mechanism. Or is the Framework only applicable to the pre-art. 7 phase? And was the idea to focus for that phase on the most central and core aspect, that is the rule of law, which also encompasses (some) fundamental rights and essential freedoms as well as fundamental aspects of democracy.

In its 2014 Communication[8] the Commission said that rule of law is one of the three pillars of the Council of Europe, alongside democracy and human rights. However, it indicated also that the rule of law is basic for the protection of fundamental values, and is a prerequisite for the protection of fundamental rights. The framework sets out to address and resolve a situation where there is a systemic threat to the rule of law. What is defined as rule of law and does that include human rights and if so which rights: legality, legal certainty, prohibition of arbitrariness of the executive powers, independent and impartial courts, effective judicial review including respect for fundamental rights, and equality before the law. So indeed, some human rights are included in the definition of rule of law. These rights are: access to courts, and we may assume: the presence and availability of effective remedies, so that fundamental rights must be justiciable, and courts must be able to effectively ensure and enforce the enjoyment of fundamental rights. And furthermore: equality. Democracy as such is only mentioned as a corollary of powers of the courts: their role in ensuring freedom of expression, assembly and rules governing the political and electoral process.

For human rights aspects the rule of law Framework aims therefore not so much at all individual rights (apart from equality and access to courts) but at the availability of and respect for a full scale system of an effective judiciary which may effectively control the observance of democratic freedoms and fundamental rights.

Is absence of a legal remedy always and in itself a violation? Probably not, since not all EU member states allow for judicial review of acts of parliaments, most notably the UK and The Netherlands, so occasionally human rights violations in such states may go unchecked and unpunished by the courts. However, even without legal remedy it remains then important to investigate whether such an absence, which in itself falls within the discretion of the states, is compensated sufficiently and effectively by other mechanisms which may and do ensure human rights compatibility. And these may be manifold: elections, regulatory restraint in the legislature and executive modesty, international supervision by the European Court of Human Rights, pressure by domestic ngo's etc etc. Legal mechanisms are one thing, the other is how the other non-court branches of power respect human rights.

In its Human Rights Resolution of 8 September 2015[9] the European Parliament (EP) asked the Commission to be (more) specific as to when the article 7 TEU mechanism has to be activated and will be activated. Sub 8 in its Resolution the

8 COM (2014) 158 final/2.
9 P8_TA-PROV(2015)0286.

Parliament invites the Commission to describe and define these criteria and to ensure that they will be transparently and proactively utilized and contribute in that way in preventing specific human rights violations. More in particular to define a clear danger for a serious violation as well as define serious and continuing violations, based upon the case law of the European Court of Human Rights. And the EP asked as well for an automatic activation when a criterion is met! In that respect it also allots a role to the Fundamental Rights Agency, to determine systematic or serious violations (in the plural!), which may even lead to the application of art. 258 TFEU!
The Parliament also indicated less far going tools to monitor human rights and to facilitate discussions: the rule of law and human rights scoreboards; national human rights institutions, discussion between Commission and member-states, monitoring and reporting on domestic human rights situations etc etc.
However, to briefly summarise: The Parliament indeed focused on specific issues where art. 258 TFE may play a role and on systematic and serious violations which could engage art. 7 TEU.
In its resolution of 10 June 2015[10] the European Parliament with regard to the situation in Hungary defined an introduction of the death punishment if this were to take place as a violation of the Treaties and the Charter, since the abolition of the death penalty is a milestone in the development of human rights in Europe. It suggested that such an introduction would also constitute a serious violation of art. 2 TEU with the necessity therefore to invoke the art. 7 TEU procedure! With respect to the death penalty we witness a similar approach in the recent exchanges between Turkey and the EU: introduction of the death penalty will be an impediment for an accessions and the relevant negotiations.

V. Triggering art. 7 TEU

So what will trigger the Framework and in all likelihood art. 7 TEU as well from the perspective of human rights? Not: individual breaches of fundamental rights or a single miscarriage of justice. But: threats to the rule of law which are of a systemic nature: widespread practices and specifically a lack of domestic redress because of an impediment in the effective protection provided by the courts.
So: clear indications of a systemic threat to the rule of law, as defined by the Commission (legality, legal certainty, arbitrariness, independent and effective judicial review, including respect for fundamental rights (fair trial, compliance with court decisions), and equality before the law. On June 1 2016 the Commission issued its opinion with respect to the situation in Poland.[11]
"Recent events in Poland concerning in particular the Constitutional Court have led the European Commission to open a dialogue with the Polish Government in

10 P8_TA-PROV(2015)0227.
11 http://europa.eu/rapid/press-release_IP-16-2015_nl.htm.

order to ensure the full respect of the rule of law. The Commission considers it necessary that Poland's Constitutional Tribunal is able to fully ensure an effective constitutional review of legislative acts.

The current concerns of the European Commission relate to the following issues:

- the **appointment of judges to the Constitutional Tribunal** and the implementation of the judgments of the Constitutional Tribunal of 3 and 9 December 2015 relating to these matters;
- the **Law of 22 December 2015 amending the Law on the Constitutional Tribunal**, the judgment of the Constitutional Tribunal of 9 March 2016 relating to this law, and the respect of the judgments rendered by the Constitutional Tribunal since 9 March 2016;

the **effectiveness of the Constitutional review of new legislation** which has been adopted and enacted in 2016."

On July 28th 2016 the Commission went even further and issued a recommendation[12]:

"This new step under the Rule of Law Framework follows the intensive dialogue that has been ongoing with the Polish authorities since 13 January. After the adoption of an Opinion on the situation in Poland on 1 June, the Polish Parliament adopted a new Law on the Constitutional Tribunal on 22 July. The Commission has assessed the overall situation, including in the light of the new law, and reaches the conclusion that even if certain of its concerns have been addressed by that law, important issues of concern regarding the rule of law in Poland remain. The Commission is therefore laying out concrete recommendations to the Polish authorities on how to address these concerns.

The Commission believes that there is a systemic threat to the rule of law in Poland. The fact that the Constitutional Tribunal is prevented from fully ensuring an effective constitutional review adversely affects its integrity, stability and proper functioning, which is one of the essential safeguards of the rule of law in Poland. Where a constitutional justice system has been established, its effectiveness is a key component of the rule of law.

First Vice-President Frans **Timmermans** said today: *"Despite the dialogue pursued with the Polish authorities since the beginning of the year, the Commission considers the main issues which threaten the rule of law in Poland have not been resolved. We are therefore now making concrete recommendations to the Polish authorities on how to address the concerns so that the Constitutional Tribunal of Poland can carry out its mandate to deliver effective constitutional review."*

The Commission today recommends in particular that Poland:

- respects and fully implements the judgments of the Constitutional Tribunal of 3 and 9 December 2015. These require that the three judges that were lawfully nominated in October 2015 by the previous legislature can take up their func-

12 http://europa.eu/rapid/press-release_IP-16-2643_en.htm.

tion of judge in the Constitutional Tribunal, and that the three judges nominated by the new legislature without a valid legal basis do not take up the post of judge without being validly elected;

- publishes and implements fully the judgment of 9 March 2016 of the Constitutional Tribunal, as well as all subsequent judgments, and ensures that the publication of future judgements is automatic and does not depend on any decision of the executive or legislative powers;
- ensures that any reform of the Law on the Constitutional Tribunal respects the judgments of the Constitutional Tribunal, including the judgments of 3 and 9 December 2015 and the judgment of 9 March 2016, and takes the Opinion of the Venice Commission fully into account; and ensures that the effectiveness of the Constitutional Tribunal as a guarantor of the Constitution is not undermined by new requirements, whether separately or through their combined effect;
- ensures that the Constitutional Tribunal can review the compatibility of the new law adopted on 22 July 2016 on the Constitutional Tribunal before its entry into force and publish and implement fully the judgment of the Tribunal in that respect."

Does **any** systemic violation automatically and by itself give rise to the application of the art. 7 TEU based mechanisms? I believe not. A systemic violation must also be serious and persistent. We may define seriousness as having a certain degree of gravity of the violation. Large scale violations may be relevant, or less large scale but grave violations. In that respect we may find inspiration in the case law of the EctHR, which has developed tools to deal with systemic non-compliance and therefore how to define them. That in itself is an argument to build upon its case law and find inspiration in defining systemic and large scale and seriousness. It has developed mechanisms and tools to identify such systemic violation through key judgments and pilot judgements, and subsequently by urging through the Council of Ministers to make the state remedy the situation allowing the Court subsequently to quickly dispose of new and similar cases.[13]

Analysing the before mentioned Resolution of the EP it seems that the EP in its assessment of human rights violations prioritizes and finds rights that deserve extra attention: however the list it has drawn up is relatively long: free speech and media; freedom of religion and conscience; equality and non-discrimination; protection of minorities; Roma; violence against women and gender equality; rights of children; rights of LGBTI; rights of people with a disability; age discrimination; hate crimes; rights of migrants; solidarity in the economic crisis; criminality and corruption; prison-conditions; justice; citizenship; victims of crimes. That is truly a long list, and not exhaustive of possible application of art. 7 TEU. Quite a

13 See: Response of the Court to the "CDDH report containing conclusions and possible proposals for action on ways to resolve the large numbers of applications arising from systemic issues identified by the Court", 20 october 2014, http://echr.coe.int/Documents/2014-ECHR_response_CDDH_report.pdf.

few aspects relate to equality: these aspects may be ranked under human rights but also in the definition used under the notion of rule of law.

VI. Pilot judgments of EctHR as trigger

Pilot judgments as utilized by the ECtHR may be a first step in identifying, or at least relying upon the ECtHR to determine, systemic violations for a possible application of art. 7 TEU. A pilot judgment is intended to help national authorities to eliminate the systemic or structural problem highlighted by the Court as giving rise to repetitive cases. In doing this it also assists the Committee of Ministers in its role of ensuring that each judgment of the Court is properly executed by the respondent State. Evidently, if subsequently the respondent state resolves the systemic or structural human rights problem, the issue must be considered as remedied. If not, would such a finding by the Council and subsequently the Court then be a possible starting point for EU member states to start the first steps under art. 7 TEU?

As examples of pilot judgments can be mentioned those regarding prison conditions in Bulgaria (the *Neshkov* judgment)[14] and Hungary (the *Varga* judgment)[15], each setting a time frame for the national authorities to take action in response to the finding of a violation of Article 3. The EctHR has now more than ten years of experience with this tool to target systemic and structural deficiencies, since it started doing so in the *Broniowski* case[16]. The purpose is to support the relevant State and enable the Committee of Ministers to duly supervise the remedying of systemic violations. In the meantime, the pilot-judgment procedure has become a central part of the Court's strategy to deal with systemic violations of Convention rights, one that can be expected to continue to be in regular use in future. I suggest under art. 7 TEU resort may be had to the criteria employed by the EctHR and to its case law, specifically in those pilot judgments areas in which the respondent state does not show any willingness to conform to the judgment and the recommendations by the Court and the Committee of Ministers.

VII. Conclusion(s):

1. First of all we can conclude that the 2014 Framework and art. 7 TEU do not fully match concerning the applicability of all art. 2 TEU values.
2. Primordial in the guarantees as applied so far in practice (Poland, Hungary, Romania) is the presence of an effective, independent and sufficiently powerful national judiciary which will have to secure the constitutional bal-

14 27-1-2015, Neshkov and others v Bulgaria.
15 10-3-2015, Varga and others v Hungary.
16 22-6-2004, Broniowski v Poland.

ance of the institutions but must and may also provide protection against human rights violations and is therefore crucial in preventing and punishing systemic violations. The absence of effective courts may be considered a rule of law violation but also as a violation of fair trial as such, specifically when it takes the form of the reduction of powers and /or independence of a constitutional court.

3. The EU may rely upon the EctHR for systemic human rights violations and the responses to these findings and whether a state has addressed the flaws sufficiently.
4. Incidental violations will not trigger the art. 7 TEU mechanism, unless possibly in extremely hard cases.
5. Incidental as well as systemic violations can give rise to art. 258 or 259 TFE, when specific obligations have been violated that coincide with human rights; they could occasionally also lead to the individual petition mechanism of the ECHR, and if within the scope of EU law, to application of the Charter.
6. However I assume that systemic violations of democratic freedoms and of fundamental rights concerning life and physical integrity (death penalty, as shows the discussion with Hungary and Turkey), may be and will be subsumed under the 2014 Framework, as will such violations of equality before the law.
7. Systemic is defined as meaning that a law or rule or practice allows for such violation, and is not and cannot be stopped or prevented by a national court, albeit possibly with the assistance of the ECtHR: gravity of a situation of non-compliance would also be a factor, establishing seriousness to warrant resorting to art. 7 TEU.
8. The Framework mechanism specifically with regard to human rights focuses on structural deficiencies which may be difficult to handle by the individual petitioning system of the ECHR: for instance, the curtailing of a constitutional court may, when other courts with effective powers do exist, be difficult to question by the ECtHR. In that respect the Framework sits in an area (integrity, stability or the proper functioning of the institutions and safeguard mechanisms) which falls largely outside the scope of the ECtHR and may not always be fit for an individual challenge in that international system.
9. For human rights violations the Framework and art. 7 TEU may be considered as last option: national remedies, access to the EctHR, art. 258 TFEU, inter-state petitions under the EU and the ECHR, application of the Charter and collaboration between national courts and the ECJ, discussion between the EP and national parliaments and the Commission and states, reports by the FRA, collaboration with the Venice Commission and the Council of Europe, can be seen as a variety of tools that are available to tackle or prevent systemic human rights violations. A Rule of Law Scoreboard, as an adden-

dum to the Justice Scoreboard within an European semester like framework may be an interesting suggestion in that respect.

10. A soft tool may also be the Justice Scoreboard and similar initiatives, trying to objectify data and engage the member states in an organised dialogue.[17]

11. However, as *Kochenov* and *Pech* have argued, the issue is possibly not so much monitoring or collecting data but enforcing compliance in a context where a member state is set on being in non-compliance. The EU would need tools that sit between the new Framework mechanism and the (option of) imposition of the severe sanctions embodied in art. 7 TEU. The European Semester process enables the EU to impose fines upon member states that do not comply with the budget rules. These fines may vary between 0[18] and 0.2% of GDP. Wouldn't that be a more productive mechanism, leaving the sanctions of art. 7 TEU as a true ultimum remedium?

12. No matter what, art. 7 TEU is a mechanism full of symbolism and full of political overtones. I suggest therefore to rely for human rights issues first of all on other and available monitoring and enforcement mechanisms, within and without the EU. Dialogue, benchmarks, specific cases, pilot judgments, are far to be preferred over politically charged and drastic procedures that deal with the rights of a state under the Treaties. Isn't the idea of art. 7 TEU to have a procedure but not so much having to resort to it. That is part of the motivation of the 2014 Framework which enables amicable solutions. The more instruments do exist in the pre art. 7 TEU phase, the better: art. 258, or 259 TEU; benchmarking and naming and shaming attached to it, seeking relations with legal professionals in the country concerned and seeking discussions in EU wide associations of judges, courts and constitutional courts; relying upon missions and judgements of Council of Europe institutions and organs and committees; reliance upon judgments of the ECtHR, should not to be ignored and must be pursued, leading to application of the 2014 Framework and only afterwards to application of the different stages of art. 7 TEU. But since the EU is not a unitary state the imposition of rules and principles by the EU is difficult to envisage. Even federal states are confronted with obstacles when they see themselves in a position with recalcitrant states.

17 *D. Kochenov/L. Pech*, Monotoring and Enforcement of the Rule of Law in the EU: Rhetoric and Reality, EuConst 2015, volume 11, pp. 512-540.

18 As proposed by the Commission in July 2016 for Portugal and Spain: http://europa.eu/rapid/press-release_IP-16-2625_en.htm.

Democracy – A Value common to the Member States of the European Union

*By Andreas Haratsch, Hagen**

The principle of democracy is not only a fundamental pillar of modern statehood, but according to Article 2 TEU, also one of the values the European Union is founded on. Therefore, European Union law presupposes that the Member States' legal orders are democratic, too. Essential elements of the principle of democracy are the sovereignty of the people, free elections on the basis of universal, equal and direct suffrage by secret ballot as well as a competitive multi-party system guaranteeing effective opposition rights. An absence of democratic structures in a single EU Member State deprives the European Union as a whole of its democratic foundation. Hence, there is an obligation to take action on the basis of Article 7 TEU against any violation of democratic principles by a Member State.

I. Introduction

"Indeed it has been said that democracy is the worst form of government, except for all the others forms that have been tried from time to time."[1] This remark made by *Winston Churchill* in the House of Commons on November, 11th 1947 – about seventy years ago –, has never seemed to be more true than today in times of "brexit" and a US President *Donald Trump*. Democracy does not guarantee decisions taken by the electorate being wise, sensible or at least moderate. For this reason, democracy is not the only component pathing the way to a State resembling a worldly paradise. The principle of democracy has to be supplemented by other fundamental legal guarantees, as there are the rule of law, separation of powers or human rights. Notwithstanding, no one so far has found or developed a better form of government than a democratically legitimized one. Against this backdrop, it is no surprise that European Union law considers democracy as one of the essential pillars of the European Union. According to the Preamble of the Treaty on European Union[2], democracy belongs to the cultural, religious and humanist inheritance of Europe and shall be one of the principles forming a firm basis for its future construction[3].

* *Prof. Dr. Andreas Haratsch* holds the Chair of German and European Constitutional and Administrative Law and Public International Law at the University of Hagen/Germany. He is also Director of the Dimitris-Tsatsos-Institute of European Constitutional Sciences at the University of Hagen/Germany.

1 Quoted in: *W. Churchill*, in: Langworth (ed.), Churchill by Himself: The Life, Times and Opinions in his own Words, 2008, p. 573.

2 Treaty on European Union, O.J. EU 2010 C 83/13.

3 Preamble TEU, recital 2 and 3; see also recital 2 of the Preamble of the Fundamental Rights Charter, which states that the European Union is based on the principle of democracy.

Hereafter, we will take a closer look at the legal requirements following from the principle of democracy for the Member States of the European Union. For this purpose, we will examine the legal bases of the democratic principle in European Union law. In a next step, we will analyse in detail the specific elements of democracy being indispensable in the national legal orders. Afterwards, we will try to shed light on the impact a national breach of the democratic principle might have on the European level. Finally, there will be some short reflections on the relation between democracy and other underlying principles of modern statehood.

II. The Legal Bases of the Democratic Principle in European Union Law

The principle of democracy finds several legal bases in European Union law. First, one can identify a number of Treaty provisions in the TEU, the TFEU[4] and the CRF[5] which deal with the democratic principle itself or at least with specific elements of it. Second, the principle of democracy is part of the unwritten general principles of the Union's law.

1. Treaty Provisions

When taking a look at written Treaty law, a distinction can be made between provisions directly binding and such indirectly binding on the EU Member States.

a) Provisions directly binding on the Member States

Concerning directly binding norms, one can see that already the Preamble of the Treaty on European Union addresses the democratic principle three times. In the preamble's fourth recital the contracting parties, i.e. the Member States, expressly confirm their attachment to the principle of democracy.[6] The pivotal provision, however, is Article 2 clause 1 TEU which qualifies democracy as one of the values on which the European Union is founded. The second clause of Article 2 states that the above mentioned values are common to the Member States. In consequence, respect for these values, including democracy, is a precondition of membership in the European Union according to Article 49 (1) TEU. Specifications to this general guarantee are made by Articles 9 to 12 TEU relating to democracy within the legal orders of the European Union itself and of its Member States. Of particular importance for the validity of the democratic principle in the Member States is Article 10 (2) subparagraph 2 TEU. It assumes that any Head of State or Government or any national government has to be democratically accountable to their national Parliaments or to their citizens. Article 12 TEU demands that national Parliaments have to contribute actively to the good function-

4 Treaty on the Functioning of the European Union, O.J. EU 2010 C 83/47.
5 Charter of Fundamental Rights of the European Union, O.J. EU 2010 C 83/389.
6 The "values" mentioned in Art. 2 TEU are called "principles" in the Preamble TEU, recital 4.

ing of the Union. Article 22 TEU and Articles 39 and 40 CRF[7] address municipal elections within the Member States and the elections to the European Parliament which have to be conducted according to democratic principles.

b) Provisions indirectly binding on the Member States

Besides, there also exists an indirect obligation of the Member States to follow democratic rules. The commitment of the European Union to the democratic principle according to Article 2 first clause TEU requires that all Member States qualify as democratic States.[8] The European Union can only be democratic if its Member States are. As the European legal order demands the European Council and the Council of Ministers to be democratically legitimated, the Member States are legally obliged to supply these European institutions with legitimacy.[9] The Heads of State or Government or members of Government forming the European Council and the Council must be legitimated and accountable in a democratic way.[10] The same applies to the Members of the European Commission, which – after a vote of consent by the European Parliament – are appointed by the European Council,[11] to the Court of Auditors, the Economic and Social Committee and the Committee of the Regions, which are appointed by the Council.[12] Similarly, the Members of the Court of Justice of the European Union – the judges and the advocates-general – are appointed by common accord of the governments of the Member States.[13] In all these cases, the principle of democracy obligating the European Union requires the Governments of the Member States to be properly legitimated.

2. General Principles common to the Laws of the Member States

Besides written provisions, the principle of democracy belongs to the unwritten general principles of European Union law as all Member States of the Union are democratic States.[14] As there is no space for an elaborate comparative work, in

7 Strictly speaking, the provisions of the Charter of Fundamental Rights of the European Union are no treaty provisions. But according to Art. 6 (1) subpara 1 TEU, the Charter shall have the same legal value as the Treaties.

8 *M. Hilf/F. Schorkopf*, in: Grabitz/Hilf/Nettesheim (eds.), Das Recht der Europäischen Union, 51st supplement, September 2013, Art. 2 TEU mn. 27.

9 *A. Bleckmann*, Das Demokratieprinzip im Europäischen Gemeinschaftsrecht, in: idem, Studien zum Europäischen Gemeinschaftsrecht, 1986, p. 159, 174; *M. Zuleeg*, Der Verfassungsgrundsatz der Demokratie und die Europäischen Gemeinschaften, Der Staat 17, 1978, p. 27, 43.

10 BVerfGE 89, 155, 187 – Maastricht.

11 Cf. Art. 17 (7) subpara. 3 TEU.

12 Cf. Art. 286 (2) subpara. 1 TFEU; Art. 302 (1) TFEU; Art. 305 (3) TFEU.

13 Cf. Art. 19 (2) subpara. 3 TEU.

14 *A. Haratsch*, Die duale parlamentarische Demokratie in der Europäischen Union, in: Brandt (ed.), Perspektiven der Unionsgrundordnung, 2013, p. 19, 20; *A. Bleckmann*, Das europäische Demokratieprinzip, JZ 2001, p. 53; *A. Rummer*, Die Europäische Union nach Amsterdam – Demokratie als Verfassungsprinzip der EU?, ZEuS 1999, p. 249, 251; *H.-J. Cremer*, Das Demokratieprinzip auf nationaler und europäischer Ebene im Lichte des Maastricht-Urteils des Bundesverfassungsgerichts, EuR 1995, p. 21, 37; *M. Zuleeg*, Demokratie in der Europäischen Gemeinschaft, JZ 1993, p. 1069, 1070.

the following, we can only take short glimpses into national legal orders. At any rate, the identification of general principles is considerably facilitated by international treaties which have been ratified by all EU Member States, as there are the International Covenant on Civil and Political Rights[15] or the European Convention on Human Rights[16] and its Additional Protocols.[17] Of foremost importance for the democratic principle are Article 25 ICCPR and Article 3 of Protocol No. 1 to the ECHR,[18] which both comprise the right to vote at elections to legislative bodies. Additionally, valuable advice is granted by the opinions of the "European Commission for Democracy through Law", the so-called Venice Commission, which was established by the Council of Europe.[19]

III. Elements of the Principle of Democracy

1. Sovereignty of the People

The main issue of the principle of democracy is the concept of the sovereignty of the people. All power is vested in the people and state authority must be derived from the people.[20] Article 10 (2) subparagraph 2 and Article 12 TEU assume the existence of national Parliaments. Hence, there have to be parliamentary elections in every Member State of the Union.

Besides, other elections such as presidential elections are not barred by the requirement to hold parliamentary elections. Article 10 (2) TEU illustrates that Heads of State or Government can also be accountable directly to their citizens. Also, referendums can be held on certain issues, although the principle of democracy does not demand them.

How the process of intermediation between the will of the people and state authority is organized is not determined by the principle of people's sovereignty. The electoral law in the Member States might either follow the concept of a majority voting system or the concept of a proportional representation system.[21]

15 International Covenant on Civil and Political Rights of 16.12.1966, 999 UNTS 171.

16 Convention for the Protection of Human Rights and Fundamental Freedoms of 4.11.1950, ETS No. 005, as amended by Protocol No. 14 to the Convention for the Protection of Human Rights and Fundamental Freedoms of 13.5.2004, CETS No. 194.

17 *A. Haratsch*, Die Bedeutung der UN-Menschenrechtspakte für die Europäische Union, MRM, Themenheft „25 Jahre Internationale Menschenrechtspakte", 2002, p. 29, 30 ff.

18 Protocol to the Convention for the Protection of Human Rights and Fundamental Freedoms of 20.3.1952, ETS No. 009.

19 Cf. *Council of Europe, Committee of Ministers*, Resolution (90) 6 of 10.05.1990 on a partial Agreement establishing the European Commission for Democracy through Law; *Council of Europe, Committee of Ministers*, Resolution 2002 (3) of 21.02.2002 adopting the revised Statute of the European Commission for Democracy through Law.

20 Accordingly already: *European Parliament*, Declaration of Fundamental Rights and Freedoms of 12.4.1989, Art. 17 para. 1, O.J. EC 1989 C 120/52, 55.

21 ECtHR (Plenary), Judgement of 2.3.1987 – 9267/81 (Mathieu-Mohin a. Clerfayt/Belgium), A No. 113, para. 54; ECtHR (Grand Chamber), Judgement of 8.7.2008 – 10226/03 (Yumak and Sadak/Turkey), RJD 2008, para. 110; *J. M.-Ladwig/M. Nettesheim*, in: Meyer-Ladewig/Nettesheim/von Raumer (eds.), EMRK. Europäische Menschenrechtskonvention, 4th ed. 2017, Art. 3 of Protocol No. 1 ECHR mn. 7.

At any rate, according to Article 3 of Protocol No. 1 to the ECHR, parliamentary elections must be held at reasonable intervals. This must also apply to other than parliamentary elections. There is no strict rule which period of time can be considered as reasonable. There are different rules from Member State to Member State or even within the same Member State. On one hand, election periods shall not be too long because this might lead to a petrification of political groupings in parliament which does not reflect the opinion of the electorate any more.[22] On the other hand, periods or terms shall not be too short in order not to impede the implementation of the will of the voters.[23] For sure, there is a large margin of appreciation in choosing the length of an election period. Every choice between two years and seven years might be considered as uncritical.[24] Incompatible with the principle of democracy would be a prolongation of a current parliamentary term.

The requirement of democratic connection between the will of the electorate and the head of government must not necessarily be effectuated by a formal act of election by parliament or by the people. There are quite a few EU Member States, as Latvia, Malta, Portugal, Slovakia, Belgium, Denmark, Luxemburg, the Netherlands and Great Britain, where the head of government is appointed by the head of state or the Monarch. This is acceptable, as long as it is legal practice that the head of state or Monarch has to appoint the majority leader or the government has to submit itself to a confidence vote in parliament in the wake of the appointment.[25]

2. Underlying Principles Governing the Law of Elections

Elections must meet certain requirements in order to qualify as democratic. There are five underlying principles of the European electoral heritage being essential for democracy. These are universal, equal, free, secret and direct suffrage.[26] According to Article 3 of Protocol No. 1 to the ECHR, elections shall guarantee the free expression of the individual voter's will and shall be held by secret ballot. Although it is not explicitly mentioned, according to the case-law of the European Court of Human Rights, this provision also safeguards an election by universal and equal suffrage.[27] This corresponds to the guarantee laid down in Article 25 ICCPR. Not expressly addressed by these norms, is the principle of direct suf-

22 *C. Grabenwarter*, European Convention on Human Rights. Commentary, 2014, Art. 3 Protocol No. 1 ECHR mn. 3.

23 *C. Grabenwarter* (fn. 22).

24 Cf. *J. A. Frowein*, in: Frowein/Peukert, Europäische Menschenrechtskonvention, 3rd ed., 2009, Art. 3 of Protocol No. 1 ECHR mn. 5; *C. Grabenwarter/K. Pabel*, Europäische Menschenrechtskonvention, 6th ed., 2016, § 23 mn. 108. Narrower *J. M.-Ladwig/M. Nettesheim*, in: Meyer-Ladewig/Nettesheim/von Raumer (fn. 21), Art. 3 of Protocol No. 1 ECHR mn. 8, who consider that a period of six or seven years gives reason for concern.

25 Cf. *C. D. Claasen*, Nationales Verfassungsrecht in der Europäischen Union. Eine integrierte Darstellung von 27 Verfassungsordnungen, 2013, mn. 98.

26 *Venice Commission*, Europe's Electoral Heritage, CDL (2002) 7 rev., p. 10, 19; *Venice Commission*, Code of Good Practice in Electoral Matters: Guidelines and Explanatory Report, CDL-AD (2002) 23 rev., p. 5, 13.

27 *A. Peters/T. Altwicker*, Europäische Menschenrechtskonvention, 2012, § 17 mn. 4.

frage. But, according to the Venice Commission, direct election of, at least, one parliamentary chamber by the people is one aspect of Europe's shared constitutional heritage.[28] The requirement of direct election is part of national constitutional or, at least, statutory law of each EU Member State.[29]

a) Universal Suffrage

The concept of universal suffrage demands that all citizens have the right to vote and the right to stand for election without restrictions based on ethnicity, gender, religion, education, wealth or social status. However, the right to vote and stand for election may be subject to a number of conditions. There may be minimum age, nationality or residence requirements.[30] A nationality requirement, of course, must not be applied to municipal elections and elections to the European parliament with respect to EU citizens. In any case, a requirement of sufficient language skills would be inadmissible. By all means, generally admissible limitations to the right to vote and stand for election can only be justified by legitimate reasons and must be proportionate to the overwhelming significance of the right to vote.[31]

b) Free Suffrage and Secret Ballot

Elections must be held under conditions which ensure the free formation and expression of the opinion of the people.[32] This principle applies to the period prior to an election and to the voting procedure itself. It ensures the free formation of the voter's opinion and protects him against indoctrination by the State or a private person.[33]

The requirement of secret ballot also safeguards the free expression of the voter's will. It shall reduce the danger of pressure on the voter,[34] especially the danger of a discrimination of the voter after having cast a vote. Secrecy must apply to the entire voting procedure, and particularly to the casting and counting of votes.[35]

Compulsory voting systems where voters are legally obliged to vote in elections are known in different EU Member States, namely Belgium,[36] Luxemburg,[37]

28 *Venice Commission*, Europe's Electoral Heritage, CDL (2002) 7 rev., p. 29; *Venice Commission*, Code of Good Practice in Electoral Matters: Guidelines and Explanatory Report, CDL-AD (2002) 23 rev., p. 9, 24.

29 *C. D. Claasen* (fn. 25), mn. 383.

30 *C. Grabenwarter* (fn. 22), Art. 3 Protocol No. 1 ECHR mn. 11; *Venice Commission*, Europe's Electoral Heritage, CDL (2002) 7 rev., p. 19 f.; *Venice Commission*, Code of Good Practice in Electoral Matters: Guidelines and Explanatory Report, CDL-AD (2002) 23 rev., p. 14 f.

31 *C. Grabenwarter* (fn. 22), Art. 3 Protocol No. 1 ECHR mn. 8 ff.

32 ECtHR (Grand Chamber), Judgement of 8.7.2008 – 10226/03 (Yumak and Sadak/Turkey), RJD 2008, para. 107.

33 *J. M.-Ladwig/M. Nettesheim*, in: Meyer-Ladewig/Nettesheim/von Raumer (fn. 21), Art. 3 of Protocol No. 1 ECHR mn. 16; *C. Grabenwarter*, (fn. 22), Art. 3 Protocol No. 1 ECHR mn. 5.

34 *C. Grabenwarter* (fn. 22), Art. 3 Protocol No. 1 ECHR mn. 5.

35 *Venice Commission*, Europe's Electoral Heritage, CDL (2002) 7 rev., p. 29; *Venice Commission*, Code of Good Practice in Electoral Matters: Guidelines and Explanatory Report, CDL-AD (2002) 23 rev., p. 24.

36 Cf. Art. 62 (3) clause 1 of the Belgium Constitution.

37 Cf. Art. 89 (1) of the Luxemburg Electoral Act of 18.2.2003.

Greece,[38] Italy[39] and Cyprus.[40] In some EU Member States, it is controversial whether compulsory voting might be incompatible with the principle of free suffrage. However, compulsory voting is not prohibited by a general principle of European Union law, especially considering that voters might cast an invalid or blank ballot paper.

c) Equal Suffrage

Equal suffrage guarantees equal treatment of all citizens in the exercise of their right to vote and their right to stand for election. First of all, it requires formal electoral equality. Each voter shall have the same number of votes, and weighted voting is not allowed. Further, from the principle of equal suffrage follows that votes must have an equal voting power. In a proportional voting system each voter shall have the same influence on the composition of the body elected. Under a majority voting system all candidates shall have equal chances of victory.[41]

Where elections are not being held in one single electoral district equal voting power requires constituency boundaries to be drawn in such a way that parliamentary seats represent an approximately identical number of voters or citizens. Malapportionment or "electoral geometry", as the Venice Commission calls it,[42] results in a misrepresentation of the electorate. As exact equality is not attainable, there always will be deviations. Usually, deviations up to a maximum of 10 % are regarded as acceptable. Larger deviations might be justified under exceptional circumstances, for example for reasons of minority protection.[43]

Malapportionment must not be confused with gerrymandering.[44] In the process of setting constituencies (electoral districts), gerrymandering is a practice intended to establish an advantage for a particular party or candidate by manipulating district boundaries. Constituency boundaries may be determined on the basis of geographical criteria and by administrative or historic boundary lines. When constituency boundaries are redrawn, this should be exercised on basis of objective criteria by an independent commission.[45]

38 Cf. Art. 51 (5) of the Greek Constitution.

39 Cf. Art. 48 (2) clause 2 of the Italian Constitution.

40 Cf. the Electoral Law 72/1979 of Cyprus.

41 *C. Grabenwarter/K. Pabel* (fn. 24), § 23 mn. 108.

42 *Venice Commission*, Code of Good Practice in Electoral Matters: Guidelines and Explanatory Report, CDL-AD (2002) 23 rev., p. 17 f.; *Venice Commission*, Europe's Electoral Heritage, CDL (2002) 7 rev., p. 23.

43 *Venice Commission*, Code of Good Practice in Electoral Matters: Guidelines and Explanatory Report, CDL-AD (2002) 23 rev., p. 17; *Venice Commission*, Europe's Electoral Heritage, CDL (2002) 7 rev., p. 23.

44 The term "gerrymandering" was created in reaction to a redrawing of Massachusetts state senate election districts under Governor *Elbridge Gerry*, who in 1812 signed a bill that redistricted Massachusetts to benefit his Democratic-Republican Party.

45 *Venice Commission*, Europe's Electoral Heritage, CDL (2002) 7 rev., p. 24.

d) Direct Suffrage

At least one of the chambers of parliament has to elected by direct suffrage.[46] The rule of direct suffrage also applies to other legislative bodies, like Parliaments of Federate States, as well as elected bodies of local self-government.[47] However, it does not require Heads of State to be elected directly, although in some states this might be the case according to their constitution.[48]

3. Competitive Multi-party System

Democracy requires a competitive multi-party system.[49] There have to be multiple political parties across the political spectrum or candidates representing such political parties which run for election. The competition between these parties must not be influenced by the state in favour of a particular party or a particular political direction. In order to safeguard a level playing field for all parties or candidates, equality of opportunity must be guaranteed for all. Equal opportunity for parties and candidates means that the same rules apply to all candidates.[50] This entails a neutral attitude by state authorities, in particular with regard to the nomination of candidates, with regard to the election campaign, with regard to access to the media and to the coverage by the media, especially by the publicly owned media, and with regard to public funding of parties, candidates and campaigns. The concept of equal treatment can either be understood as strict equality or as proportionality.[51] Strict equality means that political parties are treated without regard to their present strength in parliament or the number of votes. It must necessarily apply to the use of public facilities for the election process. Proportional equality can be applied when allocating radio and television air-time or public funds.[52]

In order to ensure a free competition between political parties and candidates, certain political human rights must be respected.[53] This is especially true of free speech and freedom of the press, and of freedom of assembly and association for political purposes, especially during election campaign periods.[54]

46 *Venice Commission*, Code of Good Practice in Electoral Matters: Guidelines and Explanatory Report, CDL-AD (2002) 23 rev., p. 9.

47 *Venice Commission*, Europe's Electoral Heritage, CDL (2002) 7 rev., p. 29; *D. Richter*, in: Dörr/Grote/Marauhn (eds.), EMRK/GG. Konkordanzkommentar, 2nd ed. 2013, Chap. 3 mn. 46 ff.

48 *Venice Commission*, Europe's Electoral Heritage, CDL (2002) 7 rev., p. 30.

49 *W. Heintschel von Heinegg*, in: Vedder/Heintschel von Heinegg (eds.), Europäisches Unionsrecht, 2012, Art. 2 TEU mn. 8.

50 *Venice Commission*, Europe's Electoral Heritage, CDL (2002) 7 rev., p. 23.

51 *Venice Commission*, Europe's Electoral Heritage, CDL (2002) 7 rev., p. 23.

52 *Venice Commission*, Europe's Electoral Heritage, CDL (2002) 7 rev., p. 23.

53 *Venice Commission*, Europe's Electoral Heritage, CDL (2002) 7 rev., p. 16; *D. Richter*, in: Dörr/Grote/Marauhn (fn. 47), Chap. 3 mn. 38.

54 *Venice Commission*, Law on Parliamentary Elections of the Republic of Azerbaijan, CDL-INF (2000) 17, p. 2; *Venice Commission*, Europe's Electoral Heritage, CDL (2002) 7 rev., p. 16.

4. *Majority Rule and Guarantee of Effective Opposition*

Another integral part of democracy forms the majority rule.[55] Parliament decisions shall be taken by the majority, and a parliamentary system of government is characterized by the fact that the government will usually have the support of the majority.

However, democracy must not degenerate into a dictatorship of majority. The majority rule must be accompanied by a guarantee of effective opposition. The Venice Commission considers that there are certain categories of parliamentary opposition and minority rights that are of particular importance and should be generally recognized. These are procedural rights of participation, special rights of supervision and scrutiny of the government, rights of veto or delay for certain decisions of a particularly fundamental character, the right to demand constitutional review, and protection against persecution and abuse.[56]

IV. The Consequences of National Breaches of the Principle of Democracy

Having identified these specific elements being indispensable to qualify a Member State as democratic, there has to be a look at the consequences of a breach of the principle of democracy by a Member State. A defective democratic legitimation of national parliaments or national Governments inevitably results in a defective democratic legitimation on the European level.[57] A decision taken by the European Council or the Council of Ministers is democratically defective if one member of these bodies lacks democratic legitimation.[58] For each member of a collegial body has to be properly legitimated.[59] An absence of democratic structures in a single EU Member State thus deprives the European Union as a whole of its democratic foundation.[60]

Via the European Union, the absence of democratic structures in one Member State even causes democratic defaults within the legal orders of all other EU Member States. Did an improperly legitimated Council of Ministers, together with the European Parliament, adopt an EU regulation or an EU directive, the Member States would be obliged to apply or to implement an improperly legitimized act within their national legal orders.[61]

55 *A. Nussberger/E. Özbudun/F. Sejersted*, Report on the Role of the Opposition in a Democratic Parliament, adopted by the Venice Commission, at its 84th Plenary Session, CDL-AD (2010) 025, p. 7.
56 *A. Nussberger/E. Özbudun/F. Sejersted* (fn. 55), p. 22 ff.
57 *M. Zuleeg* (fn. 14), JZ 1993, p. 1069, 1072 f.; *A. Haratsch*, in: Brandt (fn. 14), p. 19, 35.
58 *A. Haratsch*, in: Brandt (fn. 14), p. 19, 35.
59 Cf. VerfGH NW, OVGE 39, 292, 294, citing BVerfGE 38, 258, 271 – Magistratsverfassung Schleswig-Holstein; BVerfGE 47, 253, 275 – Gemeindeparlamente; BVerfGE 52, 95, 130 – Schleswig-Holsteinische Ämter.
60 *A. Haratsch*, in: Brandt (fn. 14), p. 19, 35.
61 *A. Haratsch*, in: Brandt (fn. 14), p. 19, 36.

For the non-observance of the principle of democracy on the level of a Member State results in a democratic deficiency on the level of the European Union, there is a legal obligation to take action against any violation of the democratic principle by a Member State. The means of choice should the mechanism according to Article 7 TEU.

V. The Correlation between Democracy and other Fundamental Values

As mentioned at the beginning, democracy in itself is not the only legal principle to safeguard a legitimate and moderate system of government. Democracy needs to be supplemented by other underlying principles of modern statehood, as there are the rule of law, the principle of separation of powers and the protection of human rights. These principles do not only stand in a relationship of supplement but might also compete against each other. Just recently, the Hungarian Government tried to outplay the rule of law by the principle of democracy when conducting a referendum on the reception of refugees in Hungary.[62] The argument was that Hungary would not be obliged to abide by European Union law if the Hungarian people voted against it in a referendum. This notion is not correct. Democracy does not axiomatically trump the rule of law. The same applies to the relation between human rights and democracy. It is not possible to deprive a group of people, such as foreigners for instance, of their inalienable human rights by an act of parliament or by means of a referendum. In the Hungarian case, the rule of law represented by the primacy of EU law over national law must prevail. The only conceivable exception might be made if a certain provision of European Union law were in breach of an element of the inviolable core content of a Member States constitutional identity. This national reservation to the primacy of European Union law was established by several national constitutional courts, including the German Federal Constitutional Court.[63] In the Hungarian case however, evidently the core content of the national constitutional identity was not touched.

VI. Conclusion

Democracy is an essential part of Europe's cultural heritage. Its implementation is a central means in order to prevent suppressive regimes and to achieve freedom. Democracy is unthinkable without free elections and without people who firmly believe that their voices are heard and their votes matter. It is the duty of the EU Member States and of the European Union itself to fight anti-democratic activities

62 The Hungarian referendum related to the European Union's migrant relocation plans was held on 2.10.2016. Although more than 98% voted against the relocation plans, the referendum was invalid because the turnout was to low; cf. the results published by the Hungarian National Election Office: http://www.valasztas.hu/en/ref2016/481/481_0_index.html.

63 Cf. BVerfGE 123, 267, 353, 387 – Lisbon.

and to further the awareness of the importance of democracy. But despite these pathetic words on a great idea, the essence is about little things you have to keep a vigilant eye on. As I commenced my presentation with a quotation by Winston Churchill, please allow me to conclude with another Churchill quote. In October 1944, he gave a short summary what is the essence of one of the most powerful ideas emanated from human mind: "At the bottom of all the tributes paid to democracy is the little man, walking into the little booth, with a little pencil, making a little cross on a little bit of paper – no amount of rhetoric or voluminous discussion can possibly diminish the overwhelming importance of that point."[64]

64 Quoted in: *W. Churchill*, in: Langworth (fn. 1), p. 100.

Part II:
Liability of Member States

The nature and requirements for liability of a Member State under Article 7 TEU

*By Luboš Tichý, Prague**

The aim of this article is to define and analyse liability of the EU member state pursuant to provision, which has not been applied yet and its character is primarily preventive. However this provision as sanction for breach of a duty by Member State is nothing exceptional in comparison with federal states and international organisations. Fundamental principles of European law and severity of violation shall be observed while the liability is assessed. European delict as a violation of fundamental European values (EU law principles) consists of penal essential elements including wrongful conduct, protected object and harmful as result on the object. Issues of culpability, attribution and justification shall be relevant as well. Particular offenses of member state against values might be prosecuted pursuant to article 258 et seq. TFEU.

I. Introduction

The aim of this paper is to define the liability of a Member State under Article 7 of the Treaty on European Union (TEU). It intends to define the meaning and purpose of the rule in Article 7 establishing a mechanism of sanctions for the wrongful conduct of a Member State, which I call European delict. Therefore, I will define this concept and describe the liability of a Member State for such an act in relation to other liability regimes under the EU law.

Article 7 TEU is a normative expression of a specific liability relationship which is based on a public offense (wrong, tort) called European delict endangered by a significant sanction.[1] Committing of a European delict and as well as the imposition of (not easily enforceable) sanctions are vital for the functioning of the European Union. They are undoubtedly important also for the affected Member State

* Professor at the Charles University, Prague.

1 The importance of Art. 7 is that it is oriented in constitutional situations in the Member States and that the violation of certain values (principles) amounts to a sanction from the EU. Art. 7 thus ensures frameworks in which the Member States have to agree how to conduct themselves among and towards each other. In other words, Art. 7 TEU may, within the meaning of Art. 2 TEU, support the argument that primary law provides for an instrument to ensure homogeneity in the EU. Federal states and international organisations use similar sanction mechanisms. For instance, the Statute of the Council of Europe contains a provision in Art. 8 governing the requirement of an enforcement mechanism against Member States (Art. 8: Any Member of the Council of Europe which has seriously violated provisions of Art. 3 may be temporarily suspended of its rights of representation and requested by the Committee of Ministers to withdraw within the meaning of Art. 7. If such Member does not comply with this request, the Committee may decide that the Member State ceased to be a Member of the Council of Europe as from such date as the Committee may determine). Homogeneity as an EU-principle means similarity of certain legal principles both among the Member States as such and towards the EU.

itself. Although I do not consider it to be the "Barroso's nuclear option"[2] there is no doubt that both the European delict and the sanctions are enormously politically charged.[3] However, my task here is not to politically evaluate the EU law rule in question, but rather its legally doctrinal interpretation. Therefore, the political context needs to be incorporated only into a legal argument.

In this paper I firstly lay down the purpose of the regulation of European delict (ad II) which was firstly contained in the Treaty of Amsterdam for reasons which now appear fully legitimate. The motive for the introduction of a special sanction mechanism was the necessity to efficiently secure the foundations of then European Communities prior to the accession of new Member States in 2004. However, breaches of fundamental values by "old" Member States were also recorded.[4]

Theoretical analysis of European delict is contained in Part III which also addresses basic elements of liability of a Member State with a constitutional dimension. These elements have similar nature as in criminal, administrative law or international law but also in the context of the EU as it is applied in other cases, for instance by Art. 258-260 or Art. 126 TFEU.

Conduct of a Member State may not be sanctioned although it formally fulfils all elements of Art. 7 TEU provided that such conduct does not contravene the law. Factors which include particular danger and the exclusion of liability of a Member State are analysed in Part IV.

Liability regime stipulated by Art. 7 TEU is not the only one in EU law. The Union may sanction a Member State in a number of other cases as well. This paper aims to not only to discuss the sanction (liability) regime in EU law but also to analyse in detail the concept of liability stipulated by Art. 258 TFEU as well as the interaction of these two regimes. The key issue is namely a possible subsidiarity of Art. 7 and Art. 258 TFEU and the possibility to sanction a Member State for violation of the fundamental values contained in Art. 2 TEU also within the liability regime stipulated by Art. 258 TFEU, which despite its milder sanctions may be due to its decision-making mechanism more efficient than the regime foreseen by Art. 7 TEU.

Final part (VI) then summarises all conclusions I drew in this paper.

Finally, it should be noted that my interpretation is to some extent rather a brave venture as it is one of the few attempts to interpret Art. 7 TEU in connection with Art. 2 TEU as a basis of a liability system.

2 See also the speech of *J. Barroso* delivered in the European Parliament on 11 September 2013, SPEECH/13/684, p. 11. We need a middle ground between diplomacy and infringement proceedings and the radical choice of suspending the rights of Member States.

3 The violation of fundamental values undoubtedly undermines the mutual trust among the Member States on the one hand and between the Member States and the EU on the other.

4 See III. 2. f).

II. The purpose and conception of Article 7 TEU

1. The purpose

Article 7 TEU is a provision of unique, exceptional character. It codifies a public law institute of constitutional liability of a Member State for delict (wrongful act) committed by it against the ideological foundations of the community (EU) of which it is a member and which serves to preserve the fundamental features of this community. The determination of this liability by the European Union institutions, for which Article 7 contains rules, is thus a certain test of the "state of health of the EU."

The purpose of the rule in Article 7 TEU is the protection of the substance of the EU, which is expressed in the fundamental values enshrined in Article 2 TEU.[5] These values, which undoubtedly also need to be perceived as fundamental principles of EU law, are exhaustively listed. Considering the nature of the liability of a Member State, such listing is essential, even though defining individual values is not an easy task.

I see the fundamental mission of Article 7 TEU in its preventive function. Perceptible sanctions represent a very serious threat for potential wrongdoers. The deterrent effect of these sanctions has an impact at both the European and national levels. At the European level, the Member State, sentenced for committing the delict and subject to suspension of certain membership rights, is threatened by the adoption of measures against which the Member State cannot defend itself due to the absence of the judicial control. Its position may thus change for the worse, which may also be evident at the national level. The convicted state may be also threatened by legal actions, such as an action for compensation for a loss, etc. Therefore, the losses as a result of sanctions can be of an immense nature. The application of Article 7 is in this context a major threat to the Member State. Thus it should be discouraged deterred from committing the violation and, respectively, it should be compelled (motivated) to respect the EU values.

2. Conception

A relatively broadly defined subject-matter of the European Union delict is the essence of the rule contained in the analysed article. Besides that Article 7 also contains a rule of determination of a member state liability for the European delict which represents a kind of the EU constitutional procedural law. Finally it con-

5 The Union may be seen as a community of values. Some authors refer to it as a framework of values, with values serving as an instrument of integration thus marking the progress from an economic community to a community of values (*Chr. Calliess,* Europa als Wertegemeinschaft – Integration und Identität durch europäisches Verfassungsrechts?, JZ 21/2004, p. 1034, 1038). Values may be classified based on their significance, as done by *Chr. Calliess* (see above). Values may also be divided into leading values (Leitwerte), fundamental values (Grundwerte), and individual values (Einzelwerte). All of these values are mandatory rules.

tains the definition of the sanctions for the European delict. However I do not deal with these two aspects in this paper.

a) Principles of the liability for European delict

aa) Compliance with principles of a State governed by the rule of law: wrongfulness, ne bis in idem, prohibition of retroactivity

Wrongfulness is a general requirement of a European delict (see III. 2. e)), which reflects the fact that the EU law connects with its commitment a threat of imposition of a sanction.

The rule of law principle[6] is preserved as Art. 7 TEU stipulated the prohibition of certain conduct and thus lays down the wrongfulness in its material elements.

It is generally accepted that conduct aimed against protected interests (legal goods) other than the values enumerated in Art. 2 may not be deemed a European delict; although, as already mentioned (see above), their delimitation, or the qualification of their relation to other legal goods, is difficult.

The principle *ne bis in idem* is applicable. This principle excludes the sanction or liability of a Member State for the same conduct even though that conduct is contained in a set of the Member State's other lawful expressions of will.

The prohibition of retroactivity means the exclusion of the possibility to judge the conduct of a Member State at the time of the adoption of the decision more strictly than it would be judged at the time of the expression's articulation resulting from a change in practice that occurred in the between commitment of the tort and the decision on it.

bb) Role of the principle of proportionality

Proportionality includes three concepts: suitability, necessity and proportionality in a narrow sense. It is relevant not only when determining the sanction, but above all in the assessment of wrongfulness.[7]

Suitability means that when assessing the conduct of a Member State, the preventive objective of Art. 7 TEU should be reflected or the functions of the respective Member State, in particular those regarding its territorial integrity, maintenance of public order and protection of national security, should be respected. National security should remain a matter reserved solely to each Member State.

Necessity means the assessment of the mandatory character of the rule the respective Member State breaches and the intensity in which it negatively affects fundamental values.

6 The CJEU stresses the fundamental, essential value of the principle of the rule of law, consisting of the principle that the acts of EU institutions are subject to judicial review in regard to their compliance not only with the treaty but also with "general principles of law including fundamental rights" (e.g. CJEU, C-50/00 P (Union de Pequeños a Gricutores), ECLI:EU:C:2002:462, ECR 2002, I-06677, mn. 38 and 39, CJEU, joined cases C-402/05 P and C-415/05 P (Kadi), ECLI:EU:C:2008:461, ECR 2008, I-06351, mn. 316.)

7 *J. Schwarze*, Europäisches Verwaltungsrecht, 2. ed. 2005, p. 830.

Proportionality in a narrow sense means assessment of the wrongfulness against the prognosis of the current state and future development of the EU.

On the other hand, it is necessary to abide by the principle of uniform application of EU law as one of the principles of great significance to the value of a legal community. This also includes consensus, legitimation, integration and security.

The duty to respect fundamental values may not depend on the internal organization of Member States. After all, the principle of equality is also one of the fundaments of EU law.

Elements existing behind the above-mentioned terms have key importance for a successful integration process. Homogeneity means equivalence of certain legal principles both between Member States and in relation to the EU. It is an expression of consensus between the Member States as a fundamental requirement for the functioning of the EU.

cc) Meaning of the principles of solidarity

From the generally valid moral postulate, a constitutional principle of the EU evolved, which is an objective feature of relationships within this community. It represents the implementation of the jointly-defined objectives. Solidarity, although often dependent on the political and social events, must be applied uniformly within the whole social environment. The EU common welfare is realized through a set of national interests, which must be once again applied in harmony with the EU objectives.[8] The principle of solidarity has undoubtedly a control function as well and correlates in this regard with the principle of loyalty. However, solidarity[9] does not mean immediate reciprocity, and it certainly has nothing to do with altruism.

dd) Function of the principle of loyalty

Speaking clearly in favor of the concept of Art. 7 TEU, is the principle of loyalty as standard of the conduct of Member States and of the EU,[10] respectively their individual duties within the meaning of Art. 4 par. 3 TEU. This norm has constitutive effects even in situations on which the applicable provisions do not mention the duty of loyalty. The duty of loyalty particularly means respect of the primacy of EU law and represents a prerequisite for the functioning of the EU, particularly

8 *P. Gussone,* Das Solidaritätsprinzip in der Europäischen Union und seine Grenzen, 2006, p. 243.

9 Solidarity, in the sense of the principle of solidarity, is based on reciprocity. It is an obligation associated with an expectation of consideration. Solidarity, as one-sided obligation of an altruistic nature, could lead to a weakening of the functioning of the EU, which is based on reciprocal solidarity (*P. Hipold,* Solidarität im EU-Recht: Die "Inseln der Solidarität" unter besonderer Berücksichtigung der Flüchtlingsproblematik und der europäischen Wirtschafts- und Währungssunion, EuR 4/2016, p. 373). Solidarity within the meaning of EU law has a particularly distinctive content that differs from the usual concepts of solidarity. The problem of refugees is directly related to the principle of solidarity. By its violation, respectively by the absence of such principle, some Member States have begun to build barriers on their borders to prevent the entry of refugees into their territories, which has completely disputed the principle of solidarity. This is particularly the case of Hungary.

10 *A. Hatje,* Loyalität als Rechtsprinzip in der Europäischen Union, 2001, p. 79.

the need of the uniform application of EU law and thus an element of the principle element of the legal community. From the duty of loyalty follows also an obligation of mutual trust within the Member States and the EU.[11]

ee) Role of the principle of subsidiarity

Besides the primary meaning of Art. 7 TEU as a prevention instrument, we should think about the application of the provision with respect to the liability of a similar nature enshrined in Art. 258 TFEU, i.e. liability for infringement of the Treaty.[12]

The main factual difference between these two liabilities lies in delimitation of the protected interest (legal goods, see III. 2. c).

While a conduct deemed as an infringement of the Treaty is understood as a breach of any legal provision and not exclusively in primary law, in case of the European delict the interest is the protected values. As I will point out (see III. 2. e)), an attack on the values represents primarily a violation of the specific provisions of particular EU law.

Since the EU should exhaust all remedy instruments, it should use the procedure according to Art. 258 TFEU prior to the activation of the procedure anticipated by Art. 7 TEU, with the exception of the cases, where the alleged delict was caused by a breach of the European legal norms outside the system of Union law.

b) Types of delicts and its stages

aa) European delict as a material delict (a tort amounting to an unlawful effect) and formal delict (a tort subsisting in an unlawful conduct)

Two types of an unlawful conduct must be distinguished with regard to its effect: firstly, an unlawful conduct amounting to an unlawful effect which is completed upon formation of the unlawful effect. As an example may serve a situation when police or other armed forces repeatedly unlawfully suppress a lawfully held manifestations. In contrast to this, formal delict does not require an effect and is committed upon issuance of a certain act (e.g. adoption of laws limiting free press without enforcing them).

bb) Disruptive delict, threatening delict or preparation of a delict

In terms of possible consequence or effect I distinguish disruptive delict and threatening[13] delict. This classification is similar to the classification of material and formal delicts. As a violation of fundamental values may be deemed enact-

11 The principle of loyalty can be regarded as a measure of the unlawfulness of conduct contrary to the values in Article 2 TEU.

12 See ad V.

13 *F. Schorkopf*, in: Grabitz/Hilf/Nettesheim (eds.), Das Recht de Europäischen Union, 59th supplement 2016, Art. 7 TFEU, mn. 21.

ment of an act restricting the powers of a constitutional court or oversight over certain sectors of state administration although these measures clearly lack any specific results. In case of threatening torts is the level of materialisation of its results, i.e. the effect on protected goods, lower. As desirable is seen the assessment of the level of harmfulness of the conduct (see III. 2. g)), which is, in essence, preparation of a delict, as a separate delict. This is, for instance, the case of an advanced stage of conduct of a Member State within the meaning of Art. 7 (1) TEU, i.e. the case of creation of conditions leading to breach of values enumerated in Art. 2 TEU. Such conduct must be in a stage approaching the commission of a dangerous threat. Apparently it presupposes "clear danger of violation of fundamental values".[14] This subject matter covers the existence of clear risk of a serious violation of fundamental values. That risk must be eminent, doubtless and immediate.[15] As a consequence it means to undertake a prognosis.[16]

Art. 7 (1) TEU thus governs a specific threatening tort instead of preparation of a disruptive tort.

Unlike the concept of the disruptive delict under Art. 7 (2) TEU has the concept of the threatening delict pursuant to Art. 7 (1) only one and not two forms of threatening result. Thus, the conduct representing the risk of a persistent violation shall not be considered an European delict.

cc) Continuation of an unlawful conduct (delict)

Continuation of an unlawful conduct (delict)[17] designates a conduct of a Member State whose elements (attacks) fulfil the set of elements of a European delict and that were executed in same or similar manner or in within a certain time frame. Continuation[18] means in case of European delict for instance enactment of implementing legislation enabling the adoption of concrete measures restricting freedom of speech while this framework restriction was foreseen by a statute. From the procedural point of view which is relevant due to the case law of the CJEU

14 This notion was introduced by the Lisbon Treaty, after the experience with the “Austrian case“ with the participation of the FPÖ in the Austrian cabinet. (e.g. *G. Winkler*, Europa quo vadis, ZÖR 2000, p. 231; *F. Schorkopf*, Verletzt Österreich die Homogenität in der Europäischen Union?, DVBl 2000, p. 1036; *W. Hummer*, Das Ende der EU-Sanktionen gegen Österreich – Präjudiz für ein neues Sanktionsverfahren?, The European Legal Forum 2000, p. 77; *W. Hummer/W. Obwexer*, Die Verhängung der „EU-Sanktionen“ und der mögliche Ausstieg aus ihnen, ZÖR 2000, p. 269; *S. Schmahl*, Die Reaktionen auf den Einzug der Freiheitlichen Partei Österreichs in das österreichische Regierungskabinett, EuR Heft 5, 2000, p. 819).

15 *Ph. Voet van Vormizeele,* in: von der Groeben/Schwarze/Hatje (eds.), Europäisches Unionsrecht, 7th ed. 2015, Art. 7 TEU, mn. 10.

16 *F. Schorkopf* (fn. 13), Art. 7, mn. 21.

17 While an instantaneous breach, understood as a breach of an obligation by an act not having a continuing character, occurs at the moment when the act is performed, even if its effect continues (ARSIWA, Art. 14(1)), a continuing breach occurs when the event occurs and extends over a period during which the event continues and remains not in conformity with that obligation (ARSIWA, Art. 14(2)).

18 It is understood that the difference between completed and continuing acts is very relative. A continuing wrongful act itself can cease: the prisoners can be released. In essence a continuing wrongful act is one which has been commenced but has not been completed at the relevant time. Where the continuing wrongful act has ceased, for example by releasing the prisoner or withdrawing police forces, the act is considered as no longer having continuing character for the future.

regarding Art. 258 TFEU individual attacks[19] may be seen as separate delicts with their own identity.

dd) Ongoing (persistent) delict

Ongoing tort designates a conduct of a Member State in which the Member State incited the unlawful state and subsequently maintains it. Typical is that in this case is predominantly sanctioned the maintenance of the unlawful state. Ongoing tort is seen as a one action lasting for as long as the unlawful state is maintained. For instance a Member State adopts a law supressing the freedom of media or limiting the controlling function of the constitutional court. Classification of such conduct as a single tort bears relevance for their sanctioning as infringement under Art. 258 TFEU.

c) Participation and accomplicity

Participation of several Member States in commission of a European delict may take various forms. Member States may be fully expressly or tacitly engaged in specific measures. It is also possible to consider a fort of participation in which some Member States participate next to the main wrongdoer by supporting him or partial execution of his measures.
The first case may be exemplified on actions of members of Visegrad group contravening the decisions of the Council on refugee quota.[20] Another form of support is submission of a claim contravening fundamental values which other Member States join as intervening parties.
While in the case is the accomplicity as grave as the commission of the tort and thus each Member State bears whole liability for the consequences, in case of support of such action it amounts only to accessory as it is less grave.

III. The European delict and the requirements of liability of a Member State pursuant Art 7 (1), (2) TEU

1. General introduction

Rules contained in Art. 7 (1) and (2) TEU, i.e. regulation of European delict, may be characterised with help of several criteria which may provide us with a better understanding which may be useful for instance when determining liability of a

19 The character of a composite act is such that the original act of the Member State, which inaugurated the series of actions leading to the breach, cannot be the same as when the act is deemed to have matured or been accomplished.

20 It is clear that all four countries of the Visegrad Treaty and Rumania violated Council Decision EU 2015/1523 of 14.9.2015 (which lays down temporary international protection measures in favour of Italy and Greece) and Council Decision EU 2015/1601 of 22.9.2015 (with the same designation). Some states have even challenged this decision at the CJEU.

Member State for a European delict. Thus we determine the scope of application of this provision as connection point with the conduct of Member States. Classification of an unlawful conduct used in administrative law used for qualification of a European delict as serious and ongoing (persistent) violation of fundamental EU values.

This paper is based on the thesis that liability regime pursuant to Art. 7 (1) and (2) TEU is a liability regime *sui generis* established in the scope of public law. In other words, even though this relationship is referred to as liability, it differs from its private law counterpart. This is for several reasons. Firstly, it falls solely within the scope of public law and has no relationship to the liability under the private law whatsoever. The private law liability regime in EU law applies when assessing liability of the EU or a Member State for damage under Art. 340 TFEU. The concept of liability for European delict differs from this type of liability. Liability under Art. 340 TFEU is a liability for damage. Liability for European delict lacks this element of liability for damage.

As to its nature the liability of the Member State for breach of the values pursuant to Art. 7 TEU is constitutional liability. It aims to protect fundamental common values of the EU enshrined in Art. 2 TEU. Even though liability for European delict has features strongly aimed at prevention, which is similar to the concept of liability in private law, it differs from the liability in private law which is to protect an individual, its material and immaterial interests.

Breach of fundamental values referred to as European delict, constitutes an unlawful conduct that differs from a tort under private law, which is defined as a purpose-oriented conduct, intentional or negligent, and failure to exercise due care. European delict does not fall within the scope of administrative or criminal law. Both civil and criminal law presuppose fault of the tortfeasor, while in the case of European delict is fault irrelevant.

Liability under Art. 7 TEU differs from administrative and criminal liability as well as from liability in private law by one more element. In contrast to administrative, criminal and private law, causality plays a minor role in the regime of liability under Art. 7 TEU. This is also due to the fact that physical impact in form of damage (harm, injury) does not play a relevant role in liability for European delict. Thus it is not necessary to examine the causality between action and its impact.

2. *Material scope of European delict*

a) Conduct

"Conduct" designates any activity of a Member State in the field of legislature, administration or judiciary. It is irrelevant whether the respective conduct took form of an act, implementing legislation, court judgment, administrative decision or a factual activity nor whether the Member State acted in the scope of shared

competence (Member State together with the EU) or exclusive competence – autonomously or within the scope of EU law.[21]
Functional analysis of such conduct with respect to the final result is relevant. In other words, a number of measures does not need to be primarily aimed against the fundamental values, many of them have a clearly different purpose. A negative impact on the fundamental values may be even a by-product of such measures.
As already mentioned above, a breach may also occur as a result of conduct of a Member State which may take form of action but also a form of omission, hence in principle any form of a disregard of bans and orders which are based on fundamental values or legal rules and which execute or implement them. Disregard of instructions, i.e. failure to comply with one's duties, thus takes form of omission, conduct breaching a ban takes form of action.

b) Protected object

Objects of the violation (also protected objects) are generally considered to be relationships, interests and values, which are often referred to as the legal assets protected by law.
The subject matter of the European delict includes six protected objects. However, these do not have to be to affected cumulatively; affecting just one of them is sufficient. All six fundamental values are covered. But a violation of mere one of them might be considered an European delict.[22]
A protected object therefore includes individual fundamental values enumerated in Article 2 TEU.[23] Their concrete expression, however, is found in a number of legal acts in a variety of legal sources, and even in other non-legal forms. The main relevant fact is that they are included in the primary EU law.[24]

c) Protected goods

Protected are legal relationships as well as rights serving as a basis for the above values.
However, protected are also actual objects such as newspapers, schools, institutions and other which are a physical manifestation of protected values.
Some torts require a specific consequence in form of negative changes on the protected good (see II. 2. b) aa)) which may be intangible such as legal relationships,

21 Communication from the Commission to the Council and the European Parliament on Art. 7 of the Treaty on European Union. Respect for and promotion of the values on which the Union is based, COM (2003) 606 final, 1.1.

22 *F. Schorkopf* (fn. 13), Art. 7, mn. 21.

23 EU integration is based on values. These values also express an identity since the integration creates a certain common system. That is why the EU, like every community, is based on shared fundamental values (*Chr. Calliess*, Europa als Wertegemeinschaft – Integration und Identität durch europäisches Verfassungsrecht?, JZ 21/2004, p. 1044).

24 See also Communication from the Commission to the Council and the European Parliament on Article 7 of the Treaty on European Union, COM (2003) 606 final, see fn. 22.

reputation, name, etc. These specific consequences or specific impact may be considered also in the case of a European delict. For instance, the limitation of fundamental rights (such as freedom of expression, freedom of assembly etc.) already contains the tort elements. In other words, a legislative measure limiting these may constitute a breach of protected goods such as values contained in Art. 2 TEU without having to implement this measure first. Newspapers do not need to be actually censored, prohibited or confiscated nor other measures have to be taken. In other words, a Member State has already committed a European delict without having to implement any such restriction or prohibition. The implementation and the extent of actual measures may contribute to the specification of the intensity of unlawful conduct of the Member State, however, it is not a necessary element of liability of the European delict.

d) Instrument used in the commission of the tort

The term "instrument" covers all measures adopted for the purpose of attack on protected values and thus violation of the protected values. It includes factual activity aimed at suppression of manifestation, legal provision conflicting with the principle of rule of law, measures restricting human rights etc.

e) Wrongfulness

Wrongfulness is a normative expression of the fact that a Member State has breached an obligation established for the protection of fundamental values. The Member State's conduct is therefore inconsistent with the fundamental interests (see the protected object) of the EU. Wrongfulness is necessarily understood according to the interpretation of individual values, not only in the context of EU law, as the legal system, but also in connection with the Member State's commitments stemming from non-EU legal sources. Wrongfulness may exist as a violation of national or international law as well; thus in legal regimes which also govern the values contained in Article 2 TEU.

Wrongfulness can therefore be seen as a violation of (mandatory) standards which are found in various sources of law (see II. 2. a) ee)). These rules are contained in EU law in unwritten and written primary law, in secondary law, and in the regulation of fundamental rights[25], not only in the Charter of Fundamental Rights of the EU, but also in the ECHR. These rules may also be the norms contained in the national law of a Member State, especially those of constitutional character. Finally, contradiction with the norms of public international law, which contains the regulation of fundamental values, is also relevant.

An aspect of wrongfulness is present when its sole or primary purpose is a breach, restriction or other effect on these values without the existence of such purpose

25 Fundamental human rights are expressions of the existing core of common values and represent unmistakable, originally common values, and, at the same time, the inner condition of modern democracy (*U. Haltern*, Europarecht und das Politische, 2005, p. 554).

(for the exclusion of liability see IV) that would justify such conduct in the benefit of other relevant interests whose relevance would be comparable to the relevance of fundamental values which they contravene.
Legal norms that Member States had to observe in specific situations are the main criteria used to qualify illegality, as their contents are sufficiently specific and mandatory.

f) Result

According to the vast majority of opinions of the doctrine of public law, in order to qualify conduct as unlawful, as in the case of European delict, another requirement is necessary: the breach of, or at least the threat to, an individual object. Such object is a fundamental value of the EU and the consequence of its breach. The result is thus a mandatory element of the European delict. Depending on whether the conduct of a Member State directly affected the object, or just threatened it, it can be distinguished disruptive and threatening delict (see II. 2. b) bb)).
Breach of respect of human dignity (for example Arts. 1-5 of the Charter of the European Union). As a failure to respect human dignity qualifies for instance introduction of investigative methods amounting to torture albeit by suspected terrorists. Another example may be humiliating conditions of employment of foreign workers, including failure to adhere to basic hygiene standards and other conditions.
There is a number of Member State's actions which may amount to a breach of freedom (Arts. 6-19 of the Charter) and thus to a European delict. These include for instance reduction of police forces (for instance through salary reductions) leading to the formation of no-go zones or general concerns about personal safety. As a European delict qualify also mass publications of personal data, removal of its control combined with the existence of corruption and thus the absence of oversight. Also enactment of an act prohibiting change of one's religion or prohibition to form and join trade unions or other civic groups may constitute a European delict.
Failure to adhere to principles of democratic society may have different forms such as an electoral system preventing free competition of political parties or irregularities in communal elections.
Differences in remuneration of men and women for the same work may constitute a massive breach of the principle of equality (discrimination). This breach can be established in a number of EU Member States. Intensive and widespread breach of the principle of equality may amount to qualification of the conduct of the Member State as amounting to a European delict.

The breach of principle of rule of law[26] as one of the most complex values under Art. 2 TEU may be a frequent case of European delict.[27] For instance, limitation to the legislative procedure which must be transparent under any circumstances, amounts to a European delict. Legislation[28] as a result of failure to comply with proper drafting principles amounts to the reduction of legal certainty and so do frequent amendments which are a widespread phenomenon in a number of Member States.[29]

Circumvention or abuse discretion in administrative proceedings and failure to penalise a decision resulting from dysfunctional administrative judiciary is another example of a breach of principle of rule of law. Political influencing judicial review of respect of fundamental human rights for instance through vulgar criticism by the head of state, is another example of breach of fundamental values.

Systematic and widespread appointment of former clerks to administrative courts may result in decreased independence of administrative judiciary. Even more controversial are cases of shifting in which disciplinary powers regarding conduct of judges of constitutional courts were shifted on the parliament or decisions modifying hearings of cases pending before a constitutional court.[30] A clear breach of presidential duties is a refusal to accept the oath of a judge of a constitutional court and so is the refusal to appoint members of the cabinet as foreseen by the constitution or refusal to appoint the president of a constitutional court.[31]

Another broad and complex issue is violation of human rights, including fundamental market freedoms. In this case, the CJEU already held Hungary[32] liable in proceedings under Art. 258 TFEU.[33]

26 On the situation in Hungary, see the resolution of the European Parliament P8_TA(2015) 0227 from 10.6.2015. In its decision, the Commisssion emphasied a systematic threat to the principle of the rule of law (para 10).

27 Cf. *V. Reding*, "A new Rule of Law initiative", SPEECH/14/202 from 11 March 2014, (para. 1) and communication from the Commission to the European Parliament and the Council COM (2014) 0158 final from 11 March 2014, A New Framework to strengthen the Rule of Law.

28 Resolution of the European Parliament on the situation in Hungary regarding enactment of a number of laws (ECLI:EU 2012 C/199 E/154 f., ECLI:EU 2013 CE 33/17 ff., P7_TA (2012) 0053 from 16 February 2012 and 2012/22130 (INI), P7_TA (2013) 0315 from 3 July 2013. Another initiative of the European Parliament in the form of a recommendation to implement the Commission notice from 2003, P7 _TA (2013) 0315, 24.

29 See also the Cooperation and Verification Mechanism, seen as a certain tool for the protection of the rule of law, which was introduced in December 2006, before Bulgaria and Romania joined the EU, and which had certain supervisory powers at its disposal to ensure the rule of law structures in these candidate countries. Hereto *D. Kochenov/L. Pech*, Upholding the Rule of Law in the EU: On the Commission´s “Pre-Article 7 Procedure” as a Timid Step in the Right Direction, European Issues no. 356, 12th Mai 2015, p. 2.

30 See the contribution of *M. Wyrzykowski*.

31 See *M. Wyrzykowski* (fn. 30).

32 See the Decision of the European Parliament on the situation in Hungary (2015/2700 of 10.6.2015), which not only lists the individual problems, but also contains a statement that the European Parliament sees “a systematic threat to the rule of law in Austria” (para 10). The European Parliament referred to the procedure proposed before applying Art. 7 TFEU (“pre - Article 7 procedure”). See *V. Reding* "A New Rule of Law Initiative", SPEECH/14/202, 11.3.2014, p. 1.

33 The European Commission decided to open infringement proceedings against Hungary under Art. 258 TFEU (cf. CJEU, C-286/12 (Commission v Hungary), ECLI:EU:C:2012:687 on equal treatment of judges and prosecutors in respect of their old age pension.

g) Gravity and persistency (harmfulness)

In determining whether a delict has occurred, European legislators start with the material concept of a tort. Apart from fulfilment of formal elements, fulfilment of its material elements presupposes the fact that the State's conduct exhibits a material element, i.e. it constitutes a serious[34] and persistent[35] violation of the protected object[36]. Only then may a State's conduct be deemed wrongful (European delict). As material element of a tort is understood a conflict with the objective of the EU legal system. Gravity and persistency[37] must be met cumulatively and thus, to a certain extent, resemble a qualified breach within the meaning of a case of the CJEU in the matter of liability for damage caused by the EU or by a Member State under Art. 340 TFEU (see III. 1.).[38] The gravity namely corresponds with a material and imminent breach in the mentioned case law. However, the duration of the breach as another material element constitutes another deviation from this standard.[39]

It must be so great that it will ultimately damage even one of the fundamental values. Only the systemic behaviour of the relevant leadership authorities, even through the tolerance of the number of violations, fulfils European delict. Thus, a breach is only permanent (persistent) if the unlawful situation is maintained for a longer period of time and the Member State concerned insists on a breach of homogeneity. In the Commission´s view, indications of permanent violation are given when a Member State is convicted several times in a short period of time by international courts or by extrajudicial bodies.[40]

34 As *Wilms* mentioned, the concept of "serious breach" is based on CJEU case law in the field of non-contractual liability (*G. Wilms*, Rules on Values, Homogeneity and their Enforcement in other Multilayer Systems 58). The extent that an institution disregards the limits of discretion is relevant for determining the seriousness of the breach.

35 As to the term of "persistent breach", there are cases where the Commission sued a Member State for its administrative practice under Art. 258 TFEU. The leading case is C-494/01 (Commission v Ireland), ECLI:EU:C:2005:250, ECR 2005, I-3331. The Irish citizens in this case complained over a period of 3 years about a number of incidents involving the deposit of waste in violation of the provisions of the waste directive.

36 See also the examples listed as serious and persistent breaches in the Commission Communication of 15.10.2003 (COM (2003) 606 final, 1.4.3 and 1.4.4 on page 8).

37 There are three criteria developer by the European Court of Justice in determining whether an infringement of EU law has occurred in the field of administrative practice acts of a Member State: structural character, scale, time of duration, and seriousness (*G. Wilms* (fn. 34), p. 59).

38 A number of cases of violation of fundamental rights were the object of other proceedings under Art. 258 TFEU. In certain cases, the Member State ceased the violation. The situation in Poland was a reason for first use of the Pre-article 7 TEU procedure established by the Commission in March 2014. The Commission issued the first rule of law opinion, meaning the first step in the Pre-article 7 TEU procedure, against Poland. The case of limiting media pluralism occurred in Italy, Hungary and Poland. Hungary and Poland hampered the work of NGOs. The efforts of curbing the independence of the courts happened in Italy, Romania, Hungary and Poland. The fundamental rights of emigrants were violated by France. France ceased the evacuation and expulsion of Romas after the Commission announced that it would start an infringement procedure. Italy, in the end, foiled several cases to concentrate media power, to avoid "biased" judges, and to curb the powers of the constitutional court to have laws *ad personam* adopted.

39 See also the examples listed as serious and persistent breaches in the Commission Communication of 15.10.2003 (COM (2003) 606 final, 1.4.3 and 1.4.4 on page 8).

40 See the Commission Communication of 15.10.2003 (COM (2003) 606 final), 1.4.4.

3. Personal scope

Personal scope delimitates the scope of application of Art. 7 with respect to specific wrongdoers whose behaviour is attributable to the Member State. Liable is any person whose actions may be attributed to the Member State. It includes state authorities such as courts, public institutions, civil servants as well as third parties factually acting on behalf of the respective Member State.
In this aspect it is permissible to accept the case law of the CJEU when assessing conduct of Member State pursuant to Art. 258 TFEU. Conduct of bodies of the Member State must be undoubtedly strongly attributed to the Member State, attributed therefore must be any relevant conduct on regional level.[41] Irrelevant is whether the national law stipulates the independence of the national body or whether is subject to central authority. In this respect is decisive the duty of loyalty of the respective Member State.

4. Territorial scope

Territorial scope designates the area in which European delict may take place or in which may materialise its consequences.
It may include not only the territory of the breaching Member State, but also the territory of another Member State or even a third State in which the breaching Member State acted or on which materialised consequences of unlawful conduct.

5. Temporal scope

Temporal scope designates the time period in which may be applied Art. 7 TEU. Relevant is commencement of this period, i.e. the date of effect of the TEU as amended by the Lisbon Treaty. A Member State thus may qualify as an offender of a European delict provided all elements of the tort were met after this date. Retroactivity is impermissible.

IV. Circumstances justifying Member State's conduct

1. Attribution in the context of the EU legal system, material concept

The conduct of a Member State may meet the formal requirements of a tort without being considered a European delict, provided that it is lawful. This may be due to circumstances preventing the respective Member State from respecting the fundamental values. As a result, the respective Member State may rely on distress or self-help.

41 CJEU, C-8/88 (Germany/Commission), ECLI:EU:C:1990:241, ECR 1990, I-2321; CJEU, C-129/00 (Commission/Italy), ECLI:EU:C:2003:656, ECR 2003, I-14637.

Certain circumstances, in particular events independent from the respective Member State, may have diverse characteristics and intensity with respect to their consequences. However, in their assessment it is notably important to reflect their relation to the respective Member State when examining the Member State's conduct. Consequently, it is necessary to assess the Member State's relation to them with respect to its possible influence on their occurrence, as well as the manner in which the circumstances were tackled. An assessment of a formation and existence of these circumstances in the wrongdoer's sphere, particularly where there is the closest connection, will also be relevant. Situations when these circumstances lay in the sphere of the EU, or are otherwise beyond the wrongdoer's control, will be thus assessed differently.

Three circumstances may preclude wrongfulness, namely force majeure, distress, and necessity. All of them denote cases where, at least in some sense, a Member State is compelled to commit an act that does not conform with an obligation. The term force majeure differs from the other two circumstances in that it implies that the Member State's act is due to something beyond its control. That act is essentially involuntary.

Distress is distinct from force majeure into ways. First, it precludes the wrongfulness of voluntary acts. Whereas force majeure requires material and immaterial impossibility, in distress, the Member State has no real choice other than to breach an obligation.

2. Distress

Distress[42] may be deemed a state in which the protection of an interest protected by EU law remains possible only upon interference with another protected interest. These circumstances must constitute a danger for values listed in Art. 2 and must be direct and imminent. The Member State has no obligation to tolerate such danger; however, its conduct when overcoming such danger may not amount to a consequence that is equally severe or even more severe than the consequence that would otherwise occur. An excess must be considered a circumstance reducing the level of wrongfulness, although excessive conduct may not be a justifying fact.

The source of danger to the fundamental values is irrelevant. It may be external forces as well as civil unrests or natural disasters. Terrorist attacks or a threat of their occurrence may constitute distress or, as mentioned above, *force majeure*. Restrictions of certain fundamental human rights or even certain functions that are typical for the rule of law are permissible if in the interest of safety of the population. However, such restriction must be proportionate to the threat. The duration of restrictive measures must be proportionate as well.

42 Distress has been described as a material source or extra-legal blueprint of all legal defenses.

Similar regime may also apply to a Member State providing help even when in the state of distress or provides help to another Member State that is in the state of distress, for instance with a restriction of the right to property when accommodating displaced persons in a refugee crisis.
Distress in a broad sense also includes self-help or distress since precautions aimed against unpredictable forces or circumstances may be deemed defence. Restriction of certain rights is thus to protect fundamental values, such as the duty to provide help to refugees, minorities or religious groups.

3. Consent

Consent of affected subjects constitutes another circumstance justifying an otherwise illegal conduct of a Member State, for instance when restricting the right to property as already mentioned. However, the consent may not be coerced when fundamental rights or values are not adhered to. Consent may not be based on a manipulation with free will.
Unlike in criminal law, EU constitutional law may therefore reduce the importance of consent of the injured party as a justification of an unlawful conduct of a Member State. In other words, even though the opinion polls indicate that the majority of the population approves the behaviour of the respective Member State, that, in fact, conflicts with the fundamental values, such approval does not render such conduct legal, i.e. in accordance with fundamental European values. The same applies to consent of a representative body (parliament) to such conduct.
Thus it is clear that legitimising reasons, i.e. facts excluding unlawfulness, must follow from objective circumstances such as the state of war and other exceptional circumstances.

V. Liability regime under Art. 7 TEU, its role in EU law and its relation to liability for a breach of the Treaties under Art. 258 TFEU

1. Liability system of the EU

I perceive liability of a Member State, on which I will focus in this section, as fulfilling a secondary obligation, which arises after a violation of primary obligation under EU law. Secondary obligation is a penalty imposed by an EU institution, either by the European Commission, the CJEU, or, as in the case of liability under Art. 7 TEU, by the Council. Although it is rarely even mentioned, there are plenty of liability regimes in EU law. Some of them have their basis in private law, but most of them are based in public law liabilities. These individual subsystems do not stand completely independent next to each other, but should create a certain unity. They are based on the same doctrinal foundations in spite of the differences in details when formulating the requirements of liability. These systems

are comparable even in terms of structure. Although there are system-immanent particularities based on the specific task of each subsystem, all of them pursue both the prevention and remedy function.
From the conceptual point of view is the closest liability regime that is based in Art. 258 TFEU liability of a Member State for breach of the Treaties. Given is rising use[43] it is necessary to focus on this regime and compare it with the liability regime under Art. 7 TEU, especially with regard to the possibility to use it as a procedural apparatus that is much more flexible and efficient than the approach under Art. 7 (2)-(4) TEU.

2. *Tort liability under Art. 258 TFEU and its comparison with the liability regime stipulated by Art. 7 (1) and (2) TEU*

a) Comparison of both regimes

aa) Purpose

Liability regime established by Art. 258 TFEU aims to ensure proper functioning of the EU and national regimes within the Member States pursuant to expectations expressed in EU law. It aims at maintenance and preservation of legality. The liability under Art. 258 TFEU is non-fault liability.[44] It is not only to deter and prevent but also to mend and to make the Member State cease its wrongful conduct (tort).
It is beyond dispute that both regimes are similar in this respect. The liability regime under Art. 7 TEU also aims to maintain order. It sanctions breach of primary duties stipulated by EU law in the broadest sense (see III. 2.). The source of law whether it is the Treaties (Art. 258 TFEU) or values (Art. 7 or Art. 2 TEU) is irrelevant. The difference is in material elements, i.e. gravity of the wrongful conduct of a Member State which is reflected in Art. 7 TFEU. A breach of fundamental values namely presupposes a grave tort, which is emphasized by the extent (intensity) of the conduct (see serious and persistent breach), while Art. 258 TFEU permits penalisation of a tort with any degree of gravity with the exception of minor misdemeanours.

bb) Main features

In case of infringement under Art. 258 TFEU, the respective tort may subsist in any "measure" of the respective Member State, its type or character are irrelevant. It is irrelevant whether the Member State committed the breach with an act, regulation, contract, judgment, administrative instrument or an informal conduct.[45]

43 *U. Ehricke*, in: Streinz (ed.), EUV/AEUV, 2009, Art. 258 TFEU, mn. 4.
44 Cf. CJEU, C-451/92 (Commission/Germany*)*, ECLI:EU:C:1995:260, ECR1995, I-2189, mn. 21.
45 K. -D. *Borchardt*, in: Lenz/Borchardt (eds.), EU-Verträge, ed. Art. 258 TFEU, mn. 6.; *U. Karpenstein,* in: Grabitz/Hilf/Nettesheim (eds.), Das Recht der Europäischen Union, 59th Supplement 2016, Art. 258 TFEU, mn. 65.

The actions may take place in legislature, administration or judiciary. European delict does not differ in this respect (see above).
Art. 258 TFEU protects the legal order and legal relationships established pursuant to it. The tort under Art. 258 TFEU includes written or unwritten law, primary, secondary or tertiary law as well as general principles of law, contracts with third States and international organisations.[46] Art. 7 TEU does not differ in this respect. The object protected is more abstract, but in essence the same.

cc) Exclusion of liability

The CJEU in its case law under Art. 258 TFEU adopts a rather strict approach to defence objections of Member States. For instance, it disregards obstacles stipulated by national law of Member States[47] or a reference to an infringement by another Member State as well, which the Commission tolerated,[48] irrelevant is also an objection that EU bodies failed to comply with their duties.[49] A claim stating the breach was marginal[50] or an argument that the Member State compensated injured parties for its unlawful conduct or at least promised such compensation were also unsuccessful. The CJEU assesses a defence of *force majeure* even in situation in which was adherence to EU law objectively impossible.[51] The CJEU does not require an absolute impossibility, it nonetheless maintains the circumstances to which the Member State refers as *force majeure* must be based on circumstances that are fully independent of the Member State's will, unusual and unpredictable and thus rendering the prevention of their consequences impossible despite all reasonable efforts.[52] These cases constitute, in fact, distress (see IV.).
Even though the CJEU nor theory address the distress, certain facts in these cases may be undoubtedly seen as one. The level of strictness of the CJEU when assessing defences is high, yet given the gravity of the breach it appears adequate. In principle, it corresponds with assessment of similar defence of a Member State in case of a European delict (see IV.).

46 In its Communication of 19 March 2014, COM (2014) 158 final/2, the Commission inaccurately defines the subject matter of the action, respectively proceedings under Art. 258-260. It defines this subject too narrowly when it claims that it must infringe a specific provision of EU law. It is generally and undeniably accepted (*Cremer*, in: Calliess/Ruffert (eds.), EUV/AEUV, 5th ed., 2016, Art. 258 TFEU, mn. 33; *U. Ehricke,* in: Streinz (fn. 42), Art. 258 AEUV, fn. 6; *W. Frenz,* Handbuch Europarecht, vol. 5, 2011, mn. 2542 ff; *U. Karpenstein,* in: Grabitz/Hilf/Nettesheim (fn. 44), mn. 25; *C. Nowak,* in: Leible/Terhechte (eds.), Encyklopädie Europarecht, Vol. 3, § 10, mn. 38, that the infringement also includes, as a subject matter of the proceedings, the infringement of general legal principles and treaties with third states and with international organizations, etc.

47 Cf. CJEU, C-450/00 (Commission/Luxembourg), ECLI:EU:C:2001:519, ECR 2001, I-7069, mn. 8; CJEU, C-503/04 (Commission/Germany), ECLI:EU:C:2007:432, ECR 2007, I-6153, mn. 38.

48 Cf. CJEU, C-232/78 (Commission/France), ECLI:EU:C:1979:215, ECR 1979, 2729, mn. 9; CJEU, C-118/07 (Commission/Finland), ECLI:EU:C:2009:715, ECR 2009, I-10889, mn. 48.

49 CJEU, C-45/07 (Commission/Greece), ECLI:EU:C:2009:81, ECR 2009, I-701, mn. 26.

50 CJEU, C-456/05 (Commission/Germany), ECLI:EU:C:2007:755, ECR 2007, I-10517, mn. 22.

51 CJEU, C-404/97 (Commission/Portugal), ECLI:EU:C:2000:345, ECR 2000, I-4897, mn. 39 ff.; CJEU, C-441/06 (Commission/France), ECLI:EU:C:2007:616, ECR 2007, I-8887, mn. 27.

52 CJEU, C-297/08 (Commission/Italy), ECLI:EU:C:2010:115, ECR 2010, I-1749, mn. 85; CJEU, C-334/08 (Commission/Italy), ECLI:EU:C:2010:414, ECR 2010, I-6869, mn. 46 ff.

dd) Member State liability is non-fault (strict) liability

Fault is not an element of liability for breach of the Treaties under Art. 258 TFEU[53] and neither are intent[54] or negligence[55] Similarly in the case of European delict under Art. 7 TEU fault is not the requirement of the liability of a Member State.

ee) Attribution

Liability shall be attributed to the Member States regardless of whether the respective body or the respective official were entitled to act or not. Irrelevant is also whether these persons abused their powers or disregarded instructions given by their superiors.[56]
Majority of case law as well as the doctrine hold that adjudicating activity of a court of a Member State does not infringe the Treaties as such and thus the conduct may not be attributed to the Member State even though a judgment conflicts with the Treaties. The reason is the independence of the judicial branch executing such power which the Member State may not influence and thus pressure it to adjudicating that would be in line with the EU law.
As mentioned above, we do not share this view with respect to European delict committed by Member States since the concepts of attribution differ substantially in both regimes.
It is possible to argue that conduct of the court may be attributed to the respective Member State. It is the task of the Member State to ensure the courts adjudicate in accordance with the principle of rule of law and other fundamental values. In order to achieve this, the Member State is required to employ its educational systems. A sanction imposed for a judgment contravening EU law on the respective Member State should serve as a warning as well as an impetus.

b) Does the principle of subsidiarity apply?

It follows from the above that both types of liability are similar in their main features. Thus it is inevitable to consider their mutual relationships as being subsidiary. Such an approach may be derived from the purpose and regime of sanctions as an instrument to procedurally and institutionally ensure both regimes of liability.
Art. 258 TFEU permits this approach in case of an attack of a Member State which may be qualified as an infringement as well as breach of values within the meaning of Art. 2 TEU, when there is a serious breach (for instance violation of

53 CJEU, C-385/02 (Commission/Italy), ECLI:EU:C:2004:522, ECR 2004, I-8121, mn. 40.

54 CJEU, C-574/10 (Commission/Germany), ECLI:EU:C:2012:145, mn. 49; CJEU, C-68/11 (Commission/Italy), ECLI:EU:C:2012:815, mn. 63.

55 CJEU, C-297/08 (Commission/Italy), ECLI:EU:C:2010:115, ECR 2010, I-1749, mn. 82.

56 CJEU, C-334/08 (Commission/Italy), ECLI:EU:C:2010:414, ECR 2010, I-6869, mn. 39.

the principle of rule of law) yet the element of duration is absent even though such a breach exhibits the elements of an ongoing (persistent) tort.

Nonetheless and in the light of the principle of audiatur et altera pars it is necessary to adhere to the principle of identity of the action in every stage of proceedings as required by case of the CJEU. This is not an issue in case of a persistent tort. Yet it requires the Commission (or another Member State) to initiate new proceedings.

c) Criticism of the proposed approach

Lastly, it is necessary to assess the arguments which may be brought against such proposition. Expected may be a statement designating it as an abuse of power since both the objective and the concept of Art. 7 TEU differ substantially from the concept of liability under Art. 258 TFEU. The concept of European delict aims at grave misconduct of a Member State attacking the very foundations of the EU. This is also reflected in the distinctive regime of Art. 7 TEU which aims at participation of the respective Member State in in decision-making of the EU and at its rights as a Member State. In this case, the decision is bound to be made not by EU institutions as it is the case under Art. 258 TFEU, but by the Member States as such. Ultimately it is also possible to argue that the introduction of the institution of European delict after forty years of functioning of Art. 258 TFEU (former Art. 226 TEC, or Art. 169 TEEC) was not designed to replace this proven scheme.

These as well as other objections are easy to disprove. A more lenient approach (given the sanctions under Art. 258 TFEU) may be adopted under the above conditions, particularly in initial stages of the wrongful conduct. Furthermore, this approach has one breaking advantage corroborated by the principle of rule of law: it is subject to a court review the case under Art. 7 TEU is not.

In case of recidivism it is permissible to initiate new proceedings under Art. 258 TFEU or launch proceedings under Art. 7 TEU. However, this is not possible in cases when the respective Member State refused to abide by the judgment of the CJEU or carries on with its tortious conduct. This is prevented by the principle of ne bis in idem.

VI. Liability qualification according to Art. 7 TEU and its position in the liability system of the EU – Summary

Liability of a Member State for a breach of the values stated in Art. 2 TEU is constitutional law liability, which has specific sanctional character.

It is being brought closer together with other liabilities of the Member States under the EU liability system by the brevity of the merits of European delict, which is the basis of liability.

Liability according to Art. 7 TEU differs from the others liability subsystems primarily by delimitation of the protected interest and sanction system.
Protected interest concerns the basis of the EU system; the sanctions system is, in principle, an independent enforcement regime that is, again in principle, exempted from the control powers of the CJEU. Sanctions fundamentally differ by their nature from sanctions in other liability subsystems.
The merit of the European delict and its liability are mostly similar to breaches of the Treaty according to Art. 258 TFEU. The Article 7 TEU is *lex specialis* to Articles 258 and 259 TFEU concerning the material scope. It does not exclude opening infringement procedures for the violation of the Members State's obligations with regard to fundamental values.[57]

57 *G. Wilms* (fn. 34), p. 81.

Comparative study on enforcing common values against subnational units, member states in federations and other international organizations. De societatis et de civitatis

*By Laurent Sermet, Aix-en-Provence**

The enforcement of common values against subnational units by member states in federations and other international organizations raises many fundamental questions, whose nature is much wider than positive law. It is important to determine by which elements a society does establish a political and social order. The social contract in modern society is dominated by extreme complexity. Has it ever been simple? Can law guarantee the foundations of an ordered society through its methods, its language, and its demiurge vocation? Can it define what is useful, what is fair, and what is good? Is it possible to establish a legal system without reference to legitimacy, efficiency, reason, comparison, or values? What place should be values to be given in legitimizing a legal system?

No human collectivity can be identified without shared values. According to Tönnies, two major forms of human collectivity can be distinguished by measuring the intensity of the ties between their members: community and society, or in German: *Gemeinschaft und Gesellschaft* (*societatis et civitatis*, in Latin)[1]. It is indeed their respective inclusive force that helps to distinguish them. Ethnology substituted for this opposition in two main types of social organization. These categories depend on whether it is a simple or a complex one, and according to the degree of technical and relational specialization of its members. A simple society would be highly integrated.[2]

It is recognized that values make sense and pursue a function of social inclusion, which is also the functional object of law: to make sense (*ratio legis*) and to socially including. When the system of law appropriates values, its legitimacy is strengthened. The functional relations between law and values are twofold: (1) the law enunciates values and (2) it ensures them a binding force. Law alone may not be strong enough to create social links. Citizenship is not simply orchestrated by law: it is the complex result of a common history, a language, a collective will to live together, and a shared feeling of common national destiny. The law gives citizenship a formal consistency, through a normative construction and a binding force. However the sole instrument of law cannot orchestrate humanity. The Universal Declaration of Human Rights, *per se*, does not establish "*unity of the human family*", as stated in the preamble. It merely receives and formalizes that con-

* *Prof. Dr. Laurent Sermet*, Professor of Public Law, Political Studies School/Institut d'études politiques, Aix-en-Provence.

1 *E. Durkheim*, Communauté et société selon Tönnies, *Sociologie* [En ligne], 2013, n°2, vol. 4, URL:http://sociologie.revues.org/1820.

2 For a critical analysis of simple opposed to complex society: *A. Testart*, Éléments de classification des sociétés, Errance, 2005.

viction, which results from moral, ethical, philosophical, religious and social values.

Values and law are useful tools to qualify the level of social and political integration.

Are there specific values to law? The Roman lawyer Ulpian, repeating the famous formula of Celsus in 212-213, stated that *Ius* is "*the discipline of what is right and equitable*", based on the observation that *Ius* and *Iustitia* have, in Latin, the same linguistic root. Hobbes thought that law was justified by power, not by truth or reason.

Values are not forever stable, as is the case in modern democracies, where over-complexity dominates, and human rights continue to play an inclusive role but their recurring violation cast doubt on their merits. Values are not always a social choice, but a political necessity, as the success of the sustainable development formula exemplifies. Sustainable development is a modern value as it is the only rational way to sustain for coexistence between present and future generations, for an equitable sharing of resources.

The interrelation between values and law reveal the level of social and political integration. Societies are distinguishing three levels of integration, depending on whether they are national, regional or international. These three levels are valid as the first two seem to belong, according to Tönnies, to the Gemeinschaft collectivity and the last one to Gesellschaft. The stronger their values are, the more integrating the mechanisms of their sanction are. In others words, the two first levels are of constitutional nature, either formal or informal, the latter one remains of international nature.[3] The values and their sanctions make it possible to qualify the degree of integration of each level, whether constitutional, regional or international.

We will question the relationship between law and values and specifically formulate the following questions: "Values, as accepted by the legal order – which definition?" and "Values received by the legal order – what sanctions?".

I. Defining common values, as a test for a society or a community

1. The constitutional comparative approach: the diversity of possible approaches

National values are a matter of social and political myth. They narrate a national history, a destiny, a collective wish to live together and because values give sense

3 Contra see: *P.-M. Dupuy*, The Constitutional Dimension of the Charter of the United Nations Revisited, Max Planck Yearbook of United Nations Law 1997, vol. 1, p. 33, in: http://www.mpil.de/files/pdf1/mpunyb_dupuy_12.pdf.

to the Nation, they are "narrated" by the Constitution and explained by constitutional case-law. How does the constitutional legal order articulate the link between their substance and their formalization? Four distinct scenarios will be considered.

a) Does substance equal form? Fusion, or confusion, between constitutional rights and constitutional values

In some cases, constitutional case-law shows almost a total lack of distinction between a right and a value. This approach is followed by the Constitutional Court of Slovenia[4] as to the issue of whether an act is unconstitutional and whether a referendum would eliminate such unconstitutionality: "*These were the basic issues that had to be answered in order for the Constitutional Court to then weigh, in such a position involving a collision of constitutional values, whether priority should be given to the right to request a referendum or to other constitutional values*".

In the case about a referendum on austerity measures which dealt with a collision of "constitutional values" (i.e. the right to request a legislative referendum as a constitutionally ensured the right versus right to constitutionally protected values), Judge Jan Zobec, joined by Judge Dr Ernest Petrič, both concurred that: "*The first step in the search for the answer to this question is the definition of the "weight" of the competing values*". He added that: "*The weighing (and balancing) of the competing values is a difficult and dangerous task (it can easily overstep intuition and become arbitrary). It is impossible to compare colors and smells, length and weight; likewise, individual constitutional goods are beyond metrical comparison. Balancing does not mean quantifying but establishing relations between the competing values and requires argumentative skills.*"[5]

b) The positivist approach for a clear distinction between law and values: the position of the Lithuanian Constitutional Court

In a significant decision, related to organized crime,[6] the Court highlighted a conceptualization of values received in the constitutional order, based on three components:

4 Constitutional Court, Slovenia, 17 Dec. 2012, case no. U-II-1/12, U-II-2/12, see Constitutional Court of the Republic of Slovenia, Selected decisions 1991-2015, p. 1266, in http://www.us-rs.si/media/zbirka.an.25.-.let.pdf.

5 See Constitutional Court of the Republic of Slovenia, Selected decisions 1991-2015, p. 1259.

6 "Ensuring of safety of each human being and the whole society from crimes is a duty of the state and one of its priority tasks as by the crimes one violates not only human rights and freedoms and other values protected and defended by the Constitution, but also negative impact to living conditions and subsistence level of people is made as well as the fundamentals of the life of the state and society are encroached upon. In case the state fails to take proper actions in order to prevent crimes, the trust in the state power and laws would be destroyed and disrespect in legal order and various social institutes would increase. Therefore, according to the Constitution, the state, an organisation of the entire society, which must guarantee the public interest, has not only the right, but also a duty to take various lawful measures preventing the crimes, as well as restricting and reducing crime. The measures established and applied by the state must be efficient": Constitutional Court, Lithuania, Dec. 29,

- The protection of fundamental rights and freedoms
- The legal bases of life in society, as established by the Constitution
- The State as a basis for the political organization of society

From this case, it can be inferred that the court identifies values as the essence of the law and the reason of the state. Legal order, the state and constitutional procedures are the means to allow values to be efficient.

c) The interpretative approach: law and values, an accepted distinction, suggested rather than conceptualized

A number of examples demonstrate that the notion of value is recognized and practiced by constitutional courts without establishing a theory, a doctrine of constitutional positivism or moral positivism. The use of values facilitates the reasoning of the decision.

The Polish Court, in a decision on the right to life of the foetus, decided to refer to a constitutional value, due to the lack of a written constitutional right concerning the protection of prenatally human life.[7] The significance of this decision deepens the distinction between value and constitutional right as the first does not actually need to be written in order to be enforced. The significance of this decision also lies in the fact that the lack of prior political assent on the content of the value does not mean that it cannot be received by the legal system. It can also be inferred from this decision that the value is a concept of meaning, not a formal concept, and it relates to the very essence of the law.

The South African Constitutional Court, for its part, "colorizes" the concept of constitutional rights, taking into account the values of the new political order established after the fall of apartheid. Thus it refers to the: "*founding constitutional values of human Dignity, the achievement of equality and the advancement of Human Rights and Freedoms, non-racialism and non-sexism.*"[8]

The Court infers from the constitutional values a clear interpretation in regard to the relationships between contractual liberty and constitutional values; the latter prevail over the Pacta Sunt Servanda principle.[9] It is a very similar position to that which is followed by general international law in regard to Jus cogens and treaties.

2004, n° 8/02-16/02-25/02 -9/03-10/03-11/03-36/03-37/03- 06/04-09/04-20/04-26/04-30/04 -31/04-32 / 04-34/04-41/04.

7 Constitutional Court, May 28, 1997, n° K 26/96.

8 CTC, 4 April 2007, case CCT n° 72/05, *Barend Petrus Barkhuizen vs Ronald Stuart Naper.*

9 "Under common law the principle of freedom of contract (often expressed in the maxim pacta sunt servanda) has never been absolute. Rather, it has always been subject to limiting rules intrinsic to the law of contract. […] In Barkhuizen itself this Court made it clear that freedom of contract is by no means absolute under our constitutional dispensation. It endorsed an 'approach that leaves space for the doctrine of pacta sunt servanda to operate, but at the same time allows courts to decline to enforce contractual terms that are in conflict with the constitutional values even though the parties may have consented to them'": CCT, March 24, 2014, Case CCT 61/14, André François Paulsen and others.

d) The French approach: formal values without substantial values?

Constitutional jurisprudence has given rise to the notion of the objective of constitutional standing named in French "**objectif de valeur constitutionnelle**". The notion dates back to the decision of 19 and 20 January 1981 when the Constitutional Council recognized that: "*the search of offenders and prevention of violation of public order (safety of people and property) are necessary for the implementation of principles that have constitutional standing (in French values)*"[10].

It can be said that: "*Objectives of constitutional value appear as the necessary corollary for the implementation of a constitutionally recognized right.*"[11] In reality, the objective of constitutional value means an objective with a constitutional rank, i.e. a formal concept rather than a substantial concept. As the term constitutional value is used in French, it is officially translated in English by "standing" (i.e. by the services of constitutional Council).

It is clear, however, that French constitutional law contains values of political and social nature which characterize the French constitutional singularity, whose revolutionary anchorage is obvious. These are the values of individual freedom and conscience and of equal rights, as stated by article 1 of the Declaration of Human and Civic Rights of 1789. The French approach to values valorizes universal human rights, which is somehow a contradiction given that French national identity claims to be of universal nature.

2. *The regional approach: Convergence on human rights and democratic constitutionalisation*

The first aim of regional integration was to bring national economies closer together. A harmonized and integrated law for economic exchanges, free movement of goods, of services and of persons was established on the basis of treaties and secondary legislation.

Then, a material, non-formal, change took place, for reasons of further integration. It was intended to go beyond the traditional tools of international law on which the initial economic project of regional integration was based. This development was expressed through the fiction of a material constitutionalisation. By informal constitutionalisation of regional law we mean a minimum of government, judicial review, and popular representation, as well as separation of powers

10 Constitutional Council, France, 20 January 1981, Decision n° 80-127 DC, Loi renforçant la sécurité et protégeant la liberté des personnes, Recueil, p. 15.
See also: "it is for the legislator to ensure, on the one hand, a reconciliation between the prevention of breaches of public order and the search for the perpetrators of misdemeanours, both of which are necessary in order to safeguard rights and principles of constitutional standing, and on the other hand the exercise of the rights and freedoms guaranteed under the Constitution; that these include the respect for freedom of movement, further to Article 4 of the 1789 Declaration of the Rights of Man and the Citizen, and the right to privacy, dwelling inviolability and the secrecy of private correspondence, which are protected by Article 2", Constitutional Council, France, 25 March 2014, Decision no. 2014-693 DC, Law on geolocation.

11 *B. Genevois*, La jurisprudence du Conseil Constitutionnel, Les editions STH, 1988, § 342, p. 205.

between Member states and regional Organizations and within the regional Organization.

This fiction has been clearly expressed within the European Economic Community with the *Parti Ecologiste Les Verts* judgment, which has adopted a terminology usually reserved for constitutional law, evoking a community based on the rule of law. The fiction has also been operative within the European Convention on Human Rights, qualified by the Court of Strasbourg as a: "*constitutional instrument of European public order*"[12].

a) European Economic Community and European Union: from human rights values to democratic values

In 1957, the EEC treaty contained no provisions on fundamental rights, except for the clause on equal pay for men and women for the same work (Art. 119 of the Rome Treaty). In the absence of a positive basis on human rights, the Court of Justice of the European Communities highlighted the existence of a common heritage in the form of constitutional traditions common to the Member States,[13] formalized as general principles of law of EEC law.

That informal constitutionalisation has continued through the incorporation of the "principles" of democracy and the rule of law common to the member states (ex Art. F of the Maastricht Treaty, 1992). The new Art. 2 of the Treaty of Lisbon abandoned the term "principles" and preferred the term "values": "*The Union is founded on the values of respect for human dignity, freedom, democracy, equality, the rule of law and respect for human rights, including the rights of persons belonging to minorities*".

This clause is not declaratory: compliance with these values is a condition of membership of the Union (Art. 49 TEU) and their breach may trigger the procedure of Art. 7 TEU. These values do not exist *in abstracto* but are at the same time the expression of the values of the Member States and the expression of the substantial nature of the European Union. These values are also shared by the Council of Europe.

b) Council of Europe integration on human rights and democracy values

The Council of Europe bases the values it defends on Art. 3 of its constitutive statute (May 5th, 1949): "*Every member of the Council of Europe must accept the principles of the rule of law and of the enjoyment by all persons within its jurisdiction of human rights and fundamental freedoms, and collaborate sincerely and effectively in the realization of the aim of the Council as specified in Chapter I*".

12 ECHR, 23 March 1995, 15318/89 (Loizidou v. Turkey), § 75.

13 CJCE, Case C-11/70 (Internationale Handelsgesellschaft), ECLI:EU:C:1970:114, ECR 1970, 1125: In fact, respect for fundamental rights forms an integral part of the general principles of law protected by the Court of Justice. The protection of such rights, whilst inspired by the constitutional traditions common to the Member States, must be ensured within the framework of the structure and objectives of the Community.

On the occasion of the terrorist attacks in Paris, November 13, 2015, the Parliamentary Assembly adopted a resolution to establish a "democratic response": "*These attacks were attacks against the very values of democracy and freedom in general, against the type of society that our pan-European Organization has aimed at building since the end of the Second World War.*"[14]
The "Council of Europe's values" test is used for the states acceding to it as it was the case for the Czech and Slovak Federal Republic applying for membership of the Council of Europe.[15] For the European Court of Human Rights, the membership of the Council is: "*a membership to the organization's values*"[16].

c) African integration on human rights and democracy principles

In Africa, where the transformation of the Organisation of African Unity into the African Union in 2001 was viewed as a "*visionary step towards greater integration, good governance and the rule of law in African countries*"[17], it may be observed that the values of Human rights, democracy and economic integration are accepted and interrelated. Unlike Europe, Africa is characterized by multiple regional economic integrations, some of which have overlapping territorial jurisdiction. This means that one state may be a party to several regional integrations. *Economic Community of West Africa States* (ECOWS) is one of them.
ECOWAS Protocol on democracy and good governance (2001) is particularly emblematic of the wish to establish common rules governing the political actions of Member States.[18] Art. 1 defines the *Constitutional Convergence Principles* shared by all member states. Here again, a movement of constitutionalizing regional law is at stake. It is necessarily based on values but does not refer to the term "values". Among the *Constitutional Convergence Principles*, the best known of them is the one on the prohibition of unconstitutional changes of government and undemocratic modes of access or of continuation in power (Art. 1, c.). The ECOWAS protocol is part of the same continental and pan-African principle developed by the constitutive act of the African Union, 2000 (Art. 4, p.)[19].

14 Parliamentary Assembly Resolution 2031 (2015) January 28, 2015, Terrorist attacks in Paris: Together for a democratic response.

15 Parliamentary Assembly Council of Europe, 30 January 1991, Opinion 155 (1991), Application by the Czech and Slovak Federal Republic for membership of the Council of Europe.

16 ECHR, 8 July 2008, 33629/06 (Vajnai/Hungary).

17 *S. T. Ebobrah*, Legitimacy and feasibility of Human rights. Realisation through regional economic communities in Africa: the case of the Economic Community of West Africa States, Thesis submitted in partial fulfilment of the requirements for the degree of Doctor of Laws (LLD), University of Pretoria, Faculty of Law, 30 September 2009, p. 79, in http://repository.up.ac.za/bitstream/handle/2263/27990/Complete.pdf?sequence=9&isAllowed=y.

18 *N. Kridis*, La CEDEAO et les changements anticonstitutionnels, p. 53 et s., in Les changements anticonstitutionnels du gouvernement: approches de droit constitutionnel et de droit international, Rafâa Ben Achour (dir.), Les cahiers de l'Institut Louis-Favoreu, Presses Universitaires d'Aix-Marseille - P.U.A.M., 2014, p. 170.

19 Art. 4, p. rules "condemnation and rejection of unconstitutional changes of governments".

The Community Court of Justice of the Economic Community of West African States (ECOWAS) refers to the Protocol to deliver its judgments[20]. The ECOWAS Court accepted the judicial action of a legal body, namely coffee and cocoa producers in Côte d'Ivoire, based on the provisions of Art. 1(h) of the Protocol on Democracy and Good Governance,[21] but dismissed the case.

The constitutional and quasi-constitutional approach emphasizes the preference for the values of the rule of law, democracy and human rights. Whether these norms are qualified as values or principles depend on the legal order at stake. As mentioned by the Lisbon Treaty, values are preferred whereas the ECOWAS protocol refers to principles of constitutional convergence. At the universal level the situation is very different because of the very low intensity of integration of international law.

3. *What values for universal level?*

In contrast, international law struggles to impose common values highlighting the little operational reality of an international community.

Two particularly noteworthy mechanisms, however, have been established, in addition to Chapter VII of the UN Charter relating to international peace and security.

The first mechanism is based on Art. 103 of the UN Charter which provides for States Charter's obligations to prevail over their others treaties' obligations. Thus the whole Charter provides for a superior legality, both of formal and substantial nature. Would it be possible to consider the Charter a universal Constitution?[22] Obviously the very structure of international law, based on the unsurpassable concept of sovereignty, weakens the constitutionalization process. If one common "value" had to be mentioned, it would be the prohibition principle of recourse to the threat or use of force in international relations, as stated in Art. 2 § 4 of the Charter. This UN principle is also of customary nature.[23] This first mechanism allows us the consideration that the United Nations legal order promotes if not common values, at least an UN legal order for states to cooperate. It differs from the second mechanism, which is at a truly universal level.

20 ECW/CCJ/JUD/05/09: The National Co-ordinating Group of Departmental Representatives of the Cocoa-Coffee Sector (CNDD) v. Côte d'Ivoire. That case is about excessive taxation on coffee and cocoa producers in Côte d'Ivoire.

21 "The rights set up in the African Charter on Human and Peoples' Rights and other international instruments shall be guaranteed in each of the ECOWAS Member States; each individual or organisation shall be free to have recourse to the common or civil law courts, a court of special jurisdiction, or any other national institution established within the framework of an international instrument on Human Rights, to ensure the protection of his/her rights".

22 *R. Chemain/A. Pellet* (dir.), La Charte des Nations Unies, constitution mondiale?, 2006, p. 237. This book is about the constitutionalism at stake in the international legal order which would be embodied in the concepts of "international community" or peremptory norms of international law.

23 ICJ, 27 June 1986, Military and paramilitary activities in and against Nicaragua (Nicaragua v. United States), §§ 202-209.

This second mechanism is based on Art. 53 of the Vienna Convention on the Law of Treaties (1969). It states the invalidity of any treaty contrary to a peremptory norm of public international law, recognized as a jus cogens norm (imperative) which is valid *erga omnes* (general for every State). But contrary to the Charter, this provision does not give examples of substantial rules of jus cogens. The definition of the substance of the jus cogens should be determined by States' practices and, if it may be, also determined by the International Court of Justice.[24] Jus cogens is a formal concept without prior substantialization. The current work of the International Law Commission is aimed specifically at giving it a normative content.

II. Sanctions for violating common values, as a test for a society or a community

Even if values are beyond the law, given that they nourish the essence of it, they are received by the legal system and are legalized. As such they are subjected to sanctions, formally adopted and just as binding as any rule of law.
The debate on values sanction is leading to the field of sovereignty. While the definition of values has a function of social and political identification, their sanction is declined on the ground of sovereignty and its protection. This proposition is verifiable for all three levels that we have identified: constitutional, regional, and international.
The constitutional level, dedicated to defending national sovereignty, may be analysed through the various forms of the State: unitary, regional, and federal. We can say that via sovereignty the protection of the national community is at stake. The international level protects the sovereignty of States from a very limited integration perspective. Mechanisms are rather dedicated to build a state society than an international community. The regional level seems to be the least homogeneous and divided between mechanisms of quasi-constitutional sanction or sanctions that are international in nature.

1. Comparative constitutional approach: sanctioning attempts to national sovereignty

Whether it is a unitary, regional or federal State, the non-respect of the sovereignty is defined by the nullity of the contrary acts or the constitutional prohibition of secession.

24 ICJ, 3 February 2006, Armed Activities on the Territory of the Congo (Democratic Republic of the Congo v. Rwanda) related to the prohibition of genocide.

a) The sanction of the violation of the unitary form of the State: the constitutional unity of the French people

The unitary form of the French State was particularly affirmed in the decision on the Statute of Corsica, which came to clarify the principles of French decentralization. The Government had chosen to include in Art. 1 of the law on the status of the territorial authority of Corsica a reference to the "Corsican people", as a component of the "French people". Referring to Art. 2 of the Constitution of 1958, which states that the French Republic is "*an indivisible, secular, democratic and social Republic*" which ensures the equality of all citizens before the law "*without distinction as to origin, race or religion*", the Constitutional Council considered as unconstitutional the reference to the "Corsican people"[25].

This unity was also affirmed in relation to collective linguistic rights, through the ratification of the European Charter on Regional and Minority Languages, giving rise to another important constitutional debate.

Analysing the European Charter for Regional or Minority Languages, as conferring specific rights on "groups" of speakers of regional or minority languages within "territories" in which these languages are used, the Council considered that "*the constitutional principles of the indivisibility of the Republic, equality before the law and the unicity of the French people*" were undermined. Thus, the ratification of the Charter could not take place without a prior substantial change to French constitutional values (i.e. amending the Constitution).

Sixteen years later, the threat of the constitutional sanction is still operative. In January 2014, with a large majority, the National Assembly adopted a constitutional amendment permitting the ratification of the Charter, the Senate rejected this amendment in October 2015. During the debate, the government mentioned that some Charter provisions, prior to ratification, did already comply with the French legal order.[26]

b) The sanction of the violation of the regional form of the State: the prevalence of Spanish national sovereignty over regional legitimacy

The Spanish Constitutional Tribunal addressed the issue of the limit of autonomy in a sentence delivered in June 28, 2010.[27] The tribunal stated that only the Spanish Nation could be constitutionally recognized even if the Autonomy Statute of Catalonia preamble evoked a "*Catalonian nation*". The tribunal refused to consid-

25 Constitutional Council, France, 7 May 1991, Decision 91-290 DC, Law on the status of the territorial authority of Corsica, Journal officiel de la République française – Lois et Décrets (Official Gazette), 14.05.1991, p. 6350.

26 Secretary General, Application of the European Charter for Regional or Minority Languages, Communication, Doc. 13993, 2 March 2016, http://assembly.coe.int/nw/xml/XRef/Xref-XML2HTML-en.asp?fileid=22538&lang=en.

27 Constitutional tribunal, June 28, 2010, n° 31/2010, See Xavier Arbós Marín, Aug. 15, 2010, http://www.justice-en-ligne.be/article197.html.

er that the "*national reality of Catalonia*", mentioned in the preamble of the Autonomy Statute of Catalonia, had any "*interpretive legal status*".
The Court also clarified the tension between national sovereignty and regional democratic legitimacy.[28] The attribution of "sovereignty" to the population of an autonomous community is conceived as a negation of national sovereignty except if the constitutional procedure of an autonomous community respects the national constitution. Thus, the democratic legitimacy of a regional legislative body remains a part of constitutional legality.

c) The sanction of the violation of the federal form of the State: the secession prohibition as the arbiter of common values in Canada

Federalism is quite interesting since it assumes that values are accepted by both the federal entity and the federated entity, accepted as being distinct places of sovereignty. The doctrine of collaborative federalism recognizes mechanisms, of vertical and horizontal nature, whose purpose is to consolidate constitutional values. Within the federation, as secession is prohibited, values are shared and fostered.
The Canadian Supreme Court addressed the secession issue, about a secession referendum in the province of Quebec (1998). The Court came to the conclusion that the Quebec Province did not have any power of unilateral secession neither under international law nor under constitutional law. The Court considered four separate hypotheses:

- political secession (extra legal), as negotiated between Quebec Province and the Canadian Federation;
- "imposed" secession: a unilateral democratic referendum held by the province of Quebec would amount not to immediate self-determination but rather to a legitimate "secession initiative" that would open negotiations;[29]
- International secession basis: since the people of Quebec, if ever recognized as a people, could not claim to be subjected "*to alien subjugation, domination or exploitation*", as expressed by international law, this way was closed;

28 Constitutional Tribunal, 2 December 2015, case 259/2015, Boletín Oficial del Estado, 10, 12.01.2016; www.boe.es/boe/dias/2016/01/12/pdfs/BOE-A-2016-308.pdf .

29 "The Constitution vouchsafes order and stability, and accordingly secession of a province under the Constitution could not be achieved unilaterally, that is, without principled negotiation with other participants in the federation within the existing constitutional framework. The democratic institutions necessarily accommodate a continuous process of discussion and evolution, which is reflected in the constitutional right of each participant in the federation to initiate constitutional change. This right implies a reciprocal duty on the other participants to engage in discussions to address any legitimate initiative to change the constitutional order. A clear majority vote in Quebec on a clear question in favour of secession would confer democratic legitimacy on the secession initiative which all of the other participants in the federation would have to recognise. Quebec could not, despite a clear referendum result, purport to invoke a right of self-determination to dictate the terms of a proposed secession to the other parties to the federation. The democratic vote, by however strong a majority, would have no legal effect on its own and could not push aside the principles of federalism and the rule of law, the rights of individuals and minorities, or the operation of democracy in the other provinces or in Canada as a whole", Supreme Court, Aug. 20, 1998, Reference re Secession of Quebec, n° 25506.

- *de facto* secession: this way would be justified neither by any legal basis, international or constitutional, nor by any negotiation.[30]

2. *The regional approach: The diversity of sanction mechanisms for regional integration*

a) The African Commission on Human and Peoples' Rights: classical principles of international law to serve regional integration

In a significant decision,[31] the African Commission recalled the ways in which self-determination may be exercised and the possible grounds for secession. It stated that "*self-determination may be exercised in any of the following ways - independence, self-government, local government, federalism, confederalism, unitarism or any other form of relations that agreements with the wishes of the people*". But whatever form of self-determination, national or international, might be chosen, it should respect the principles of sovereignty and territorial integrity principles.
In the present case, the demand for the secession of the Katangese people was rejected on the basis of a double test: the absence of concrete evidence of violations of human rights and the absence of evidence that the Katangese people were denied the right to participate in the government as guaranteed by Art. 13 (1) of the African Charter. The Commission held the view that Katangese peoples' congress was obliged to respect the sovereignty and territorial integrity of Zaire.

b) The case of Crimea and the Russian Federation as an integration test: the limited integration capacity of the Council of Europe

The crisis of the Crimean peninsula in 2014 undermined the fundamental values of the Council of Europe. The Parliamentary Assembly qualified, by a large majority,[32] that "*serious violation of the basic principles of the Council of Europe mentioned in Article 3 of, and the preamble to, the Statute*"[33] had occurred. Russian parliamentarians were not called to vote and the Assembly decided to suspend several rights of the Delegation of the Russian Federation: right to vote; right to be represented in the Bureau of the Assembly, the Presidential Committee and the Standing Committee; right to participate in election observation missions.

30 "Although there is no right, under the Constitution or at international law, to unilateral secession, the possibility of an unconstitutional declaration of secession leading to a de facto secession is not ruled out. The ultimate success of such a secession would be dependent on recognition by the international community, which is likely to consider the legality and legitimacy of secession having regard to the conduct of Quebec and Canada, amongst other facts, in determining whether to grant or withhold recognition. Even if granted, such recognition would not, however, provide any retroactive justification for the act of secession, either under the Constitution or at international law", Supreme Court, Aug. 20, 1998, Reference re Secession of Quebec, n° 25506.

31 Af. Comm. HPR, Communication 75/92, Katangese Peoples' Congress v Zaire (2000).

32 145 for, 22 abstentions, 21 against.

33 Parliamentary Assembly, Resolution 1990 (2014), April 10, 2014, Reconsideration on substantive grounds of the previously ratified credentials of the Russian delegation.

The annulment of the credentials of the Russian delegation was reserved in case of any de-escalation of the situation. Cancellation of credentials is a political sticking point: should the Assembly cancel credentials of the Russian authorities with the immediate consequence of the suspension of dialogue or should the Assembly maintain dialogue with Russia as consequence of maintaining of the Russian credentials? The Parliamentary Assembly preferred the latter option.[34]

The sanction mechanism of values within the framework of the Council of Europe has a clear distinct meaning as in the constitutional order: the sovereign equality of Member States 'protects' the States (here Russian Federation) against a strong sanction. Could Russia afford not to belong to the Council of Europe without great harm? Could the Council of Europe let Russia leave? The Council of Europe has at least a lot to lose in this state of play. And the principle of peaceful settlement of disputes shows the best way: dialogue and diplomacy, rather than punishment and exclusion.

Obviously weak sanctions imposed by the Council of Europe do not really encourage Russia to change its behaviour. The latest attempt was a motion for a resolution (not adopted) of the Assembly of 14 October 2016 about local elections which were held on September 18, 2016, in Crimea and Sevastopol. The issue was to declare the elections null and void based on the Latin maxim: "*ex injuria jus non oritur*"[35].

Recently Ukraine filed an application to the International Court of Justice.[36]

c) European Union: A complex skein of sanction mechanisms

The profound originality of the European construction will not be explained here. When lawyers discuss its legal nature (more than a confederation but not a federal state)[37], they all agree upon their helplessness: its nature is *sui generis*. The federative role of values is fundamental, as the mention of the new formula in the Preamble to the Lisbon Treaty mentions: "*cultural, religious and humanistic heritage of Europe*".

If the central sanctioning mechanism is found in Art. 7 TEU, the reality is much more complex. European construction is based on a delicate balance between sovereign states and the non-sovereign European Union. Thus whilst the Union

34 Parliamentary Assembly, Resolution 2063 (2015) 1, June 24, 2015, Consideration of the annulment of the previously ratified credentials of the delegation of The Russian Federation (follow-up paragraph 16 of Resolution 2034 (2015)).

35 Parliamentary Assembly, 14 October 2016, Illegal elections in the occupied Autonomous Republic of Crimea and in the city of Sebastopol, Doc. 14188.

36 See: ICJ, 16 January 2017, Terrorism financing and racial discrimination in Ukraine, (Ukraine v. Russian Federation), http://www.icj-cij.org/docket/files/166/19314.pdf.

37 Federal Constitutional Court, Germany, Second Panel, 30 June 2009, Lisbon Decision, Neue Juristische Wochenschrift 2009, pp. 2267-2295: European Union is designed as an association of sovereign states *(Staatenverbund)*. The concept of *Verbund* covers a close long-term association of states which remain sovereign, a treaty-based association which exercises public authority, but whose fundamental order is subject to the decision-making power of the Member States and in which the peoples, i.e. the citizens, of the Member States remain the subjects of democratic legitimation.

has mechanisms of sanctions the States do too, as evidenced by Article 50 TEU (State withdrawal). Preventing imbalances in relationships is what the principles of attribution of powers, subsidiarity and proportionality of their exercise (Art. 5 TEU) are concerned with.
There are also functional sanctions, unknown in international law, as evidenced by Art. 260 of the TFEU, where the State has not taken the enforcement measures imposed by a judgment of the Court of Justice (lump sum or penalty payment). A simplified procedure is used when non-transposition of Directives is concerned. These functional sanctions do not particularly concern the values of the Union but they demonstrate the high intensity of integration.

3. *The universal approach: poor definition of values equals poor sanction mechanisms*

The notion of international community with common values at the universal level is very poorly advanced as are the mechanisms of sanctioning their violation.
Art. 103 of the UN Charter provides for the setting aside of any treaty obligations contrary to UN Charter obligations.[38] This primacy applies not only to the provisions of the Charter, but also to obligations arising out of the Charter, which, according to Art. 25, are subject to the resolutions of the Security Council adopted under Chapter VII.[39] There is no dedicated procedure to allow Art. 103 to produce its effects. Treaties against the Charter and the Security Council resolutions are supposed to no longer produce their effects. It is widely accepted that Art. 103 gives a priority to the Charter, and nothing else (i.e. invalidity)[40]. How could a single State party to a treaty declare the treaty inapplicable? States remain free to expel the treaty against the Charter from the international legal order. Another obvious limitation is the power of judicial review of International Court of Justice, as the Court does not have the power to "*supervene, modify, negate or confine the applicability of resolutions of the Security Council*"[41]. The level of priority of Art. 103 over customary law is unclear.[42]

38 "In the event of a conflict between the obligations of the Members of the United Nations under the present Charter and their obligations under any other international agreement, their obligations under the present Charter shall prevail". See Article 103 Commentary, *J.-M. Thouvenin*, in: Cot/Pellet/Forteau, La Charte des Nations Unies, Commentaire article par article, 3rd edition, Économica, 2005, vol.II, p. 2133.

39 ICJ, 14 April 1992, Questions of Interpretation and Application of the 1971 Montreal Convention arising from the Aerial Incident at Lockerbie (Libyan Arab Jamahiriya v. United Kingdom), § 39, p.16.

40 See for example (based on the presumed nature of the Charter as a Constitution): *B. Fassbender*, The United Nations Charter as Constitution of the International Community, Columbia Journal of Transnational Law, vol. 36, 1998, p. 590.

41 Dissenting opinion Schwebel, ICJ, 27 February 1998, Questions of Interpretation and Application of the 1971 Montreal Convention arising from the Aerial Incident at Lockerbie (Libyan Arab Jamahiriya v. United Kingdom), p. 71.

42 See *M. Koskenniemi,* Fragmentation of international law: difficulties arising from the diversification and expansion of international law, 13 April 2006, p. 176, A/CN.4/L.682.

The Court of First Instance of the EC[43] considered that "*the obligations of United Nations Member States under the Charter prevail over any other obligation, including those under the European Convention of Human Rights and the EC Treaty*"[44], but that priority would cease when a UN Security Council resolution would undermine a jus cogens norm. Art. 103 whose international practice is very limited[45] indirectly recognizes values as it provides for a legal mechanism of hierarchy.

Art. 53 of the Vienna Convention on the Law of Treaties provides for a more accurate example.[46] It provides that any treaty contrary to a peremptory norm recognized by the international community (*jus cogens*) is null and void, having the same effect as a vice of consent, i.e. treaty invalidity (Art. 46 and ff. VCLT). That nullity is operative for any source of international law not only treaties qualified as *jus dispositivum*, as soon as it is contrary to *jus cogens*. This nullity is not operative if two norms of *jus cogens* are in conflict.

What is the complementarity between Art. 103 UN Charter and Art. 53 VCLT? The general opinion is that the clauses do not have the same object: Article 103 is dedicated to the UN legal and has any invalidity effect whereas Art. 53 VCLT, as a general norm, is dedicated to have an invalidity effect. The question about a formal hierarchy between *jus cogens* and the UN Charter remains unclear. It would be the case, if and only if, *jus cogens* was a customary norm. This qualification could be ascertained by the ICJ judgment.[47] But taking into account the current work of the International Law Commission, on *jus cogens*[48], and States observations at the 6th Commission of the UNGA, it remains difficult to state positively the full customary value of the *jus cogens*. France expressed "scepticism about the possibility of reaching a consensus on the topic"[49]. The Netherlands estab-

43 CFI, Case T-306/01 (Ahmed Ali Yusuf and Al Barakaat International Foundation v. Council of the European Union and Commission of the European Communities), ECLI:EU:T:2005:331, ECR 2005, II-03533 and CFI, Case T-315/01 (Yassin Abdullah Kadi v. Council of the European Union and Commission of the European Communities), ECLI:EU:T:2005:332, ECR 2005, II-03649.

44 Contra: about the autonomy of the European legal order in regard to international law ECJ, Case C-402/05, (Yassin Abdullah Kadi et Al Barakaat International Foundation v. Council and Commission), ECLI:EU:C:2008:461, ECR 2008, I-06351.

45 See Military and Paramilitary Activities in and against Nicaragua (Nicaragua v. United States of America), (Jurisdiction and Admissibility) I.C.J. Reports 1984 p. 440, para. 107: priority of obligations under the Charter over other treaty obligations is mentioned.

46 Under that clause: "A treaty is void if, at the time of its conclusion, it conflicts with a peremptory norm of general international law. For the purposes of the present Convention, a peremptory norm of general international law is a norm accepted and recognized by the international community of States as a whole as a norm from which no derogation is permitted and which can be modified only by a subsequent norm of general international law having the same character."
See also article 64 VCLT: "If a new peremptory norm of general international law emerges, any existing treaty which is in conflict with that norm becomes void and terminates".

47 ICJ, 3 February 2006, Armed Activities on the Territory of the Congo (New Application: 2002) (Democratic Republic of the Congo v. Rwanda).

48 ILC, 8 March 2016, First report on jus cogens, Dire Tladi, Special Rapporteur, A/CN.4/693.

49 A/C.6/69/SR.22, para.37. The United States "did not believe it would be productive for the Commission to add the topic of jus cogens to its agenda", A/C.6/69/SR.20, para. 123.

lished that "it was hard to determine a specific need among States with regard to the codification or progressive development of the notion of jus cogens"[50].
But in regard to the current work of the International Law Commission, the status of *Jus Cogens* remains a matter of uncertainty, both for its effects and its content. The first report proposes as a draft conclusion: "*Norms of jus cogens protect the fundamental values of the international community, are hierarchically superior to other norms of international law and are universally applicable*".
The path to sustain a coordinated community will remain long and arduous.

50 A/C.6/69/SR.20, para. 13.

Causation as a requirement for the Member State liability under Art. 7 TEU in conjunction with Art. 2 TEU

By Ewa Bagińska and Sylwia Majkowska-Szulc,** Gdańsk*

In the first part of the article, the requirement of a direct and exclusive causal link between the breach of the obligation resting on the State and the damage sustained by the injured party is discussed. Secondly, the authors analyze several issues connected with the New Rule of Law Framework and the 'Art. 7 Procedure'. The article argues that the scope of application of Art. 7 TEU is vital to the determination of Member State liability for the breach of EU values. The authors identify main functions of norms defining the values set by the EU Treaties in the context of individuals' rights is important. The Authors come to the conclusion that the nature of a direct and exclusive causal link in the situation of the violation of Art. 7 TEU is a serious obstacle to the liability.

The analysis of the problem determined in the title requires a systematisation of Member State liability issues for the breach of the protected values of the EU set by the Treaty on the EU. The aim of the article is to determine whether causation constitutes a requirement for the Member State liability under Art. 7 TEU and how far that responsibility extends. For this purpose the conditions of Member States liability for the infringement of EU law are presented briefly. The study includes not only the theories of causation present in the domestic systems, but also a review of the EU jurisprudence concerning causation in Member States liability cases. The authors undertake to explain how the Court of Justice understands causation, including direct or sufficiently direct causation, exclusive causation and the interferences between causation and damage. The question is to what extent the traditional, national tort law rules on causation dominated by the adequate causation theory will shape the liability of Member State under Art. 7 TEU. Correspondingly, several issues connected with the New Rule of Law Framework and the 'Art. 7 Procedure' require in-depth consideration. The authors argue that the scope of application of Art. 7 TEU is vital to the determination of Member State liability for the breach of EU values. Eventually, the identification of the main functions of norms defining the values set by the EU Treaties in the context of individuals' rights is important.

* Full Professor of Civil Law, Director of the Civil Law Department, University of Gdańsk (Poland), Member of the European Group on Tort Law.

** Associate Professor in the Department of Company Law and International Private Law, University of Gdańsk (Poland).

I. The conditions of Member States liability for the infringement of EU law

The principle of Member States liability for loss and damage caused to individuals as a result of breaches of Community law is "inherent in the system of the Treaty".[1] The key concepts underlying the Court of Justice case law on Member State liability are the supremacy of EU law, the fundamental requirement that EU law be effective and the protection of the individual in the European context. Following the *Francovich,* in *Brasserie du Pêcheur* and *Factortame III,*[2] the Court of Justice clearly recognized that in the case of breach of the EU law attributable to a Member State acting in the field in which it has a wide discretion to make legislative choices, individuals suffering loss or injury thereby are entitled to compensation, provided certain conditions are met: 1) the rule infringed must be intended to confer rights on individuals; 2) the breach must be sufficiently serious; and 3) there must be a direct causal link between the breach and the damage.[3]

Those conditions are necessary and sufficient to found a right for individuals to obtain redress. It is a matter for national law to choose the individual tort that best suits these requirements.

It is worth noting that the discussed liability is objective, which means that reparation cannot be made conditional upon 'fault' of the public organ. The Court did not differentiate between a "subjective fault" and an "objective breach". Any condition requiring fault imposed by national law for liability to arise on the part of the organ of the State to which an infringement of the EU law is attributable must be set aside to the extent that it is inconsistent with the EU law.[4] Nevertheless, various factors connected with the concept of fault could well be relevant for determining whether the breach of EU law was sufficiently serious. Consequently, reparation could not be made subject to proof of fault where the concept went beyond the requirement that the breach be sufficiently serious.[5]

Thus, the liability regime under the Court of Justice case law has its specific characteristics, which must influence the interpretation of the conditions of liability provided in the domestic legal systems. Most importantly, the Court of Justice has not made any distinction between the conditions of liability for the administrative and legislative acts. The *Bergaderm* judgment confirmed that the above-men-

1 ECJ, Joined Cases C-6/90 and C-9/90 (Francovich), ECLI:EU:C:1991:428, ECR 1991, I-5357; ECJ, Joined cases C-143/88 and C-92/89 (Zuckerfabrik), ECLI:EU:C:1991:65, ECR 1991, I-415.

2 ECJ, joined Cases C-46/93 and C-48/93 (Brasserie du pêcheur SA), ECLI:EU:C:1996:79, ECR 1996, I-1029.

3 ECJ, joined Cases C-46/93 and C-48/93 (Brasserie du pêcheur SA), ECLI:EU:C:1996:79, ECR 1996, I-1029, mn. 51; in respect of the liability of the EU see ECJ, Case C-198/03 P (Commission/CEVA Santé Animale SA and Pfizer Enterprises Sàrl), ECLI:EU:C:2005:445, ECR 2005, I-6357, mn. 63.

4 ECJ, joined Cases C-46/93 and C-48/93 (Brasserie du pêcheur SA), ECLI:EU:C:1996:79, ECR 1996, I-1029, mn 79.

5 See *N. Emiliou*, State liability under community law: shedding more light on the *Francovich* Principle, 21 European Law Review (1996), p. 399; *P. Craig*, The domestic liability of public authorities in damages: lessons from the European Community, in: Beatson/Tridimas (eds.), New directions in European Public Law 1998, p. 75.

tioned conditions should be applied in the same way, regardless of the nature of the action that caused the damage.[6]

In the discussed regime of EU liability causation is determined on the basis of principles common to the laws of the Member States. In order to identify the common principles the Court of Justice does not carry out a deep analysis of the domestic legal system, but rather looks first at these systems' general common features, and then compares these features with the objectives of the founding treaties, as well as the specific tasks and competences of the Union.[7] Were we to apply those methods to the problem of causation in the context of the liability for the violation of Art. 7 TEU, we should first recall the contents of causation in the national rules of civil liability.

II. Theories of causation in domestic laws

Causation is not a natural or scientific term, but a legal concept, which serves the attribution of legal responsibility.[8] Generally, the causation test combines the elements of the two categories, which it associates: breach of duty and damage. Any assessment of causation in tort is carried out according to tort law criteria, which are also used to evaluate the existence of
a breach of duty and damage. As Ch. von Bar rightly points out "Whether compensation is payable thus depends on a closed-system normative evaluation. Both the law and ease of approach of the problem often demand the mental separation of breach of duty, damage, and attribution of the latter to the former: but the overall view should not be lost. The final solution to a case shows that nothing which is decided in one category is without effect on the others."[9]

In European tort law the most popular method of establishing causation is the *conditio sine qua non,* or 'but-for', test.[10] The *conditio sine qua non* test identifies 'factual' causation. The subsequent question of attribution, or 'legal' cause, arises when the first test is positive (ie the answer is 'yes' to the following question: is the examined cause a condition in the absence of which the damage would not have happened?). Under the doctrine of legal causation, or adequate causation, this is no longer a scientific problem but a value judgment. Thus, despite a causal

6 ECJ, Case C-352/98 P (Bergaderm/Commission), ECLI:EU:C:2000:361, ECR 2000, I-5291, mn. 40; see *N. Półtorak*, Action for damages in the case of infringement of fundamental rights by the European Union, in: Bagińska (ed.), Damages for Violations of Human Rights. A Comparative Study of Domestic Legal Systems, 2016, p. 433.

7 See *N. Półtorak,* (fn. 6), p. 431; ECJ, Case C-120/06 P and C-121/06 P (Fabbrica italiana accumulatori motocarri Montecchio SpA – FIAMM), ECLI:EU:C:2008:476, ECR 2008, I-6513, mn. 175: As regards the question of causation see *T. Tridimas*, Liability for breach of community law: growing up and mellowing down?, CML Rev 38, 2001, p. 322.

8 See *H. Koziol*, Basic questions of tort law from a Germanic perspective, 2012, p. 132 ff.

9 See *Ch. von Bar*, The Common European Law of Torts: Volume Two, Causation or Attribution, 2000, no 442, p. 463.

10 See Winiger/Koziol/Koch/Zimmermann (eds.), Digest of European Tort Law, vol I: Essential Cases on Natural Causation, 2007, Chapter 1 passim H. Koziol, Basic questions, p. 133 ff.

link in the sense of *conditio sine qua non*, liability for the damage can be denied on the basis of very different criteria.[11] The adequacy test is the best known and most widely used in Europe as a test of attribution.

Adequate, or normal, consequences of a fact are those, which typically occur in the regular sequence of the course of events; it is not required for them to always happen. It is believed that adequate causation may be both direct and indirect. Thus, there is a causal link between damage and an event if the event indirectly created the favourable conditions or facilitated another event or a sequence of events, the last of which became the direct cause of the damage. Thus, in a multi-element causal chain, each part separately is subject to the causality test. Other abstract formulae of causal attribution also constitute the requirement that proximate or direct results of a damaging event be distinguished from distant or indirect results.

Both tests of causation ordinarily apply in the law of public authority liability. The question thus arises whether the rules on liability for the violation of the EU law include the tests of factual and/or adequate causation.

III. How does the Court of Justice understand causation?

1. Direct or sufficiently direct causation

According to European case law only *direct (immediate)* and *exclusive* causal link will trigger liability. The test of direct causation typically means that the damage must arise directly from the conduct of the State organ and does not depend on the intervention of other causes, whether positive or negative.[12] However, in the liability of the Union cases the direct causation is sometimes qualified as *sufficiently direct.*[13] For example, in the case *Idromacchine Srl* the General Court ruled that there is a causal link between the conduct complained of and the damage alleged by the claimant, when the alleged harm is a sufficiently direct consequence of the conduct, which must be the determinant cause of the harm. There is no obligation to make good every harmful consequence, even a remote one, of an unlawful situation.[14]

The EU Court has seldom given further guidance as regards the meaning of the causal requirement for liability. There are, however, some hints to be found in the case law related to the liability of the Union organs.[15] It should be recalled that the principle of public liability is also endorsed in Art. 340 TFEU (ex Article 288

11 See *H. Koziol* (fn. 10), Basic questions, p. 133 ff.

12 See *I.C. Durant*, Causation, in: Koziol/Schulze (eds.), Tort Law of the European Community, 2008, p. 68 ff.

13 ECJ, Joined cases 64 and 113/76, 167 and 239/78, 27, 28 and 45/79 (P. Dumortier Frères SA/Council), ECLI:EU:C:1979:223, ECR 1979, I-3091, mn 21 and CFI, T-279/03 (Galileo International Technology and Others/Commission), ECLI:EU:T:2006:121, ECR 2006, II-1291, mn. 130.

14 CFI, Case T-88/09 (Idromacchine Srl), ECLI:EU:T:2011:641, ECR 2011, II-7833, mn 112.

15 See *R. Rebhahn*, Non-contractual liability in damages of Member States for breach of Community law, in: Koziol/Schulze (eds.), Tort Law of the European Community, 2008, mn 9/68.

TEC) according to which 'In the case of non-contractual liability, the Union shall, in accordance with the general principles common to the laws of the Member States, make good any damage caused by its institutions or by its servants in the performance of their duties.'

Both the *Francovich* case law and Art. 340 TFEU relate to extra-contractual liability for the same kind of breaches of the EU law, the first on the part of national public authorities, and the second on the part of the Union institutions.[16] The ECJ emphasized that its own case law on the non-contractual liability of the Community under Art. 288 should "in the absence of particular justification" serve as a yardstick for shaping the rules on state liability.[17] As stated in the Brasserie du Pêcheur case,

"the conditions under which the State may incur liability for damage caused to individuals by a breach of Community law cannot, in the absence of particular justification, differ from those governing the liability of the Community in like circumstances".[18]

It seems clear that the condition of causation in actions against Member States is not a stricter one than in the liability of the Union cases.[19]

The European Courts seem to consider the *conditio sine qua non* test as being the causal test, and at the same time they also seem to require that the causal link be a direct causal link. The *conditio sine qua non* test is used in many cases. For example in the van den Berg judgment (C-164/01 P) the Court stated:

'[...] an act of the Community institutions is the cause of damage only where such damage can be attributed directly and exclusively to such act. The requisite causal link does not exist where the damage would also have occurred in the absence of the relevant act of the Community institutions'.[20]

In the judgment of 20 March 2013, *Nexans France v. European Joint Undertaking for ITER and the Development of Fusion Energy*[21], the General Court denied causation between the decision refusing the award of a contract and all the alleged heads of damage, including the loss of an opportunity to obtain the contract and the loss of the competitive advantage that the award of the contract to the applicant would have secured. The Court rules that:

'In that regard, it follows from the examination of the legality of the rejection decision that the applicant had no chance of obtaining the contract. There is there-

16 See *W. Van Gerven*, Bridging the unbridgeable: Community and national tort laws after *Francovich* and *Brasserie*, 45 The International and Comparative Law Quarterly 1996, p. 517.

17 See however critically of this view Advocate General Léger in the opinion in ECJ, Case C-5/94 (Hedley Lomas), ECLI:EU:C:1996:205, ECR 1996, I-2553 who argues that it would be "somewhat paradoxical to align state liability for breach of Community law with Article 215 rules which are judged to be unsatisfactory, unduly stringent and affording insufficient protection for the right to effective judicial relief, at least with regard to the condition concerning breach of Community law".

18 ECJ, Joined Cases C-46/93 and C-48/93 (Brasserie du pêcheur SA), ECLI:EU:C:1996:79, ECR 1996, I-1029, mn. 42.

19 See *I.C. Durant*, Causation, in: Koziol/Schulze (eds.), Tort Law of the European Community, 2008, p. 55 ff.

20 ECJ, Case C-164/01 P (G. van den Berg/Council and Commission), ECLI:EU:C:2004:665, ECR 2004, I-10225.

21 CFI, Case T-415/10 (Nexans France/Fusion for Energy), ECLI:EU:T:2013:141.

fore no causal link between the award decision and the alleged loss of opportunity and competitive advantage.[at 186]'
The method of elimination is the most common way to apply the "but for" test in the EU case law, but in omission cases the courts have generally to replace the omission by the (positive) act that should have been carried out (*method of substitution*). In cases of omissions, the court's reasoning consists generally in assessing the causal impact of the omitted action.[22]

2. *Exclusive causation*

The exclusivity criterion is strongly linked with the *conditio sine qua non* test. The fact that an act or omission is one of only several such circumstances may not in itself be sufficient for a causal connection entailing non-contractual liability under EU law, as opposed to national laws.[23] It has often been held that negative financial outcomes obtained by the applicants, such as a loss of market, bankruptcy were conditional upon a series of factors, including the conduct of a Member State.
The requirement of exclusivity of the causal link provokes the question whether the chain of causation between the action of an EU institution and the loss can be broken by the action of a Member State organ or the plaintiff himself.
In general, the case law of the Court of Justice excludes the possibility of the Union being held liable for damage having its direct cause in the allegedly wrongful conduct of a third party.[24] A Member State organ is considered a third party in this context. The ECJ has consistently held that where the loss arises from an intervention by the Member State, the Community is no longer liable.[25] This idea allows holding that if the applicants fail to demonstrate reasonable diligence to avoid or limit their losses, this very circumstance allows the Court for discounting the existence of a sufficiently direct causal link between the alleged damage and the alleged wrongful conduct of the Community.
Rebhahn observes that the European Courts apply a concept of causation, which in many Member States has long been rightly abandoned. The distinctive concept of "breach of causation" confounds the question of causation with other questions of liability (especially the aim of the rule) in a way that is as unhappy as unwise. According to a modern concept of tort law the former problem of breach of causation and the "effective" cause now are dealt with under other titles.[26]
Under the EU case law a national court may inquire whether the injured person showed reasonable diligence in order to avoid the loss or damage or limit its extent and whether, in particular, he availed himself in time of all the legal remedies

22 See *I.C. Durant*, Causation, in: Koziol/Schulze (eds.), Tort Law of the European Community, 2008, p. 59-60.
23 See *R. Rebhahn* (fn.15), p. 179, p. 201 mn 9/70.
24 AG *Mengozzi*, Opinion of 29 October 2009 in Case C-419/08 P (Trubowest Handel GmbH and Viktor Makarov/Council and Commission), mn 101.
25 *R. Rebhahn* (fn.15), mn 9/71.
26 *R. Rebhahn* (fn.15), mn 9/72.

available to him.[27] The likelihood that a national court will make a reference for a preliminary ruling or the existence of infringement proceedings pending before the Court of Justice cannot, in itself, constitute a sufficient reason for concluding that it is not reasonable to have recourse to a legal remedy. Furthermore, it seems that the liability of a Member State is not precluded by exceptional and unforeseeable events when the Member State violated an obligation of result. Moreover, no direct link is established when the misconduct of the Union is followed by the autonomous decision of another (domestic) authority.[28]

One of the recent cases where the breach of causation was explained and applied is *Trubowest Handel GmbH and Viktor Makarov v. Council and Commission*. The Court of Justice held that in the Union liability case it is necessary to verify whether, at the risk of having to bear the damage himself, the person adversely affected had demonstrated reasonable diligence in avoiding or limiting the extent of the damage. The causal link may be broken by negligence on the part of the person adversely affected, where that negligence proves to be the *determinant cause of the damage.* [29]

3. *Interferences between causation and damage*

Furthermore, we should note that the consideration of the damage itself often influences the overall causal analysis. As regards the type of recoverable damage, generally personal injury and death are more easily attributable than damage to property, and that property damage is more easily attributable than pure economic loss (which recoverability is principally very limited across Europe).

It could be argued that the direct causation test is not only used to establish the existence of the causal link, but also to establish the existence of the damage. Three examples can be cited for reference.

Firstly, in *Frederick Farrugia* the claim for alleged non-material damage was rejected by the Court of First Instance, because 'the applicant has failed to prove *actual and certain damage* by showing that, had the Commission not rejected his application for a fellowship on erroneous grounds concerning his nationality, that application fulfilled the prescribed conditions for it to be taken into consideration and accepted'.[30]

A second example is the Grand Chamber judgment of 14 October 2014, C-611/12 (Giordano v Commission)[31]. The court ruled that „the [erroneous] rejection by the General Court of the appellant's argument that he would have exhausted his quota [for Bluefin tuna fishing] is solely relevant for assessing the extent of the harm

27 In Brasserie and Factortame, mn 84; ECJ, Case C-445/06 (Danske Slagterier/Bundesrepublik Deutschland), ECLI:EU:C:2009:178, ECR 2009, I-2219, mn. 59, 64.

28 Eg. when the decision of English authorities to arrest an official having benefited from unlawful cooperation of the European Commission. See *I.C. Durant* (fn. 12), p. 69, 71.

29 ECJ, Case C-419/08 P (Trubowest Handel GmbH and Viktor Makarov/Council and Commission) ECLI:EU:C:2010:147, ECR 2010, I-2259, mn 61.

30 CFI, Case T-230/94 (Farrugia/Commission), ECLI:EU:T:1996:40, ECR 1996, II-195, mn 46.

31 ECJ, Case C-611/12 (Giordano/Commission), ECLI:EU:C:2014:2282.

alleged, but not the very existence of such harm, the certainty of which is not called into question by uncertainty as to its precise extent".
Thirdly, in Nexans France v. European Joint Undertaking for ITER and the Development of Fusion Energy the General Court held "it is appropriate to consider first of all whether a causal link may be established between the heads of damage alleged by the applicant and that decision and whether those heads of damage are established and may lead to an award of damages." with three heads of damage being sought, only the last one – lost opportunity to win the tender was rejected due to the lack of causation, instead of lack of reparable damage. "it follows from the examination of the legality of the rejection decision that the applicant had no chance of obtaining the contract There is therefore no causal link between the award decision and the alleged loss of opportunity and competitive advantage."

4. (Lack of) Conclusion

In the light of the above remarks a question arises whether the direct or sufficiently direct causation is something different to adequate causation theory, which is a dominant theory in most European states. A conclusion that follows from the above remarks is that the direct link is "less than" adequate. In some cases, we can observe that the CFI's causal inquiry combines the use of several criteria to conclude the inexistence of direct causation, moreover without applying the but for test prior to the examination of the "remoteness"[32]. Hence, 'direct' means 'not too remote" and does not mean "immediate".[33] To the EU courts themselves it is probably a variant of the *conditio sine qua non* test,[34] while to some commentators the EU concept includes the second step, ie the evaluation equivalent to the doctrine of adequacy.[35]
Hence, causation is an autonomous concept developed by the European Courts. The crux of the problem lies, however, in the fact that the EU Courts developed a fragmentary concept, by using inconsistent terminology.[36] Nevertheless, the deliberate lack of an abstract (general) formula allows for incorporating the individual circumstances of a given case as well as innumerable policy considerations, which influence the ascertainment of liability.

32 *I. C. Durant* (fn. 12), p. 69 mn 3-51.

33 *P. Machnikowski*, The liability of public authorities in the European Union, in: Oliphant (ed.), The Liability of Public Authorities in Comparative Perspective, Intersentia 2016, p. 571.

34 *I. C. Durant* (fn. 12), p. 63.

35 *U. Magnus/K Bitterich*, in: Digest of European Tort Law 1/27, mn 5, p. 94.

36 *U. Magnus/K Bitterich*, in: Digest of European Tort Law 1/27, mn 3, p. 93. In a contribution from 1997 devoted to "The concepts of damage and causality as elements of non-contractual liability", *A.G. Toth* came to the contrary conclusion that "it may be said that the Court has developed a fairly comprehensive, consistent and settled case law on damage and causality, which is unlikely to change significantly in the near future" – see *A.G. Toth*, The concepts of damage and causality as elements of non-contractual liability, in: Heukels/ McDonnell (eds.), The Action for Damages in Community Law 1997, p. 198.

IV. The role of the national rules in establishing causation

A few important questions flow from the rule that a national court must determine whether causation exists between the alleged breach of the EU law and the loss.[37] It is not entirely clear whether a national court could deny causation according to its national rules if causation would have been established for an action against the Community according to the EU rules.[38] The Court in Brasserie emphasised that "the protection of the rights which individuals derive from Community law cannot vary depending on whether a national authority or a Community authority is responsible for the damage"[39]. The commentators seem to agree that since causation is one of the three EU law conditions, it is ultimately for the Court of Justice to indicate its main elements. This implies that it is not the national rules governing causation that should be applied.[40] Moreover, from the EU point of view the requirement that the national authority organs may not treat the EU law claims less favourably than similar domestic law claims implies that – in the absence of the EU uniform substantive rules – the same level of protection must be attained at national and the EU level even if for the former the law grants a higher level of protection.[41] This dual standard may thus result in strict liability rules applied to both domestic and the EU cases.

Most often, the cases concern failure to implement EU Directives. A recent Polish judgment of 19 June 2013 might serve as an example.[42] Poland failed to implement two MiFID Directives of the European Parliament and the Council 2004/39/EC (MiFID I)14 as well as the Commission Directive 2006/73/EC (MiFID II).[43] The plaintiff was an investor who entered into a CRIS (Cancellable Interest Rate Swap transaction). CRIS is a contract by which the bank and the client undertake to exchange a nominal account and periodically exchange interest payments in two currencies. In the case at hand it was yen and Polish zloty. The plaintiff closed the transaction (cancelled the swap) prematurely, thereby incurring a huge loss of € 400,000. He sued the State for damages, alleging that he had not been properly informed and advised on the risks inherent in the CIRS contract due to the failure to implement the MiFID Directives into Polish law. The plaintiff asserted that the Directives imposed a higher level of protection of investors than the then existing Polish law. The Court of Appeal rejected the claim

37 ECJ, joined Cases C-46/93 and C-48/93 (Brasserie du pêcheur SA), ECLI:EU:C:1996:79, ECR 1996, I-1029. mn 65; and ECJ, Case C-5/94 (Hedley Lomas), ECLI:EU:C:1996:205, ECR 1996, I-2553, mn 30.

38 See *R. Rebhahn* (fn.15), mn 9/74.

39 ECJ, joined Cases C-46/93 and C-48/93 (Brasserie du pêcheur SA), ECLI:EU:C:1996:79, ECR 1996, I-1029, mn 42.

40 *I. C. Durant* (fn. 12), p. 63 and the literature cited therein.

41 *W. Van Gerven*, Bridging the gap between Community and national laws: towards a principle of homogeneity in the field of legal remedies?, 32 Common Market Law Review 1995, p. 700.

42 I CSK 392/12, OSN IC – ZD C/2014, item 58 also reported in: Bagińska/Krupa-Lipińska, Poland in: European Tort Law 2014 (2015), p. 436 f.

43 Directive 2004/39/EC of the European Parliament and of the Council of 21 April 2004 on markets in financial instruments amending Council Directives 85/611/EEC and 93/6/EEC and Directive 2000/12/EC of the European Parliament and of the Council and repealing Council Directive 93/22/EEC, OJ L 145, 30.4.2004, 1-44.

stating that there was no causal link between the delayed implementation of Directives by Poland and the conclusion of the CRIS contract (which caused damage), because EU investment rules were already partially implemented by the existing laws. The Supreme Court affirmed this judgment and stated that the requirement of State liability stemming from EU case law and concerning direct causal connection between the breach of the obligation resting on the State and the damage sustained by the injured party is equivalent to the adequate causation test prescribed by Art. 361 § 1 of the civil code. In that regard, the *conditio sine qua non* requirement was lacking in the given case. The extent of differences between the protective rules of the non-implemented Directives and the existing Polish regulations were not considerable. Therefore, the failure to implement the Directives could not be considered as a factual cause of the plaintiff's damage. In other words, plaintiff did not prove that he would not have entered into the CRIS contract transaction had the Directives been timely implemented. First, the Directives did not forbid this type of contracts and, second, there was no evidence that the bank would have refused to enter into that concrete transaction.

V. New Rule of Law Framework and the 'Art. 7 Procedure'

In the past years, the European Commission has been confronted with systemic threats to the rule of law in some Member States. In 2012 President Barroso said in the annual speech to the European Parliament that the European Union needed a better developed set of instruments, something more than the alternative between the 'soft power' of political persuasion and the 'nuclear option' of Article 7 TEU. In response, the Commission adopted in March 2014 a new Rule of Law Framework[44] which has three stages: Commission assessment, Commission Recommendation and follow-up to the Commission Recommendation. On the one hand the communication acknowledged that the precise content of the principles and standards stemming from the rule of law may vary in different Member States, depending on each Member State's constitutional system. On the other, the Court of Justice of the EU case law, the European Court of Human Rights case law, as well as documents of the Council of Europe, including the expertise of the Venice Commission, define the core meaning of the rule of law as a common value of the EU in accordance with Art. 2 TEU. Consequently, the following rules shall be observed: legality, legal certainty, prohibition of arbitrariness of the executive powers, independent and impartial courts, effective judicial review in-

44 Communication from the Commission to the European Parliament and the Council, A new EU Framework to strengthen the Rule of Law, Brussels, 19.3.2014, COM (2014) 158 final/2.

cluding respect for fundamental rights, equality before the law. Legality implies a transparent, accountable, democratic and pluralistic process for enacting laws.

Source: 1 European Commission's Press release, Commission adopts Rule of Law Opinion on the situation in Poland, Brussels, 1 June 2016, p. 3.

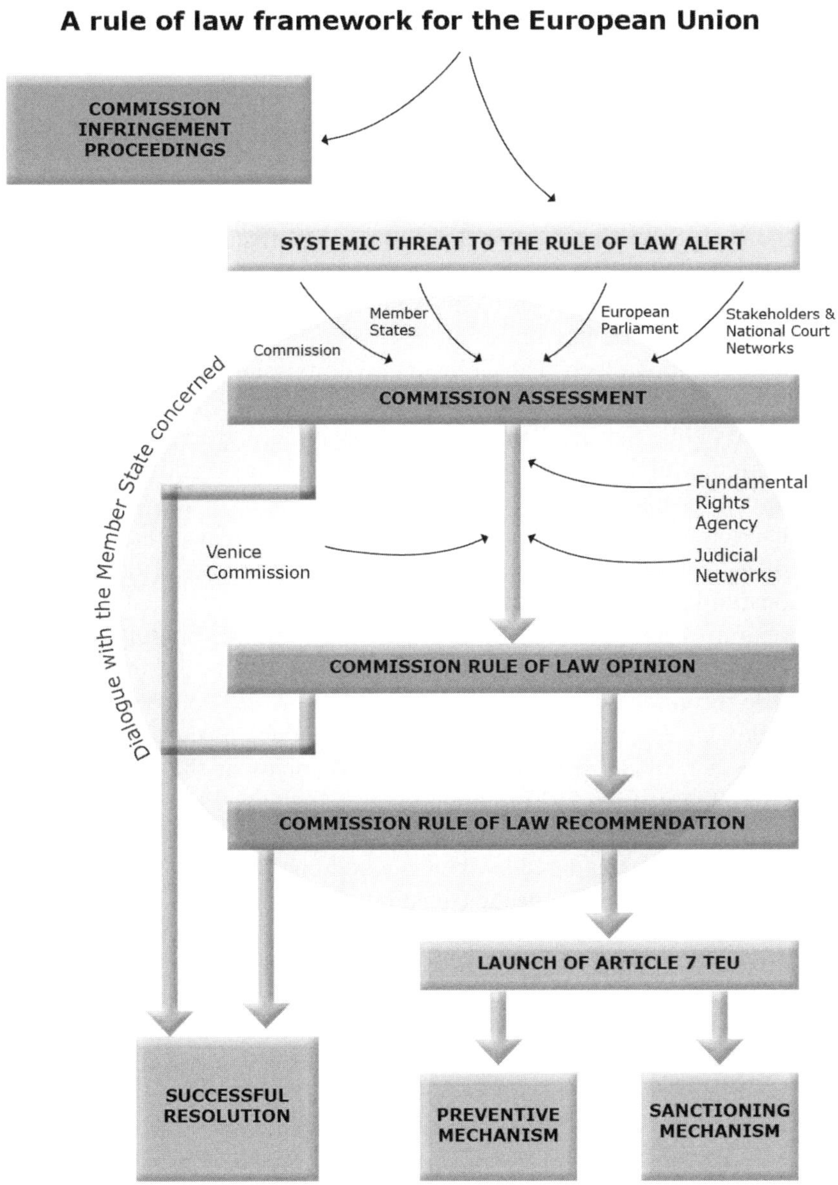

Art. 7 TEU has introduced two mechanisms to ensure compliance of Member States' conduct with the values on which the European Union is founded. These are mechanisms of prevention and of sanction, being noted that conditions for the use of both mechanisms are directly related to the violation of the EU values. The mechanism of prevention applies when "there is a clear risk of a serious breach by a Member State of the values referred to in Article 2".[45] On the other hand, the sanction mechanism applies in the situation of "the existence of a serious and persistent breach by a Member State of the values referred to in Article 2".[46] Since the adoption of Art. 7 TEU in 2009 neither the preventive nor sanctioning mechanism have not been resorted to till June 1, 2016 when the Commission has adopted Rule of Law Opinion on the situation in Poland.[47] The opinion consisted of three main problems: 1) The appointment of judges to the Constitutional Tribunal; 2) The functioning of the Constitutional Tribunal; 3) Effectiveness of constitutional review of new legislation (media law and other laws).

It does not mean that any other problems were not identified. On January 13, 2016 College Orientation Debate on recent developments in Poland and the Rule of Law Framework[48] took place. The College of Commissioners discussed developments in Poland concerning not only the Constitutional Tribunal but also the governance of the Public Service Broadcasters. Furthermore, the European Parliament in its resolution of 13 April 2016 on the situation in Poland called on the Polish Government to fully implement the recommendations of the Venice Commission and sharing the Venice Commission's opinion highlighted that the Polish Constitution as well as European and international standards require that the judgments of a Constitutional Court be respected.[49]

After the adoption of an Opinion on the situation in Poland, on July 27, 2016 Commission Recommendation of regarding the rule of law in Poland has been adopted. It made recommendations to the Polish authorities on concerns which related to the following issues: 1) the appointment of judges of the Constitutional Tribunal and the lack of implementation of the judgments of the Constitutional Tribunal of 3 and 9 December 2015 relating to these matters; 2) the lack of publication in the Official Journal and of implementation of the judgment of 9 March 2016 and of the judgments rendered by the Constitutional Tribunal since 9 March 2016; 3) the effective functioning of the Constitutional Tribunal and the effectiveness of Constitutional review of new legislation, in particular in view of the law on the Constitutional Tribunal adopted by the Sejm on 22 July 2016. The Commission has recommended that the Polish authorities take appropriate action to

45 Art. 7 (1) TEU.

46 Art. 7 (2) TEU.

47 European Commission's Press release, Commission adopts Rule of Law Opinion on the situation in Poland, Brussels, 1 June 2016, p. 3.

48 European Commission – Fact Sheet, College Orientation Debate on recent developments in Poland and the Rule of Law Framework: Questions & Answers, Brussels, 13 January 2016.

49 European Parliament resolution of 13 April 2016 on the situation in Poland, 2015/3031(RSP).

address the systemic threat to the rule of law as a matter of urgency.[50] It is worth noting that in case of no satisfactory follow-up within the time limit set, resort can be had to the Art. 7 Procedure.

Formally, the procedure under Art. 7 TEU can be triggered by one third of the Member States, by the European Parliament or by the European Commission. Firstly, the Council, after obtaining the consent of the European Parliament, must act with a decision of 4/5 of its members to determine that there is a clear risk of a serious breach of the rule of law or to address recommendations to the Member State concerned. Before adopting the decision mentioned above the Council must hear the Member States concerned. Secondly, the European Council must act by unanimity, after obtaining the consent of the European Parliament, to determine the existence of a serious and persistent breach of the rule of law. Accordingly, the Member State concerned must first be invited to present its observations. Finally, the Council must act by qualified majority to sanction a Member State for a serious and persistent breach of the rule of law as well as to revoke or amend these sanctions.[51] In the light of Art. 354 TFEU, the Member of the European Council or the Council representing the Member State in question shall not take part in the vote, and the Member State concerned shall not be counted in the calculation of the majorities for these determinations.

VI. The scope of application of Art. 7 TEU

For clarity of argumentation some arrangements connected with Art. 7 TEU should be laid down. First of all, it is advisable to assume the scope of application of Art. 7 TEU, including its *rationae personae* and *rationae materiae*. As far as the *rationae personae* of Art. 7 TEU is concerned it is clear that the addressees of the obligation imposed on the basis of Art. 7 TEU are Member States. In general, the breach of EU values must be committed by a Member State itself. It should be added that the notion of 'state' in the EU law includes all kinds of bodies qualified as an 'emanation of the State'.[52] As a consequence the breach of EU values under Art. 7 TEU can be imputable to all national institutions or bodies which constitutes 'emanation of the State'. In addition, the respect of the EU values is a *sine qua non* condition of accession of new member state to the EU.[53] The reasoned proposal in order to activate the preventive mechanism can be issued by one third of the Member States, by the European Parliament or by the European Commission[54] while the reasoned proposal in order to activate the sanctioning

50 Commission Recommendation of 27.7.2016 regarding the rule of law in Poland, Brussels, 27.7.2016, C(2016) 5703 final, p. 7, 8, 21.

51 Art. 7 (2-5) TEU.

52 ECJ, Case C-188/89 (Foster and others), ECLI:EU:C:1990:313, ECR 1990, I-03313.

53 Art. 49 TEU.

54 Art. 7 (1) TEU.

mechanism can be issued by one third of the Member States or by the Commission and after obtaining the consent of the European Parliament.[55]
Secondly, the aim of the procedure is to ensure the observance of EU values in Member States, so the provision imposes obligations on Member States. The breach of EU values imputable to a state may consist of a positive act or of an omission.[56] For instance, the Commission imputes to Poland the breach of EU values connected with the appointment of judges of the Constitutional Tribunal and the lack of implementation of the judgments of the Constitutional Tribunal of 3 and 9 December 2015 relating to these matters, moreover the lack of publication in the Official Journal and of implementation of the judgment of 9 March 2016 and of the judgments rendered by the Constitutional Tribunal since 9 March 2016. In this context, the relationship between Art. 7 TEU and Art. 258 TFEU is worth mentioning. The infringement procedure based on Article 258 TFEU is an important instrument in addressing certain rule of law concerns, but it can be launched by the Commission only where these concerns constitute simultaneously a breach of a specific provision of EU law. Yet, there are situations of concern which fall outside the scope of substantive EU law and therefore cannot be considered as a breach of obligations under the Treaties but still they pose a systemic threat to the rule of law. Taking into account these kind of situations, the preventive and sanctioning mechanisms provided for in Article 7 TEU may apply. Consequently, it should be stressed that the *rationae materiae* of Art. 7 TEU is not confined to areas covered by EU law, but empowers the EU to intervene also in areas where Member States act autonomously.[57] It is justified by the fact that "if a Member State breaches the fundamental values in a manner sufficiently serious to be caught by Article 7, this is likely to undermine the very foundation of the EU and the trust between its members, whatever the field in which the breach occurs".[58]
Art. 7 TEU provides sanctions in case of the determination of the existence of a serious and persistent breach by a Member State of the values referred to in Article 2. The sanction consists in the suspension of certain rights deriving from the application of the Treaties to the Member State in question, including the voting rights of the representative of the government of that Member State in the Council.[59] It should be noted that the Treaty obligations continue to be binding for the Member State in question also after its voting rights have been suspended.[60]

55 Art. 7 (2) TEU.

56 *B. de Witte/G. N. Toggenburg*, Respect for Human Rights as a Condition for Membership of the European Union, in: Peers/Ward (eds.), The European Union Charter of Fundamental Rights, 2004, p. 71.

57 Communication from the Commission to the European Parliament and the Council, A new EU Framework to strengthen the Rule of Law, Brussels, 19.3.2014, COM (2014) 158 final/2, p. 6.

58 Communication from the Commission of 15 October 2003: Respect for and promotion of the values on which the Union is based, Brussels, 15.10.2003, COM (2003) 606 final.

59 Art. 7 (3) TEU.

60 Art. 7 (3) TEU the last sentence. Also: *B. de Witte/G. N. Toggenburg*, Respect for Human Rights as a Condition for Membership of the European Union, in: Peers/Ward (eds.), The European Union Charter of Fundamental Rights, Hart Publishing, 2004, p. 72.

Paradoxically, the role of the Court of Justice in cases covered by Art. 7 TEU is limited. In the light of Art. 269 TFEU the Court of Justice decides on the legality of an act adopted by the European Council or by the Council pursuant to Art. 7 TEU solely at the request of the Member State concerned by a determination of the European Council or of the Council and in respect solely of the procedural stipulations contained in Art. 7 TEU. *A contrario*, the Court of Justice does not possess jurisdiction to examine whether the substantive conditions for the application of Art. 7 TEU have been fulfilled. Thus, it seems clear that consequently the Court of Justice does not have jurisdiction to state on the interpretation of Art. 7 TEU within the preliminary ruling procedure.[61] That is the reason why Art. 7 TEU cannot give rise effectively to any liability of Member State towards individuals especially in case of breach of rule of law principles by the Member State concerned.

VII. Functions of norms defining the values set by the EU Treaties in the context of individuals' rights

One of the legal problems of the analysis concerns the normative theory of EU law with a particular focus on the structure and function of norms defining the values set by the EU Treaties. Adapting Robert Alexy's theory of fundamental rights[62] to the theory of EU law, the theory of values, together with the theory of purposiveness and the theory of principles of European Union law may be understood as one of the three theories of the normative theory of EU law in general.[63] EU primary law indicates in the Art. 2 TEU the general and overarching values of the European Union which are: respect for human dignity, freedom, democracy, equality, the rule of law and respect for human rights, including the rights of persons belonging to minorities. The list of EU values is supplemented by an explanation that these values are common to the Member States in a society in which pluralism, non-discrimination, tolerance, justice, solidarity and equality between women and men prevail.[64] The identification of legal norms specifying the protected values of the European Union, as well as the scope of the responsibility and hypothetic liability for the breach of the protected values involve not only the literal, but also systemic and functional interpretation of EU Treaties.

The concept of a legal norm is not the same as the concept of a legal provision such like Art. 2 or 7 TUE. The individual provisions of the Treaties may not contain all the elements necessary for formulation of the legal norm determining the appropriate standards of conduct for fulfilment of the values set by the EU

61 *M. Broberg/N. Fenger*, Preliminary References to the European Court of Justice, 2nd edition, 2014, p. 110.

62 *R. Alexy*, Theorie der Grundrechte, 1994 (Erstauflage 1986).

63 *R. Alexy*, Teoria praw podstawowych, tłum. Bożena Kwiatkowska i Jerzy Zajadło, Wydawnictwo Sejmowe, Warszawa 2010, p. 421.

64 Art. 2 TEU. Consolidated version of the Treaty on European Union, OJ C 202, 7.6.2016, p. 13-388 (EN).

Treaties, but it is possible to identify them in other provisions of the Treaties. The legal norms defining the values set by the Treaty on the EU are of the fundamental importance for the European Union's legal order. Among the values of the European Union these are the values which are superior towards the other values of the European Union. The formal fundamentality of the legal norms defining the values of the EU Treaties results from the position of the EU Treaties in the hierarchy of the sources of law. However, the legal norms determining the values of the European Union are of the fundamental nature in the substantive meaning, because they are the substantive grounds for the action of the EU institutions in case of a breach of protected values by a Member State in the field of shared competences or competences not conferred upon the Union in the Treaties which are remained with the Member States. The values adopted in the EU Treaties also provide the substantive basis for formulation of the principles of EU law. The content-related fundamentality is confirmed in the universality of the values of the EU Treaties which do not relate to the specific areas of law but appear in all areas of EU law. This demonstrates the abounding and dynamically developing content of norms specifying the values of the European Union.

Moreover, the norms of the EU Treaties specifying the values of the European Union determine the competences of the EU institutions to take action in order to achieve a satisfying state of protection of the EU values. This applies to the competences conferred upon the European Union by its Member States, the competences "not conferred" upon the European Union, as well as the category of the potential competences of the European Union. Therefore, actions of the European Union are based on the principle, according to which the right to a protected value grants the right to a measure. This solution confirms the major importance of the protected values for the whole EU legal order. As a result, the protected values indicated in Art. 2 and Art. 7 TEU constitute the substantive legal basis for the European Union's activities, both in situations where specific provisions of the Treaties contain the norms of competency as well as in the absence of the specific norms of competency.

Obviously, Art. 7 TEU is too abstract and too general to constitute a sole basis for the Member State liability towards individuals, but it does not mean that it is irrelevant. If the breach of EU values imputable to a state causes damage, specific EU rules on state liability should apply depending on the specific rights concerned.[65] The norms specifying the values of the European Union, especially in Art. 2 and 7 TEU effectuate the following main functions: systematizing function, stabilizing function, interpretative function, repressive function and evolutionary function. Firstly, the systematizing function manifests when the norms determining protected values of the EU bring order to all the EU law norms so that the EU law becomes EU legal system. Norms indicating protected values constitutes a paradigm

65 *B. de Witte/G. N. Toggenburg*, Respect for Human Rights as a Condition for Membership of the European Union, in: Peers/Ward (eds.), The European Union Charter of Fundamental Rights, Hart Publishing, 2004, p. 71.

from which other norms may be interpreted. Secondly, the stabilizing function of Art. 2 and 7 TEU prevents the EU legal system and the Member States legal orders from destabilisation and disintegration. In this context, the standards defining EU values can serve as a criterion for assessing the admissibility of the national regulation at stake. In addition, the interpretative function may be expressed by the national judge ruling in any case under influence of the EU decision stating the breach of EU values by the Member State concerned. Furthermore, the repressive function demonstrates that EU values protection constitutes an obligation, which signifies a kind of constraint. Legal norms indicating protected values constitutes a formal basis expressing the will of a subject of law so that the subject is obliged to suit the legal norms determining protected values. Accordingly, Art. 7 TEU provides the basis to impose sanctions to the Member State concerned. Finally, the evolutionary function also reveals, because once a high court of the concerned Member State rules taking into consideration the decision or judgement, national judges will gradually recognize Member State liability and the evolution will influence the development of law in the given area.

Until the stage of the preventive mechanism inclusive it is hard to imagine the liability of the Member State towards individuals. However, it does not constitute any obstacle for the liability of a Member State on the basis of the traditional rules which are applied in case of a breach of EU law. Paradoxically, even after the stage of launching the sanctioning mechanism the liability does not seem obvious, especially if the breach of causation concept is applied by the national judge. In case of any doubts concerning Art. 7 TEU the Court of Justice may decide about the liability of a given Member State within the preliminary ruling procedure initiated by a national judge in a state liability case pending before a national court.

Therefore, these are mainly the national judges, using both EU and national law, who will decide whether the European Union will be the Union of values or the Union of survival irrespective of the fact that a Member State has caused damage by the breach of EU values accompanied by a breach of a substantive EU law granting rights to an individual. In order to determine whether there is a sufficiently serious breach of EU law, all the factors which characterize the situation before the national court must be taken into account. According to the case law of the Court of Justice, the factors which may be taken into consideration in this regard include, inter alia, the degree of clarity and precision of the rule breached, the extent of the margin of appreciation which the infringed rule leaves, the intentional or unintentional nature of the breach or the injury caused, the excusable or inexcusable nature of a possible error of law, the fact that the attitudes taken by an EU institution may have contributed to the adoption or the maintenance of national measures or practices contrary to EU law, as well as the failure of the court in question to fulfil its obligation to make a reference for a preliminary ruling under Art. 267 TFEU. However, it must in any event be pointed out that the breach of EU law is sufficiently serious where it occurred in manifest disregard of the

Court's case law on the matter.[66] For instance, the Court of Justice in case C-385/12 Hervis stated Hungarian tax legislation establishing an exceptional tax on the turnover of store retail trade contrary to EU law. Notwithstanding the judgment mentioned the Polish Government has prepared the proposal of a legal act introducing an analogue tax in Poland. The entry into force of the act was suspended on the sole ground that the European Commission has started an investigation on the planned tax.

Another approach to the problem of unlawfulness is to make a case of infringement of the Charter of Fundamental Right. The CFR is, as a rule, addressed to the institutions of the EU, and it applies to the Member States only when they are implementing Union law (Art. 51(1) CFR). The Charter may not extend the field of application of Union law beyond the powers of the Union or establish any new power or task for the Union, or modify powers and tasks as defined in the Treaties (Art. 51(2) CFR).[67] The notion of 'fundamental' rights used in the Charter slightly differs from the notion of 'human' rights mentioned as one of the EU values in Art. 2 TEU. One of the explanations is that 'human rights' are broader and all-encompassing, whereas the term of 'fundamental rights' allows for a distinction between rights belonging to 'everybody' or only to 'EU citizens'.[68] In addition, the scope of application of the Charter is limited by the condition of existence of substantive EU law, whereas Art. 2 TEU, interpreted for the purpose of Art. 7 TEU, applies in all areas including these covered by shared competences.

From the point of view of the subject of this work, it is important to note that, according to the *Schöppenstedt* formula, the condition of the liability is not only the qualified violation of the law, but also a violation of specific legal standards – *a superior rule of law for the protection of the individual.* For a superior rule of law the ECJ recognised primarily the provisions of the founding treaties, as well as general principles of law developed by the CJEU, such as the principle of equality, the protection of legitimate expectations, and the protection of the acquired rights.[69] The *Schöppenstedt* formula has been modified in *Bergaderm vs. Commission.*[70] The Court of Justice rejected the understanding of the discussed requirement in accordance with the German *Schutznorm* doctrine because it would, in practice, make it impossible or extremely difficult to obtain effective reparation for loss or damage resulting from a breach of EU law by the legislature. Thus, the rule does not have to be a superior rule of law, but it should confer rights on individuals. The existence of a right conferred on individuals by a rule of law implies that the breach of such a rule is sufficiently serious.[71] The element

66 ECJ, Case C-168/15 (Milena Tomášová), ECLI:EU:C:2016:602, points 25-27.

67 *N. Półtorak* (fn. 6), p. 429-430.

68 *F. Hoffmeister*, Enforcing the EU Charter of Fundamental Rights in Member States: How Far are Rome, Budapest and Bucharest from Brussels?, in: von Bogdandy/Sonnevend (eds.), Constitutional Crisis in the European Constitutional Area: Theory, Law and Politics in Hungary and Romania, 2015, p. 204.

69 ECJ, joined Cases C-104/89 and C-37/90 (Mulder), ECLI:EU:C:2000:38, ECR 2000, I-203, mn 15.

70 ECJ, Case C-352/98 P (Bergaderm/Commission), ECLI:EU:C:2000:361, ECR 2000, I-5291.

71 ECJ, Case C-611/12 P (Giordano/Commission), ECLI:EU:C: 2014:2282, mn. 40. See *N. Półtorak* (fn. 6), p. 432-433.

crucial for the assessment of the condition of sufficient seriousness of the breach is the *discretion* available to the institution. This notwithstanding, the discretion is also evaluated in the context of causation.[72]

VIII. Conclusion

The modern evolution of national laws on civil liability have not modified the shape of causation as developed by the Court of Justice, which still demands proof of a direct and exclusive causal link between the breach of EU law and the damage. However, a claim arising from a European delict committed by a Member State will always be heard by a national court. From the viewpoint of a civil court causation concerns attribution, and thus attribution questions necessarily invoke innumerable policy considerations which influence the ascertainment of legal causation. In conclusion, at least one of the conditions of Member State liability for the breach of EU law, namely the missing requirement of a direct and exclusive causal link between the breach of the obligation resting on the State and the damage sustained by the injured party, makes a case for liability in damages hardly possible.

Considering various functions performed by Art. 7 TEU it is too general and abstract to constitute a necessary and sufficient element of a delict. A violation of common values is followed by a concrete act or omission, which can be regarded a direct cause of loss to an individual. The test of directness, although it is a minimum requirement of liability, is hence put into question.

72 ECJ, joined Cases C-120/06 P and C-121/06 P (Fabbrica italiana accumulatori motocarri Montecchio SpA – FIAMM), ECLI:EU:C:2008:476, ECR 2008, I-6513, mn. 144. The Court held „with regard to the causal link, the Court of First Instance failed to observe the requirement that the damage must be a sufficiently direct consequence of the conduct of the institution concerned. There is no automatic link between the DSB's decision of 25 September 1997 and the introduction of the increased customs duty at issue, since the United States authorities, in the exercise of their discretion, decided in principle to impose the duty and determined the products upon which it would be charged and its rate when, in particular, they could have accepted the compensation offered by the Community.".

Wrongfulness and Fault as Requirements of the „European Delict“ under Art. 7 TEU?

*By Ulrich Magnus, Hamburg**

The article surveys and compares the the requirements of Art. 7 TEU with the concepts of wrongfulness and fault as particularly used in private tort law. Several questions call for discussion: Can the violation of Art. 2 and 7 TEU be rightly termed delict? In which sense? Does the private law concept of wrongfulness add anything to the understanding and interpretation of the Art. 7 TEU mechanism? Does the notion of fault? Finally, some conclusions can be drawn.

I. Introduction

On the one hand probably nobody would object if one simply stated that wrongfulness and fault are typical legal terms of private law, in particular of private tort law, and of criminal law, too. However, usually they have no direct place in general public law and European community law. Even Art. 340 (2) TFEU on the extra-contractual liability of the European Union for its organs does not mention them as requirements of liability. On the other hand, wrongfulness and fault could be considered as general ingredients of any kind of liability irrespective whether liability encounters in private law, public law or criminal law and irrespective whether a private person, a state or state agency shall be made liable.
The following text examines whether wrongfulness and fault, as understood in private law, have any meaning for what Lubos Tichy has nicely termed the "European Delict" under Art. 7 TEU.

II. The "European Delict" under Art. 7 TEU

First, some words on the "European Delict" under Art. 7 TEU. For enabling the comparison with its private law counterparts it must be defined what the "European Delict" is. It may be shortly described as a serious breach by a Member State of the European values enshrined in Art. 2 TEU. The delict has two levels of realisationrealization on which the Member State in question can become, so to speak, liable and can face escalating reactions and sanctions by the Community.[1]

* Professor (em.) of Civil Law, Private International Law and Comparative Law, University of Hamburg; Judge (ret.) at the Court of Appeal, Hamburg; Affiliate of the Max-Planck-Institute for Foreign and Private International Law, Hamburg.

1 See thereon *P. V. van Vormizeele*, in: von der Groeben/Schwarz/Hatje (eds.), Europäisches Unionsrecht, 7th ed. 2015, Art. 7 EUV mn. 4; *M. Ruffert*, in: Calliess/Ruffert (eds.), EUV/AEUV, 5th ed. 2016, Art. 7 EUV mn. 7 et seq.; *F. Schorkopf*, in: Grabitz/Hilf/Nettesheim (eds.), Das Recht der Europäischen Union, 59th supplement 2016, Art. 7 EUV mn. 19 et seq. In the past, Art. 7 TEU had been discussed with regard to Austria when the rightwing party FPÖ entered into the government coalition; see thereto *W. Hummer/W. Obwexer*, Die Wahrung

To arouse measures on the first level, Art. 7 (1) TEU requires "a clear risk of a serious breach by a Member State of the values referred to in Article 2." Even on this level sanctions of different weight are possible: either diplomatic contacts, recommendations or the determination of a risk of breach of the values enshrined in Art. 2 TEU. On the next level, stronger sanctions[2] become available if the competent EU-organs "determine the existence of a serious and persistent breach by a Member State of the values referred to in Article 2."[3] This regulation has borrowed from Art. 6 of the United Nations Charter[4] which allows the exclusion of a UN-Member State "which has persistenly violated the Principles" of the Charter and from Art. 8 of the Statute of the Council of Europe[5] which allows the suspension and finally also the exclusion of a Member State "which has seriously violated" the fundamental principles and rights which the Statute provides for.[6] Also many other international state cooperation or integration movements know of similar provisions.[7] However, in particular the risk concept in Art. 7 TEU that allows an early intervention in the forefront of a breach is a true European invention and creature.[8]

Art. 7 TEU requires that the Member State must violate or threaten to violate the values mentioned in Art. 2 sent. 1 TEU, namely: "respect for human dignity, freedom, democracy, equality, the rule of law and respect for human rights, including the rights of persons belonging to minorities."[9] The term "values" seems to be the abstract and abbreviated expression for the principles named in Art. 2 TEU. It comprises but the listed principles and is apparently no separate concept that

der "Verfassungsgrundsätze" der EU – Rechtsfragen der EU-Sanktionen" gegen Österreich, EuZW 2000, S. 485; *F. Schorkopf*, Verletzt Österreich die Homogenität in der Europäischen Union?, DVBl 2000, S. 1036; further *C. Calliess*, Europa als Wertegemeinschaft – Integration und Identität durch europäisches Verfassungsrecht?, JZ 2004, S. 1033.

2 In particular the suspension of EU-membership rights, see Art. 7 (3) TEU.

3 Art. 7 (2) TEU.

4 "A Member of the United Nations which has persistently violated the Principles contained in the present Charter may be expelled from the Organisation by the General Assembly upon the recommendation of the Security Council.".

5 "Any Member of the Council of Europe which has seriously violated Article 3 may be suspended from its rights of representation and requested by the Committee of Ministers to withdraw under Article 7. If such Member does not comply with this request, the Committee may decide that it has ceased to be a Member of the Council as from such date as the Committee may determine.".
The quoted Art. 3 runs as follows: "Every Member of the Council of Europe must accept the principles of the rule of law and of the enjoyment by all persons within its jurisdiction of human rights and fundamental freedoms, and collaborate sincerely and effectively in the realisation of the aim of the Council as specified in Chapter I.".

6 See the Communication from the Commission to the Council and the European Parliament on Article 7 of the Treaty on European Union. Respect for and promotion of the values on which the Union is based, COM (2003) 606 Final p. 6.

7 See the remarks by *F. Schorkopf*, in: Grabitz/Hilf/Nettesheim (fn. 1), Art. 7 EUV mn. 18 (with the examples of the MERCOSUR, the African Union, the Commonwealth and the Andean Pact).

8 See the Commission's Communication COM (2003) 606 Final p. 7.

9 Art. 2 sent. 1 TEU.

reaches further than the included principles. It appears also to be clear that only a grave breach or risk of such a breach will allow the application of Art. 7 TEU.[10]
In 2003, the Commission published a Communication[11] on the interpretation of Article 7 TEU which intended to give some guidelines concerning the application of the provision. At first glance, the value of these guidelines may appear doubtful since actually only the European Court of Justice is competent to authoritatively interpret the Union Treaty. However, the Court has no full competence to decide on the legality of measures adopted under Art. 7 TEU but only "in respect solely of the procedural stipulations contained in that Article" (Art. 269 TFEU). The reason is that the decision whether a Member State has violated or threatens to violate the fundamental values of the Union shall be rendered by the other Member States represented by the Council (after assent of the European Parliament). In this respect they – and not the CJEU – sit as judges over the behaviour of the 'accused' Member State and they decide by – a qualified – majority. Therefore, the Commission's Communication covers an area outside the jurisdiction of the CJEU and gives guidelines for the interpretation of Art. 7 TEU. They are thus helpful and provide at least an impression of the intentions behind this provision. The Commission's Communication rightly stresses that the mechanism under Art. 7 TEU is a political one[12] which grants the Council a rather wide though not unlimited discretion.
Several open questions surround the Council's discretion which are only scarcely, if at all, discussed. First, it is doubtful whether the Council has discretion only with respect to the selection of the appropriate sanction or also with respect to the principles listed in Art. 2 TEU and the question whether their breach was serious. Since the values of Art. 2 constitute fundamental principles of EU law which are relevant in many instances it seems inadequate that the Council should have discretion to give these principles from case to case different meanings. Insofar there is, and should be, no Council discretion.
It is more difficult to answer whether the Council should have discretion in the assessment of the seriousness of the breach. The seriousness of the breach is foremost a question of law. Should it be a matter of political discretion as well? In my view the answer is no. Political discretion is apt for the selection of the sanctions and even there a clear order exists that first soft sanctions should be chosen and that any sanction must be in proportion to the weight of the violation of one or more fundamental principle. The rule of law principle binds the EU organs as well as the Member States. As far as possible the decision of the Council should be based on legal principles and avoid discretionary, let alone arbitrary elements. This insight should actually lead to a further necessary consequence, namely the

10 See the Commission's Communication COM (2003) 606 Final p. 7 ("go beyond specific situations and concern a more systematic problem"); also *M. Ruffert*, in: Calliess/Ruffert (fn. 1), Art. 7 EUV mn. 5; *F. Schorkopf*, in: Grabitz/Hilf/Nettesheim (fn. 1), Art. 7 EUV mn. 32.

11 Communication of 15 October 2003: COM (2003) 606 Final; see already supra fn. 6.

12 Com (2003) 606 Final, p. 5 et seq.

ultimate decision whether a Member State seriously breached one or more of the Art. 2 TEU values should lie in the hands of the CJEU. The Court decides on the compliance with these values, in particular with the rule of law principle, also in other relationships.[13] The neutrality of the Court would safeguard that the decision is further removed from the realm of the political field. The competence of the Court would also avoid the certain merger of judicial and administrative function which a decision by the Council on both the serious breach and the consequential sanctions presently constitutes. In addition, the competence of the CJEU would provide a remedy against the verdict of the Council. The realisation of this proposal would be easy, namely consisting of the deletion of Art. 269 TFEU.

Furthermore, it is doubtful whether or not the Council should have discretion to pursue breaches of the Art. 2 values. There is probably discretion as to the point of time when to take measures. But the rule of law principle requires that measures are to be taken when there is a clear risk of a serious breach.

The Council certainly has discretion in selecting the respective measures. The Council, after assent of the European Parliament, may determine that there is a clear risk of a serious breach or that there is a serious and persistent breach but the Council is not tied to do so. It is the Council's discretion to prefer mere diplomatic reactions without any express decision under Art. 7 TEU. The Communication of the Commission on Art. 7 TEU further explains that the risk of breach or the breach itself must "go beyond specific situations and concern a more systematic problem."[14] This has to be understood that single violations as such cannot trigger Art. 7 TEU. However, if violations of the fundamental values of the Union occur on a regular basis they may amount to a serious breach. The circumscription "systemic deficit" has been coined for this constellation.[15]

A "clear risk of a serious breach" requires that first signs of such a breach have become visible.[16] The Commission mentions in its Communication two examples for such a risk: firstly, a Member State adopts legislation that allows procedural guarantees to be abolished in wartime; secondly, first signs of racist or xenophobic policies have become apparent.[17] It appears to be common ground that it does not matter whether the breach was caused by legislative, governmental, administrative or judicial activities of the Member State in question.[18]

With respect to the "serious and persistent breach" the Communication stresses that the seriousness depends on several factors, including the purpose and result

13 See, e.g., ECJ, Case C-90/95 (De Compte/Parliament), ECLI:EU:C:1997:198, ECR 1997, I-1999; ECJ, Case C-222/86 (Unectef/Heylens), ECLI:EU:C:1987:442, ECR 1987, 4097; ECJ, Case C-169/80 (Gondrand Frères), ECLI:EU:C:1981:171, ECR 1981, 1931; ECJ, Case C-98/78 (Racke), ECLI:EU:C:1979:14, ECR 1979, 69 where the CJEU exposed different aspects of the rule of law principle.

14 COM (2003) 606 Final, p. 7.

15 *A. von Bogdandy/M. Ioannidis*, Das systemische Defizit – Merkmale, Instrumente und Probleme am Beispiel der Rechtsstaatlichkeit und des neuen Rechtsstaatlichkeitsaufsichtsverfahrens, ZaöRV 2014, p. 283 ff.

16 COM (2003) 606 Final, p. 7.

17 COM (2003) 606 Final, p. 7.

18 See COM (2003) 606 Final, p. 5 ("[…] whatever the field in which the breach occurs."); in particular with respect to the principle of the rule of law, *A. von Bogdandy/M. Ioannidis* (fn. 15), p. 283 ff., 288 ff.

of the breach, its effect on specific social classes, in particular if "they are vulnerable, as in the case of national, ethnic or religious minorities or immigrants."[19] Furthermore, the simultaneous violation of several of the values mentioned in Art. 2 TEU may provide evidence for the seriousness of the breach.[20] In order to be persistent the breach "must last some time."[21] Repeated and systematic single breaches, condemnations for the ignorance of the mentioned values by national or international courts such as the European Court of Human Rights, any failure to take remedial actions can demonstrate a persistent breach.[22]

However, on no occasion mentions the Commission's Communication an express requirement of wrongfulness or fault with respect to the application of Art. 7 TEU.

III. The requirements and function of wrongfulness and fault in civil liability law

In private liability law and in particular in tort law it is no question that wrongfulness and fault play an important role.[23] Although both terms also encounter in the law of contractual liability as well as in criminal law, I will limit the following to private tort law. If there is at all a parallel to the "European Delict" under Art. 7 TEU, it is more likely to be found in tort law.

In tort law wrongfulness and fault are in principle core elements. Nonetheless, it must be stated at the outset that modern tort law – probably almost everywhere on the globe – knows of torts which do not formally require wrongfulness and fault. Today, strict liability is the second leg of tort law.[24] The different legal systems usually provide for strict liability if an activity is so dangerous that the observance of normal care would not prevent the occurrence of damage caused by that activity.[25] The most prominent example is tortious liability for traffic accidents: many, though by far not all countries,[26] have introduced strict liability for owners of motor vehicles which cause damage to persons or goods. Here, responsibility for a certain risk, damage and causation form the exclusive basis of liability. The risky activity of driving is entirely legal and even the absence of fault does not relieve from liability. One can argue that at least the result of the dangerous driving, the

19 COM (2003) 606 Final, p. 8.
20 COM (2003) 606 Final, p. 8.
21 COM (2003) 606 Final, p. 8.
22 COM (2003) 606 Final, p. 8; *P. V. van Vormizeele*, in: von der Groeben/Schwarz/Hatje (fn. 1), Art. 7 EUV mn. 10; *M. Ruffert*, in: Calliess/Ruffert (fn. 1), Art. 7 EUV mn. 5; *F. Schorkopf*, in: Grabitz/Hilf/Nettesheim (fn. 1), Art. 7 EUV mn. 32 ff.
23 See e.g., under a broad comparative perspective, *H. Koziol*, Comparative conclusions, in: Koziol (ed.), Basic Questions of Tort Law from a Comparative Perspective, 2015, p. 782 et seq.
24 See thereon *B. Koch/H. Koziol*, in: Koch/Koziol (eds.), Unification of Tort Law: Strict Liability, 2002, p. 395 ff.; *H. Koziol*, in: Koziol (fn. 23), p. 802 ff.
25 See the references in the preceding fn.
26 Countries that have not introduced strict liability for traffic accidents are, e.g., the Netherlands and Great Britain.

damage, is wrongful in the sense that the law does not allow it but disapproves of it. However, it is a certain inconsistency – reminding of Shakespeare's Shylock – that the activity is allowed though its result is forbidden. In any event, strict liability dispenses entirely with fault.

1. Wrongfulness

Despite the foregoing it is for sure that wrongfulness plays a prominent role in all private tort law systems.[27] Its regular definition in this field says that wrongfulness requires that something has been done or occurred that was forbidden by law. It is not a question of fact but a legal judgment that an activity of whatever kind must be in contradiction to what the law requires. It is the general rule that nobody should be held liable for what society accepts as legal. Therefore, legitimate self-defence or reasonable defence of others as reaction to an incriminated activity is allowed.

However, at a second glance, the point of reference of wrongfulness varies among legal systems and sometimes even within a single system.[28] Some systems link wrongfulness to the conduct of the tortfeasor and require that the conduct must be against the law.[29] Other systems primarily connect wrongfulness with the result of conduct that must infringe rights protected by the law.[30] Some mix wrongfulness with fault.[31] Taking again the example of a road accident caused by a car driver, it can be said that driving on the road is certainly not against the law but that running down a pedestrian certainly is. At least the result, the injury of the pedestrian, is an obvious violation of the fundamental rule of law of *neminem laedere*. In many of such accidents it will be the case that the driver also neglected a certain traffic rule, drove too fast, overlooked a traffic sign, did not take the necessary attention etc. Then, both the conduct and the result offended the law and were wrongful. It thus appears that there is a certain necessary link between wrongfulness and the social acceptability of conduct. For, to use another example, if you sit in the metro and get infected by the flu of the person sitting next to you, such infection is usually judged as socially adequate and a general risk but not as wrongful. You may change your seat but you are not allowed in legitimate self-defence to expell the other person from the train or even attack him or her. Also, yet another example, where a patient validly agrees to an operation the bodily injury that is the necessary consequence of the operation is no longer a wrongful result because it is now justified by the consent.

27 Explicitly *H. Koziol*, in: Koziol (ed.), Unification of Tort Law: Wrongfulness, 1998, p. 129.
28 See – on a broad comparative basis – *H. Koziol*, in: Koziol (fn. 27), p. 129 ff.
29 This is the leading view, for example, in Austria: see *E. Karner*, in: Koziol/Bydlinski/Bollenberger (eds.), ABGB-Kurzkommentar, 4th ed. 2014, § 1294 mn. 4.
30 This is, for instance, the leading view, in particular of the courts, in Germany; see, e.g., BGH NJW 1996, 3205; BGH NJW 2014, 3788.
31 For instance, the French legal system; see *O. Moreteau*, France, in: Koziol (fn. 23), p. 59 ff.

The differences between the different conceptions of wrongfulness do not matter too much in practice. As indicated, very often both the conduct and its result offend legal norms. Nonetheless should the difficulties with the point to which wrongfulness should refer be avoided as far as possible. According to suggestions particularly under a comparative point of view,[32] instead of the two-step-distinction between wrongfulness and fault one should distinguish between three different levels or steps: first, the unjustified infringement of a protected right; secondly, the neglect of a statutory or judge-made objective duty of care; thirdly, subjective blameworthiness, for instance, lacking capacity, mental illness. While in the traditional sense the first element regularly constitutes wrongfulness and the third fault, the middle element can be and is seen as part of either wrongfulness or of fault or of both. The terminology "wrongfulness" and "fault" should however not obscure the more refined requirements that are essentially necessary in order to establish tortious liability in private law.[33] I will nevertheless use the terms in their traditional sense that wrongfulness means the violation of the objective law and fault the subjective responsibility.

In contrast to fault, wrongfulness or unlawfulness is generally not classified in different degrees. The decision on wrongfulness is an either-or-decision. An activity or result either offends the law or is lawful, for instance is justified because the victim had validly consented to the injury. Gradations are unnecessary and unusual. Nonetheless can one speak of grave and slight violations of law. However, the degree of seriousness or weight of the violation of the law does not influence the judgment on wrongfulness as such.

At least where tort law is concerned with compensation of damage, wrongfulness generally fulfills the function to separate allowed infringements which do not entail liability from forbidden ones which lead to liability if the necessary further conditions of liability are met. The requirement of wrongfulness thus functions as a limit to liability. It safeguards that causation alone does not suffice to establish liability.

Wrongfulness can also have repercussions on the burden of proof. Where a protected interest has been infringed it is often presumed that the infringement was wrongful; then, the tortfeasor and author of this infringement must prove any ground of justification.[34]

2. *Fault*

Few legal systems define "fault" by statute: it is either intention or negligence.[35] Most systems just use the term "fault" leaving it to the courts to define the no-

32 See *H. Koziol*, in: Koziol (fn. 27), p. 130 ff.; *H. Koziol*, in: Koziol (fn. 23), p. 782 ff.

33 Strongly in this direction *H. Koziol,* in: Koziol (fn. 23) p. 784.

34 This is for instance the case under Austrian (OGH SZ 61/270; OGH ZVR 1992/177; OGH JBl. 1995, 658) and German law (BGHZ 74, 9; BGH NJW 1996, 3205).

35 For definitions see, for instance, § 1294 ABGB, § 276 BGB, Art. 1104 Spanish Codigo civil; in a certain sense also the former Art. 1383 French Code civil, now Art. 1241.

tion.[36] Generally, fault is understood as the individual blameworthiness with respect to a tortious activity.[37] The background of the fault concept is the still valid idea of individual responsibility. A person should be held liable – in principle only – if he or she could be blamed for the damage or harm resulting from the own activity or omission.

Almost all legal systems know of different degrees of fault, at least of intent and negligence and usually also of gross negligence as a specifically strong case of negligence and sometimes even of slight negligence.[38] The different degrees form a continuum with slightest negligence (*culpa levissima*) at the one end and direct intent (*dolus directus*) at the other. In many legal systems in certain cases either liability as such or/and the amount of damages depends on the degree of fault or blameworthiness.[39] Generally the rule is: the higher the degree of fault the stricter the consequences of liability.

Intent is one of the forms of fault. It requires that the tortfeasor aims at the detrimental result or is at least content with it (*dolus eventualis*). Negligence is the neglect of the general standard or duty of care that is owed in the circumstances. Most legal systems apply an objective standard of care which the liable person must have failed to observe.[40] It is generally no excuse that a person individually did not meet that standard. The law expects that everybody behaves in a prudent and reasonable way adapted to the circumstances of the case.

Only few truly individual features of the tortfeasor are regarded as relevant and allow for a more subjective assessment of fault, in particular the lack of capacity and mental handicaps. Besides these general excuses, only under exceptional circumstances can the tortfeasor be excused, for instance because he or she reacted in the agony of the moment in an understandable though nevertheless detrimental way.[41]

The fault concept functions as a further limit to liability for damage that a person has caused. Only where a person's individual conduct did not comply with the socially expected behaviour is liability regarded as justified.

Also the fault concept can have repercussions on the burden of proof. This burden is reversed in certain situations. "The conclusion […] seems to be that the reversal of the burden of proof regarding fault is – at least in the field of extra-contractual liability – an improper or 'cold' way of metamorphosing fault based liability into strict liability […]".[42]

36 This is in particular the case with Common law countries.

37 See *P. Widmer*, Comparative Report on Fault as a Basis of Liability and Criterion of Imputation (Attribution), in: Widmer (ed.), Unification of Tort Law: Fault, 2005, p. 340.

38 See *P. Widmer*, in: Widmer (fn. 37), p. 353.

39 See the examples given by *P. Widmer*, in: Widmer (fn. 37), p. 354 ff.

40 See *P. Widmer*, in: Widmer (fn. 37), p. 348 ff.

41 See for instance BGH NJW 1976, 1504 (tortfeasor sharply braked his car when unexpectedly a tire exploded; the hard braking made the car skid and led to a collision; the Federal Court denied a fault of the driver who acted in the agony of the moment wrongly but excusably). For a short comparative survey on possible exculpations see *P. Widmer*, in: Widmer (fn. 37), p. 355.

42 *P. Widmer*, in: Widmer (fn. 37), p. 356 ff.

IV. Transferability to the "European delict"?

In the following part I will examine whether the notions of "wrongfulness" and "fault" have any meaning in respect of the "European delict" under Art. 7 TEU. Are they necessary elements of the liability under that provision?

1. Is the "European Delict" a delict?

However, a first question is whether the "European delict" is at all a delict in the sense that private tort law attaches to the term. I take it for granted that the term "delict" is meant here to refer to private law and not to criminal law. Is the violation of Art. 7 TEU comparable to delict conceptions of private tort law? Private tort law in its widest sense imposes private sanctions (compensation awards, injunctions) against socially unwanted behaviour. In its narrow sense private tort law primarily aims at fixing the conditions under which damage has to be compensated that a person caused to another. It is evident that the "European Delict" under Art. 7 TEU does not comply with this narrow definition of tort because the ultimate sanction under Art. 7 TEU is not compensation of damage but the suspension of certain rights the involved Member State actually enjoys under EU law.

However, the wide definition of private tort law could fit the mechanism under Art. 7 TEU. Art. 7 TEU clearly aims at the prohibition of unwanted behaviour by a Member State, namely the serious breach of the values mentioned in Art. 2. In this respect, such behaviour of a Member State has some similarity with a tort under private tort law which also requires the breach of norms which in essence intend to enforce certain principles, though in particular the maxim of *neminem laedere*. Therefore, in a rather specific sense it may be justified to speak of a "European Delict" under Art. 7 TEU.

It is thus a challenging question whether the conceptions of the private law terms wrongfulness and fault can be and should be transferred to Art. 7 TEU and whether they can add anything to the interpretation of this Article. Both terms shall be dealt with separately, starting with wrongfulness.

2. Wrongfulness

a) Breach of values

As mentioned above neither the text of Art. 7 TEU or of Art. 2 TEU nor the Commission's Communication on the interpretation of Art. 7 TEU mentions the notion "wrongfulness". However, as stated supra, the term wrongfulness basically requires that an activity (including omissions)[43] was against the law and creates a

43 *P. V. van Vormizeele*, in: von der Groeben/Schwarz/Hatje (fn. 1), Art. 7 EUV mn. 10; *M. Ruffert*, in: Calliess/Ruffert (fn. 1), Art. 7 EUV mn. 5; *F. Schorkopf*, in: Grabitz/Hilf/Nettesheim (fn. 1), Art. 7 EUV mn. 30; *M. Pechstein*, in: R. Streinz (ed.) EUV/AEUV, 2nd ed. 2012, Art. 7 EUV mn. 13.

state of affairs that violates specific rules of law. Art. 7 TEU requires that the fundamental values of "human dignity, freedom, democracy, equality, the rule of law and respect for human rights" have been violated.[44] The Member State in question must have acted and shown activities in a way that seriously endangers or already infringed these values. The activity can be any measure or omission of the state either by way of legislation, administration, governmental acts or even judicial practice.[45] Indeed, the breach of the values listed in Art. 2 TEU can be termed a special wrongful behaviour of the respective State. It is clear here that both the conduct of the state in question and the outcome of its activities must seriously infringe the values listed in Art. 2 TEU. If this is the case one could speak of wrongfulness in the specific sense that the activities of the Member State violate one or more values of the EU and are thus against the law.

Whether this violation corresponds to the wrongfulness-concept of private tort law may be doubted because these values are rather broad and to a certain extent vague principles which require concretisation. Which is the precise content, for instance, of the rule of law? It could be argued that the values are too uncertain so that they do not allow a clear judgment on when they are violated. However, it is common ground that the values can be – and to a large extent already have been – concretised.[46] The relative vagueness of the values of Art. 2 TEU does thus not conflict with their qualification as binding law which can be violated.

Another field of doubt whether the notion of wrongfulness has any meaning for the "European Delict" under Art. 7 TEU is the fact that, as mentioned, wrongfulness usually does not distinguish different degrees.[47] Conduct or its result is either wrongful or lawful. There is no serious or slight wrongfulness. Yet, Art. 7 TEU requires a *serious* breach. On the other hand, the consequences of a breach of law and in particular a breach of the values protected in Art. 2 and 7 TEU can be massive, if, for instance, a Member State would abolish the independence of all courts making judges mere helpers of the political regime. The seriousness of the breach of values thus relates to the extension of the consequences and effects of the breach. Art. 7 TEU certainly requires more than slight and limited consequences of the breach. For single violations with small effects the normal remedies against breaches of Community law are available and sufficient.

It is therefore not impossible to compare a breach of the values of Art. 2 TEU with wrongfulness in private tort law and private law at all in the sense that the objective law has been – and must be – infringed. Like in tort law it is a precondition for sanctions under Art. 7 TEU.

44 As listed in Art. 2 sent. 1 TEU.

45 See the references in fn. 17.

46 See, e.g., *M. Ruffert*, in: Calliess/Ruffert (fn. 1), Art. 7 EUV mn. 5; *M. Hilf/F. Schorkopf*, in: Grabitz/Hilf/Nettesheim (fn. 1), Art. 2 EUV mn. 20.

47 See supra under III.1.

b) Grounds of justification?

As mentioned above, in private law wrongful acts and results of such acts can be justified for special reasons such as self-defence and the like. It must be asked whether there are also certain grounds for justification of a breach of the values of Art. 2 TEU. Can the parallel to private law and especially to private tort law be extended even to this aspect?

The answer is probably: no. The private law defences of self-help, consent etc. evidently have no place and meaning here. It is hardly imaginable that a Member State can be given the permission to violate the values of Art. 2, for instance the rule of law, in order to defend its own state interests. These values are so fundamental that their violation cannot and should not be justified even in a state of necessity or emergency. The Commission's Communication lends support to this view. As mentioned above it refers to the example of the legislative abolition of procedural guarantees and its actual use in wartime as an example for a serious breach of the values of Art. 2 TEU.[48] This example demonstrates that even in a state of emergency or necessity as in wartimes, the fundamental values of the Union must be respected. Some discretion exists merely with regard to the seriousness of the breach. In somewhat overstretching the parallel to private law it could be said that even a minor breach of the values of Art. 2 TEU remains a wrongful violation of the objective law but may be excused for certain reasons. This brings us to the area of fault.

3. *Fault*

As already indicated, neither Art. 7 TEU itself nor the Commission's Communication on this provision does in any respect mention fault as a requirement for the application of this Article. However, the condition that the breach of the values of Art. 2 TEU must be serious may provide an element that comes close to fault as precondition of liability under Art. 7 TEU.

The serious breach reminds to a considerable extent of the "sufficiently serious breach" of Community Law under the *Francovich*-doctrine of the CJEU[49] as explained in the *Dillenkofer*-decision of the Court[50] and further developed in many later decisions.[51] In respect of the seriousness of the breach the parallel to this case law is much more evident – and probably much more helpful – than the parallel to Art. 6 of the United Nations Charter and of Art. 8 of the Statute of the

48 COM (2003) 606 Final, p. 7.

49 ECJ, Joined cases C-6/90 and C-9/90 (Andrea Francovich/Italian Republic), ECLI:EU:C:1991:428, ECR 1991, I-5357.

50 ECJ, Joined cases C-178/94, C-179/94, C-188/94, C-189/94 and C-190/94 (Dillenkofer/Bundesrepublik Deutschland), ECLI:EU:C:1996:375, ECR 1996, I-4845 mn. 23 ff.

51 For a summary of these decisions see *N. Reich/A. N. Scholes/J. Scholes*, Unterstanding EU Internal Market Law, 2015, p. 626 ff.; *P. Machnikowski*, in: K. Oliphant (ed.), The Liability of Public Authorities in Comparative Perspective, 2016, p. 559 ff., 569 ff.; also *U. Magnus*, in: Tichý/Hrádek (eds.), Odpovednost státu zu legislativní újmu. Staatshaftung für legislatives Unrecht, 2012, p. 79 ff., 105 ff.

Council of Europe which were models for Art. 7 TEU and which provide for sanctions if their fundamental principles were either persistently or seriously violated.[52]

In *Dillenkofer* the CJEU defined a "sufficiently serious breach" of Community law in general in the following way: "[…] a breach of Community law is sufficiently serious if a Community institution or a Member State, in the exercise of its rule-making power, manifestly and gravely disregards the limits on those powers" or, where there is no or almost no legislative discretion, "the mere infringement of Community law may be sufficient."[53] Basically the same rules apply in the field of administration[54] and judicature.[55] In *Köbler*[56] the CJEU stated that in particular the following factors should be considered when assessing whether a breach of Community law manifestly infringed the applicable law and whether such breach was sufficiently serious: "the degree of clarity and precision of the rule infringed, whether the infringement was intentional, whether the error of law was excusable or inexcusable, […]."[57] In particular the latter factors strongly resemble fault elements.[58] Even though fault is no formal requirement of liability under *Francovich* or under Art. 340 (2) TFEU, elements of fault (intent or negligence, excusable or inexcusable error of law) play a considerable and sometimes decisive role.[59]

In parallel to the private law concept of fault it could thus be argued that a breach of values is serious if a reasonable EU-legislator, administrative or judicial authority would not have committed it. Such a legislator, administrative or judicial body would not seriously violate – or violate at all – the fundamental values of the Union. In private law this fault standard is, as mentioned, an objective one which in principle does not take account of individual shortcomings. The most prominent and practically most important excuses are the lack of capacity and mental handicaps.[60] It is evident that these excuses have neither a place in public law nor in Community law when public bodies act. The citizen has a right that public authorities act lawfully and do not violate fundamental values. Even if the authority acted in an excusable error of law this should not hinder sanctions in order to stop any further disrespect for the fundamental values of Community law.

The fault concept of private law thus suits only partially the needs of the here involved Community law. Only its objective side seems to be acceptable for the

52 See supra under II.

53 ECJ, Joined cases C-178/94, C-179/94, C-188/94, C-189/94 and C-190/94 (Dillenkofer/Bundesrepublik Deutschland), ECLI:EU:C:1996:375, ECR 1996, I-4845, mn. 25.

54 See for instance ECJ, Case C-470/03 (A.G.M.-COSMET Srl/Suomen valtio and Tarmo Lehtinen) ECLI:EU:C:2007:213, ECR 2007, I-2749, mn. 80 ff.

55 ECJ, Case C-224/01 (Köbler/Republik Österreich), ECLI:EU:C:2003:513, ECR 2003, I-10239, mn. 32 ff., 51 ff.

56 See preceding fn.

57 ECJ, Case C-224/01 (Köbler/Republik Österreich), ECLI:EU:C:2003:513, ECR 2003, I-10239, mn. 55.

58 See in this sense for the parallel problem in Art. 340 TFEU *M. Jacob/M. Kottmann*, in: Grabitz/Hilf/ Nettesheim (fn. 1), Art. 340 AEUV mn. 87 ff.; also *M. Gellermann*, in: Streinz (fn. 43), Art. 340 AEUV mn. 29; *M. Ruffert*, in Calliess/Ruffert (fn. 1), Art. 340 AEUV mn. 28.

59 See the references in the preceeding fn.

60 See supra under III.2.

purposes of Art. 7 TEU. Fault appears to play a role only in the sense of the violation of an objective duty to observe the values of Art. 2 TEU. This resembles the French "faute" concept which merges wrongfulness and fault. It has the consequence that Art. 7 TEU in essence provides for strict liability with respect to violations of the basic values of the EU. Fault in the sense of individually imputable responsibility with certain possible excuses is inappropriate for the applicability of Art. 7 TEU. In view of the weight and importance of the values listed in Art. 2 TEU, their objective violation should suffice to trigger the mechanism of Art. 7 TEU. Elements of fault in the sense of individual blameworthiness may however come into play with regard to the selection of the suitable sanction. Insofar it must be borne in mind that Art. 7 TEU already establishes a specific sequence of sanctions: (1) recommendation, (2) statement that there is a clear risk of a serious breach respectively the existence of a serious breach, (3) suspension of EU-Membership rights. It must be further remembered that, to be serious, the breach must anyway be sufficiently massive in its consequences and effects. One single administrative act, though in breach of one or more of the values of Art. 2 TEU, would not suffice if it concerned only one or few persons and irrespective whether or not the breach was intentional and inexcusable. As the Commission in its Communication stated the breach must occur or threaten to occur on "a more systematic" basis.[61]

For the choice of the appropriate reaction, the traditional fault concept may however render useful services. Where a Member State breached the values of Art. 2 TEU unintentionally and perhaps because of an excusable error of law, the sanction should be mere diplomatic warnings or a mere recommendation as envisaged in Art. 7 (1) TEU. However, the longer a Member State continues to infringe a value addressed in Art. 2 TEU the harder the sanction should be. Insofar, intention and the excusability of an error of law should matter for the further steps to be taken under Art. 7 TEU.

V. Conclusions

There are some evident conclusions:

- Wrongfulness in the special form that one or more of the values listed in Art. 2 TEU are violated or threatened to be violated is necessary for the application of the mechanism of Art. 7 TEU.
- The violation or risk of violation must reach a certain massiveness and be of "a more systematic" nature. In a certain parallel to private duties of care it could be said that the violation must be such that a reasonable EU-Member State exercising its legislative, governmental, administrative or judicial function would not have committed it.

61 See the Communication of the Commission COM (2003) 606 Final, p. 7.

- Fault plays no role in triggering the mechanism under Art. 7 TEU but fault elements have relevance for the selection of the appropriate sanction this provision allows for. The more the Member State in question can be blamed for the violation of the values of Art. 2 TEU, the stricter the sanctions should be.
- The CJEU should be given competence to decide in the last instance whether a Member State accused under Art. 7 TEU in fact committed a serious breach of the values enshrined in Art. 2 TEU.

In general, the private law concepts of wrongfulness and fault do not fully fit as requirements for the 'liability' of a Member State under Art. 7 TEU. Nonetheless, they offer some helpful considerations for the interpretation and application of this provision.

Balancing Values and Interests in the Art. 7 TEU Procedure

*By Michael Potacs, Vienna**

Art. 7 TEU protects the values provided in Art. 2 TEU. But the thresholds for the use of Art. 7 TEU are extremely high. Moreover Art. 7 TEU gives discretionary power to the Council at all levels of its procedure. To exercise this discretion the violation of the values must always be balanced against the interest of the mutual trust of the Member States and a suspension of rights must regard further interests like the possible consequences on the rights and obligations of natural and legal persons. All these requirements demonstrate that Art. 7 TEU should obviously more threaten than be applied.

I. Introduction

In accordance with Art. 2 TEU the EU is founded „on the values of respect for human dignity, freedom, democracy, equality, the rule of law and respect for human rights, including the rights of persons belonging to minorities". This commitment to the values of the Union shall undoubtedly express the development of the EU from an economic association to a "Community of Values"[1]. The confession in Art. 2 TEU of course has a political function which should not be underestimated. But it has also a legal dimension as already the references to Art. 2 TEU in the provisions of the determination and sanction procedure of Art. 7 TEU and the accession process in Art. 49 TEU demonstrate. Therefore, with good reasons, the commitment in Art. 2 TEU can be described as the "basic norm"[2] or (using the wording of the Commission) "the very foundation"[3] of the EU.
Nevertheless, it must be conceded that the values provided in Art. 2 TEU are formulated quite abstract and vague. Therefore, to some extent, they open a scope for political assessments.[4] That could be a reason why the Commission seems to have some doubts whether the infringement procedure of Art. 258 TFEU is the appropriate instrument for the persecution of a violation of Art. 2 TEU.[5] But it also has to be conceded that the proceeding of Art. 7 TEU has not been used up to now. The Commission just enacted a "Framework to strengthen the Rule of Law"

* Professor of Austrian and European Public Law, WU Vienna (IOER).

1 See *F. Schorkopf*, in: Grabitz/Hilf/Nettesheim (ed.), Das Recht der EU, 2010, Art. 7 TEU, mn. 12.

2 *M. Potacs*, Wertkonforme Auslegung des Unionsrechts?, EuR 2016, p. 164, 175.

3 Communication from the Commission to the Council and the European Parliament on Article 7 of the Treaty on European Union. Respect for and promotion of the values on which the Union is based, 15.10.2003, COM (2003) 606 Final, p. 3.

4 *J. Schwarze*, in: Schwarze (ed.), EU-Kommentar, 2013, Art. 2 TEU, mn. 4.

5 See Communication from the Commission to the European Parliament and the Council. A new EU framework to strengthen the Rule of Law, 11.3.2014, COM (2014) 158 Final, p. 6. The infringement procedures threatened by the Commission against Hungary related to violations of directives or fundamental rights and not Art. 2 TEU; see *R. Yamato/J. Stephan*, Eine Politik der Nichteinmischung – Die Folgen des zahnlosen Art. 7 EUV für das Wertefundament der EU am Beispiel Ungarns, DÖV 2014, p. 58, 61 f. See also chapter II.

to "resolve future threats to the rule of law in Member States before the conditions for activating the mechanism foreseen in Article 7 TEU would be met"[6]. This restraint is quite understandable as Art. 7 TEU provides high demands on a determination and sanction proceeding. On the one hand, the scope of Art. 7 TEU is not confined to areas covered by EU law, but empowers the EU to intervene also in areas where Member States act autonomously.[7] On the other hand, Art. 7 TEU is just applicable to "serious" breaches of the values of Art. 2 TEU. Above all, Art. 7 TEU gives discretionary power to the Council at all levels of its procedure.[8] That raises the question as to which criteria this discretion should be applied. Of course, Art. 7 TEU protects the values provided in Art. 2 TEU. But which interests have to be balanced against these values to exercise the discretion in accordance with the requirements of EU law?

II. Function of Art. 7 TEU

To answer this question, in the first instance, it seems to be useful to refer to the purpose and function of Art. 7 TEU.[9] It must be emphasized that Art. 7 does not authorize to terminate the membership in the EU.[10] This follows already from the wording of Art. 7 para. 3, which entitles to suspend just "certain" (and not all) rights of a Member State[11] and maintains the "obligations of the Member State in question"[12]. This view is also in accordance with the intention of the preamble of the TEU as well as of Art. 1 of the Treaty, namely to continue "the process of creating an ever closer Union among the people of Europe". The main interests which have to be regarded in the exercise of Art. 7 are therefore the basic interests which are connected with the maintenance of a membership in the Union.
Moreover, the function of Art. 7 TEU has to be seen against the background of the infringement proceeding of Art. 258 and 259 TFEU. As mentioned, some doubts remain whether the infringement procedure should apply to violations of the values provided in Art. 2 TEU. But Art. 258 and 259 TFEU are applicable when "a Member State has failed to fulfil an obligation under the Treaties". There seems no convincing argument against the view that the values of Art. 2 TEU create

6 Communication (fn. 5), p. 3.
7 Communication (fn. 5), p. 5.
8 Communication (fn. 3), p. 5.
9 To the history of Art. 7 TEU for example *W. Sadurski*, Adding Bite to the Bark: The Story of Article 7, EU Enlargement, and *J. Haider*, Columbia Journal of European Law 16, 2010, p. 385 ff.
10 See from general perspective *J. H. H. Weiler*, Alternatives to Withdrawal from an International Organisation: the Case of the European Community, Israel Law Review 20, 1985, p. 282 ff.
11 E.g. *K. Träbert*, Sanktionen der Europäischen Union gegen ihre Mitgliedstaaten, 2010, p. 321; *V. van Vormizeele*, in: von der Groeben/Schwarze/Hatje (ed.), Europäisches Unionsrecht, 2015, Art. 7 TEU, mn. 5.
12 *F. Schorkopf*, Homogenität in der Europäischen Union – Ausgestaltung und Gewährleistung durch Art. 6 Abs. 1 und Art. 7 EUV, 2000, p. 171.

such obligations. Therefore, the appropriate instrument to persecute a "simple" infringement of Art. 2 can be seen in the infringement proceeding.[13]

In contrast, the procedure of Art. 7 TEU is designed for exceptional cases of qualified violations of the values of Art. 2 TEU. Hence, there is not (as claimed)[14] a paradox between the demand of a "serious" breach of the values of Art. 2 and Art. 7 TEU and the request of any "respect" of those values for the accession to the EU in Art. 49 TEU as every violation of Art. 2 by a Member State faces persecution. In this system, the function of Art. 7 is with the words of the former President of the EU Commission *Barroso* the "nuclear option"[15] which should be used very carefully by balancing the "serious breach" of the values in Art. 2 TEU against the interest in the maintenance of a full membership in the Union. In order to do so, it is necessary to figure out the values of Art. 2 TEU, on the one hand, and the interests which are connected with the maintenance of a full membership in the Union, on the other hand.

III. Balancing Criteria

1. "Serious Breach" of Values

a) Values

To begin with the values of Art. 2 TEU it must again be confessed that they are without doubt quite vague and ambiguous and offer to a certain extent a scope for political realization. That is true for "human dignity, freedom, democracy, equality" as well as for "the rule of law and the respect for human rights". Nevertheless, it must be noted, that this scope cannot be completely unlimited. Otherwise Art. 2 TEU would have no legal effect and could hardly be a normative requirement in sanction proceedings in accordance with Art. 7 TEU or in the accession process provided in Art. 49 TEU. Therefore, it has to be assumed that Art. 2 TEU at least guarantees a "core collection"[16] of values, which can be more or less recognized. Some of the values of Art. 2 TEU are fundamental rights ensured in the EU Charta of fundamental rights. Their content is largely well known by the jurisdiction of the ECJ, the ECHR and domestic courts. The "rule of law" is a principle the ECJ referred to in many cases and which includes at least the requirement of legality

13 E.g. *K. Stephan*, Der Schutz der gemeinsamen Werte (Art. 2 EUV) innerhalb der EU am Beispiel Ungarns, 2014, p. 22 f; *R. Yamato/J. Stephan* (fn. 5), p. 65 f., *D. Kochenov/L. Pech*, Better Late than Never? On the European Comission´s Rule of Law Framework and its First Activation, Journal of Common Market Studies 54, 2016, p. 1062, 1065.

14 See for example *W. Hummer*, Ungarn erneut am Prüfstand der Rechtsstaatlichkeit und Demokratie. Wird Ungarn dieses Mal zum Anlassfall des neu konzipierten „Vor Artikel 7 EUV"-Verfahrens?, EuR 2015, p. 625, 629.

15 *J. M. Barroso*, State of the Union 2012 Address. SPEECH/12/596, URL: http:/Europa.eu/Rapid/press-release_SPEECH-12-596_en.htm.

16 *M. Hilf/F. Schorkopf*, in: Grabitz/Hilf/Nettesheim (ed.), Das Recht der Europäischen Union, 2013, Art. 2 TEU, mn. 20.

and a sufficient legal protection.[17] Also the value of democracy finds expression in Title II of the TEU about "Provisions on Democratic Principles".[18] All in all, the values of Art. 2 TEU are in no way meaningless; and it seems reasonable that the infringement of even one value mentioned in Art. 2 TEU can justify a procedure in accordance with Art. 7 TEU.[19]

b) "Serious Breach"

But in any case Art. 7 TEU stipulates on each level of the procedure a "serious breach" of a value referred to in Art. 2 TEU. That leads to the question of the features of such a "serious" violation. It is obvious that a "serious" infringement must have a high intensity and manifest a breach of great weight. In the literature a "serious breach" is described as a "final impairment" of the values of Art. 2 TEU which against the background of the intent and purpose of Art. 7 TEU questions the European Integration as such.[20] To fulfill this requirement the violation of the values of Art. 2 must have a "systematic" dimension[21], which means that according to Art. 2 the state shows a "systemic deficit"[22].

As the Commission pointed out, to determine the "seriousness of the breach, a variety of criteria will have to be taken into account, including the purpose and the result of the breach"[23]. Therefore, in the eyes of the Commission "for instance, one might consider the social classes affected by the offending national measures. The analysis could be influenced by the fact that they are vulnerable, as in the case of national, ethnic or religious minorities or immigrants"[24]. In any case, a "serious breach" in accordance with Art. 7 TEU can just be assumed when the particular infringement of a value of Art. 2 TEU has such a dimension that it calls the characteristic of the European Union as a "Union of values" into question. To put it in other words: a "serious breach" occurs if a member state can be qualified as "failed state" in the light of the values of Art. 2 TEU. Of course the determination of a "serious breach" in that sense leaves a wide margin of assessment.[25]

As examples for such a "serious breach" we find in the literature the systematic and continued suppression of minorities, the institutionalized discrimination of

17 See e.g. Communication (fn. 5), p. 4; *A. von Bogdandy/M. Ioannidis*, Das systemische Defizit, Merkmale, Instrumente und Probleme am Beispiel der Rechtsstaatlichkeit und des neuen Rechtsstaatlichkeitsaufsichtsverfahren, ZaöRV 74, 2014, p. 283, 288 f; *K. Sandfort*, Der Schutz der gemeinsamen Werte (Art. 2 AEUV) innerhalb der EU am Beispiel Ungarns, 2014, p. 14.

18 See also according to Art. 2 TEU *G. H. Fox/G. Nolte*, Intolerant Democracies, Harvard International Law Journal 36, 1995, p. 1 ff; *A. Verhoeven*, How Democratic Need European Union Members Be? Some thoughts After Amsterdam, European Law Review 23, 1998, p. 217 ff.

19 E.g. Communication (fn. 3), p. 8; *K. Serini*, Sanktionen der Europäischen Union bei Verstoß eines Mitgliedstaats gegen das Demokratie- oder Rechtsstaatsprinzip, 2009, p. 120; *M. Ruffert*, in: Calliess/Ruffert (ed.), EUV/AEUV, 2016, Art. 7 TEU, mn. 5.

20 See for example *F. Schorkopf*, Verletzt Österreich die Homogenität in der Europäischen Union?, DVBl 2000, p. 1036, 1038.

21 *M. Ruffert* (fn. 19), mn. 5.

22 E.g. *A. von Bogdandy/M. Ioannidis* (fn. 17), p. 298.

23 Communication (fn. 3), p. 8.

24 Communication (fn. 3), p. 8.

25 E.g. *M. Pechstein*, in Streinz (ed.), EUV/AEUV, 2012, Art. 7 TEU, mn. 19.

races, the establishment of totalitarian structures, the abolition of general, free and equal elections, the permanent disregard of the jurisdiction of courts but also large and continuous impairments of fundamental rights like the freedom of assembly or the freedom of opinions.[26] Also the repeated condemnation by international authorities are seen as indications for a "serious breach" of the values of Art. 2 TEU.[27] In this context it can be recalled that the Venice Commission (a committee of the Council of Europe) in a recent opinion gave Poland a dismal assessment. Among others, the Venice Commission criticized a Polish law which stipulates a two third majority among the judges of the Constitutional Court for most of its decisions. In the opinion of the Venice Commission these provisions are "affecting the efficiency of the Constitutional Tribunal" and, therefore, endanger "not only the rule of law, but also the functioning of the democratic system"[28].

But can such a law be qualified as a "serious breach" of the values of Art. 2 in the sense of Art. 7 TEU? Doubts arise when we take into account that many States with Constitutional Courts (as the Venice Commission admits)[29] provide qualified majorities for decisions in at least some cases. Although if the Polish law might conflict with the Polish constitution[30] it can hardly be considered as a "serious breach" under Art. 7 TEU.[31] This example might slightly demonstrate the difficulties of an assessment of a "serious breach" in practice. The problem is that normally particular measures of a state do not exceed the thresholds of a "serious breach" but together with other provisions they might step by step lead to such a breach. Of course Art. 7 TEU recognizes this problem in its para. 1 which regulates the situation of a "clear risk of a serious breach by a Member State". But also Art. 7 para. 1 TEU requires a determination of a "serious breach", which is why the problem of assessment with its wide margins still remains.

2. *Interests*

a) Mutual Trust

Even if a "serious breach" is well justified, the application of Art. 7 TEU needs a further discretionary decision, *if* a measure under this article should be taken. That leads to the interests which should be respected upon the exercise of the discretionary power under Art. 7 TEU. When we regard those interests we should differ between a basic interest which has always been taken into account in all decisions based on Art. 7 TEU and special interests which should be respected in the proce-

26 See for example *F. Schorkopf* (fn. 16), p. 1038; *K. Träbert* (fn. 11), p. 255; *K. Serini* (fn. 19), p. 125 f; *K. Sandfort* (fn. 17), p. 30.

27 *K. Ruffert* (fn. 19), mn. 6. See also Communication (fn. 3), p. 8.

28 European Commission for Democracy through Law (Venice Commission), Opinion no. 833/2015 from 11.3.2016 on Amendments to the Act of 25. June 2015 on the Constitutional Tribunal, p. 24.

29 Venice Commission (fn. 28), p. 13 f.

30 Venice Commission (fn. 28), p. 15.

31 See in this context also *E. Regan*, Are EU Sanctions Against Austria Legal?, Zeitschrift für öffentliches Recht 55, 2000, p. 325 ff.

dure of suspensions of rights under Art. 7 para. 3 TEU. To start with the basic interest as a criterion of discretion it should be recalled that in accordance with its function Art. 7 TEU generally demands a balance between the values of Art. 2 TEU and the interests which are connected with the maintenance of a membership in the EU. But what is a basic interest of an EU membership?

The answer to this question can be found in Art. 2 TEU itself with regard to the opinion of the ECJ. The Court stated in his opinion to the accession of the EU to the European Convention of Human Rights that the "essential characteristics of EU law have given rise to a structured network of principles, rules and mutually interdependent legal relations linking the EU and its Member States, and its Member States with each other, which are now engaged, as is recalled in the second paragraph of Article 1 TEU, in a 'progress of creating an ever closer union among the peoples of Europe'"[32]. This legal structure, the Court continues, "is based on the fundamental premiss that each Member State shares with all other Member States, and recognizes that they share with it, a set of common values on which the EU is founded, as stated in Article 2 TEU. That premiss implies and justifies the existence of a *mutual trust* between Member States that those values will be recognized and, therefore, that the law of the EU that implements them will be respected."[33]

This statement of the Court to the "mutual trust" might support the legal position of scholars, which derives from Art. 2 and 7 TEU a presumption of conformity with these provisions.[34] Furthermore, the "mutual trust" is a necessary condition for the functioning of the Union in its specific structure. It is the foundation of the "principle of sincere cooperation" in Art. 4 para. 3 TEU, which ensures not only efficient work of the EU Institutions but also the effective implementation of EU law by the Member States. It is unquestionable that a determination of a "serious breach" in accordance with Art. 7 TEU could undermine this "mutual trust" for the concerned Member State as well as for the rest of the Union. The consequences of such a damage should not be underestimated. Therefore, the maintenance of the "mutual trust" must always be balanced against a determination of a "clear risk of a serious breach" under para. 1 or "the existence of a serious and persistent breach" under para. 2 of Art. 7 TEU. This balance is a very responsible and quite risky task, which might explain the qualification of Art. 7 TEU as a "nuclear option"[35].

b) Suspension of Rights

The mutual trust has to be regarded as a basic interest in all decisions based on Art. 7 TEU. Further interests must be taken into account when a decision about a suspension of rights under Art. 7 para. 3 TEU is made. Under this provision the

32 ECJ, Opinion 2/13 (ECHR), ECLI:EU:C:2014:2454, mn. 167.

33 ECJ, Opinion 2/13 (ECHR), ECLI:EU:C:2014:2454, mn.168; emphasis added.

34 *A. von Bogdandy/M. Ioannides* (fn. 17), p. 298.

35 See fn. 12.

Council "may decide to suspend certain rights deriving from the application of the Treaties to the Member State in question, including the voting rights of the representative of the government of that Member State in the Council. In doing so", Art. 7 para. 3 adds, "the Council shall take into account the possible consequences of such a suspension of the rights and obligations of natural and legal persons."

But what are the rights of a Member State, which are allowed to be suspended in accordance with Art. 7 para. 3 TEU? As this provision rules expressly, the suspension might concern the "voting rights" of a Member State in the Council. Furthermore, following the meaning of the words "certain of the rights", the suspension does not comprehend all rights of a Member State and must not leave to an exclusion of the Union.[36] There is also a broad consensus that the suspension under Art. 7 para. 3 TEU might relate to financial aids for Member States.[37] Apart from that, the limit of a suspension is under discussion. Some scholars believe that the authorization of Art. 7 para. 3 TEU does not include a suspension of the participation in the European Commission or in the European Parliament.[38] Others are skeptic if the rights of Member States to bring actions before the ECJ in accordance with Art. 259 and Art. 263 TFEU can be suspended under Art. 7 para. 3 TEU.[39]

In my eyes, a wide interpretation of the suspended rights should be preferred. Such a wide interpretation is already suggested by the wording of Art. 7 para. 3 TEU which says "the rights deriving from the application of the Treaties" without any restriction. A wide interpretation is also supported by the requirement in Art. 7 para. 3 TEU that the Council must "take into account the possible consequences of such a suspension on the rights and obligations of natural and legal persons". This provision expresses that the suspension might concern rights which do not only touch the legal sphere of a Member State alone but also those of private persons. This indicates a wide meaning of the words "rights" in Art. 7 para. 3 TEU because rights as the mentioned voting right in the Council can never really affect the rights and obligations of private persons. Last but not least, also the in EU law generally accepted doctrine of the *effet utile*[40] suggests to some extent a wide understanding of "rights" in Art. 7 para. 3 as it must be assumed that the sanctions should have an effective character. In dependence of the principle of proportionality[41] therefore, the suspension of any rights "deriving from the application of the Treaties" must be basically possible in order of an effective avoidance of "serious" breaches of Art. 2 TEU. "Rights" in this wide sense are all rights of a Member State which are connected with the membership of the EU.

36 See above fn. 9.
37 E.g. *F. Schorkopf* (fn. 16), p. 1040; *K. Sandfort* (fn. 17), p. 33.
38 E.g. *M. Ruffert* (fn. 19), mn. 24.
39 E.g. *M. Pechstein* (fn. 25), mn. 19. Different view *K. Serini* (fn. 19), p. 134.
40 See *L. Tichy/M. Potacs/T. Dumbrovsky* (eds.), Effet utile, 2014.
41 E.g. *U. Becker*, in: Schwarze (ed.), EU-Kommentar, 2012, mn. 11; *M. Pechstein* (fn. 25), mn. 19.

Rights in accordance with Art. 7 para. 3 TEU therefore, include for instance the right of a Member State to "be allocated"[42] certain seats in the European Parliament, that a citizen of this Member State is appointed as a member of the Commission[43], the right to bring an action against an act of the European Union before the ECJ[44] and the right to participate in the freedoms of the internal market. The interests which have to be balanced against the violated value in a sanction proceeding under Art. 7 para. 3 TEU considering the principle of proportionality depends primarily on the "seriousness" and evidence of the breach: the more "seriously" and evidently the values of Art. 2 are violated by a Member State the more rights of that state connected with its membership can be suspended. Apart from that, the interests which have to be balanced depend on the sanction which is taken into consideration.

A suspension of the voting rights in the Council has to regard (besides the maintenance of the mutual trust) the effective implementation of the legal acts adopted without the votes of the concerned Member State in that particular state. The suspension of a full participation in the internal market (for instance by suspension of some rights of free movement) has to regard the economic impact of such a measure in view of the aim of the EU provided in Art. 3 TEU to "promote economic, social and territorial cohesion, and solidarity among Member States". As far as a suspension has consequences for the rights and obligations of natural and legal persons, they have to be taken into account in accordance with Art. 7 para. 3 TEU. That might concern the rights of Members of the Parliament due to a suspension of the right of a Member State "to be allocated" seats in the Parliament as well as the rights of persons which have already used their right of free movement when the participation in the internal market should be suspended to some extent. The requirement of the regard of the consequences for natural and legal persons is an expression of the general principle of legal security (as a part of the value of the rule of law in Art. 2 TEU). As that principle of Union law stipulates that the rights of persons basically must not be restricted retroactively, those sanctions should in general not limit existing rights of natural and legal persons.

IV. Conclusion

To conclude my considerations I may summarize: The thresholds for the use of Art. 7 TEU are extremely high.[45] That applies not only to the unanimous vote for a decision in accordance with Art. 7 para. 2 TEU. The procedure of Art. 7 TEU relates to a "serious breach" of a value of Art. 2 TEU which means an infringement of high intensity and deep impact. Moreover, Art. 7 TEU gives discretionary

42 Art. 14 para. 2 TEU.
43 Art. 17 para. 4 TEU.
44 Art. 263 TFEU.
45 *D. Dalmers/G. Davies/G. Monti*, European Union Law, 2014, p. 264.

power to the Council at all levels of its procedure. To exercise this discretion the violation of the values must always be balanced against the interest of the mutual trust of the Member States which is also a high value of the European Union. A suspension of rights of Member States must regard further interests like the possible consequences on the rights and obligations of natural and legal persons. Finally Art. 269 TFEU provides that neither the determination of a "serious breach" of Art. 2 TEU nor the exercise of the discretion under Art. 7 TEU shall be reviewed by the ECJ.[46] All these requirements demonstrate the character of Art. 7 TEU as a "nuclear option" which should obviously more threaten than be applied.

46 For details see *A. Hau*, Sanktionen und Vorfeldmaßnahmen zur Absicherung der europäischen Grundwerte, 2002, p. 188 ff.

Rule of Law: European Commission v. Poland

*By Mirosław Wyrzykowski, Warsaw**

In 2016, Poland was the subject of interest of considerable intensity. The institutions of the European Union, and the European Commission in particular, enquired into the alleged systemic problem with the implementation of the principle of rule of law that suggested that there was a 'clear risk of a serious breach of the values of the rule of law. In case such clear risk could be ascertained, Article 7 TEU procedures could be triggered once the actions specified in the *New EU Framework to Strengthen the Rule of Law*[1] have been exhausted.

Without any prejudice to the discussion of nature and mechanism of violation of the rule of law below, it is suitable to set out the terms of reference of the discussion by setting forth the Commission Recommendation of 27 July 2016 regarding the rule of law in Poland.[2] The Commission recommended that 'the Polish authorities take appropriate action to address this systemic threat to the rule of law as a matter of urgency'. In particular, the Commission recommended that the Polish authorities:

a) implement fully the judgments of the Constitutional Tribunal of 3[3] and 9[4] December 2015 which requires that the three judges that were lawfully nominated in October 2015 by the previous legislature can take up their function of judge in the Constitutional Tribunal, and that the three judges nominated by the new legislature without valid legal basis do not take up the post of judge being validly elected;

b) publish and implement fully the judgments of the Constitutional Tribunal of 9 March 2016 and its subsequent judgments and ensure that the publication of future judgments is automatic and does not depend on any decision of the executive or legislative power;

c) ensure that any reform of the Law on the Constitutional Tribunal respects the judgments of the Constitutional Tribunals, including the judgments of 3 and 9 December 2015 and the judgment of 9 March 2016, and takes the Opinion of the Venice Commission fully into account; ensure that the effectiveness of the Constitutional Tribunal as a guarantor of the Constitution is not undermined by requirements, whether separately or trough their combined effect, such as those referred to the attendance quorum, the handling of cases in chronological order, the possibility of the Public Prosecutor-General to prevent the examination of cases, the

* *Prof. Dr. Mirosław Wyrzykowski*, Faculty of Law, University of Warsaw.

1 *A new EU Framework to strengthen the Rule of Law*, Communication from the Commission to the European Parliament and the Council, COM (2014) 158/2 final, 19 March 2014.

2 COM (2016) 5703 final.

3 Case K 34/15, constitutional review of the Act on the Constitutional Tribunal of of 25 June 2015 (Journal of Laws 2015, item 1064).

4 Case K 35/15, constitutional review of the Act of 19 November 2015 amending the Act on the Constitutional Tribunal (Journal of Laws 2015, item 1928).

postponement of deliberations or transitional measures affecting pending cases and putting cases on hold;
d) ensure that the Constitutional Tribunal can review the compatibility of the new law adopted on 22 July 2016[5] on the Constitutional Tribunal[6] before its entry into force and publish and implement fully the judgment of the Tribunal in that respect;
e) refrain from actions and public statements which could undermine the legitimacy and efficiency of the Constitutional Tribunal.
The Polish authorities of the day have a rather poor track record of compliance. Whilst the Commission Recommendations have not been overtly contested as such, the parliamentary majority has had the upper hand at both securing the controversial three judges but also at securing personal control of the Constitutional Tribunal.

I. The Crisis of Constitutional Review in Poland and the Rule of Law in Peril

Before venturing into the supernatural realms of the constitutional calamity of the Constitutional Tribunal that has been so aptly captured in the Recommendation, it seems necessary to draw up its context. Indeed, political and constitutional crisis has marked Polish public life since autumn 2015 (1.). It is against this backdrop that a number of reflections on aspects of the rule of law that are implicated in the crisis will be drawn up (2.).

1. The Elements of the Crisis of Constitutional Review in Poland in 2015-2016

The actual historical stem of the problem seems unrelated to the scale of the crisis that would unfold. The crisis all began with an apparently technical and neutral piece of legislation. The Act on Constitutional Tribunal of 25 June 2015 provided for the Sejm to elect the 5 constitutional judges for whom there was a forthcoming vacation of office on the Constitutional Tribunal in 2015.[7] The Act provided that all candidates for the vacancies had to be notified within 30 days of the coming into force of the Act. The legislator thereby provided for an exception to the general rule applicable according to which the motion nominating a candidate is to be moved with the Marshal of the Sejm not later than 3 months before the vacation of office of the judge of the Constitutional Tribunal following the expiration of the term of office. The disposition was, therefore, technical and apparently innocuous though it interfered directly with the legal process otherwise regulated within the Act.

5 The Constitutional Tribunal has undertaken constitutional review of this Act, *cf.* text at notes 64 *et seq. infra*.
6 The Act on the Constitutional Tribunal of 22 July 2016 (Journal of Laws 2016, item 1157).
7 Law on the Constitutional Tribunal of 25 June 2015, Official Journal 2015, item 1064 as amended.

As it sometimes happens, the legislator was not random in its purpose. On the neutral reading, the legislation provided for the Constitutional Tribunal to be fully operational and properly manned as there was a risk of that the vacancies would not be properly filled after elections. The piece of legislation was introduced, however, within a specific and special political context. It was introduced after the presidential elections of May 2015. Andrzej Duda was to be sworn in as the new President of the Republic; whilst the presidency is supposed to be non-partisan, the new President had been supported by the Law and Justice, i.e. the major opposition party at the time. The Act replacing the Act on Constitutional Tribunal had been in preparation for a long time but was to only come into force on 30 August 2015. The Constitutional Tribunal, on the other hand, was to have 5 vacancies, which makes up a third of its membership. This means that the Parliament sought to vote all 5 justices before the forthcoming parliamentary elections. In October, parliamentary elections were held and delivered a majority to the Law and Justice party.

The Law and Justice party not only ceased to be the major opposition party but was to command the majority in the Parliament (242 members of the Sejm composed of 460 members and 61 senators in the 100 members Senate), partly because the party had decided to allow candidates of two minor right-wing parties[8] to run in its colours. This was a rather surprising and landslide victory because the political process had never delivered a non-coalition majority. The elections were held on 27 October; the President called the opening session of the new Parliament for 10 November 2015. This day marked the first day of the term of the new Parliament.

The Sejm of the previous term of the parliament (VII) elected five judges to sit on the Constitutional Tribunal. Three judges were to take office because the terms of three judges was to expire on 8 November; two judges were to take office as the terms of office of two other judges was to expire on 3 December 2015 and 5 December, respectively.

The very idea of electing five judges of the Constitutional Tribunal when the term of the Parliament was drawing to an end received no favourable welcome from the Law and Justice party. Political disapproval of this procedure, however, now received a new lease of life as the Law and Justice Party commanded majority in the new Parliament and could rely on the new President of the Republic elected in May 2015. Executive and legislative powers at hand, political and legal measures in respect to the untimely renewal of a third of membership of the constitution court would surprise no one in those circumstances. The President of the Republic refused to administer oath from the judges elected by the Sejm of the previous term of Parliament. The Parliament, on the other hand, hurriedly enacted an amendment of the Act on the Constitutional Tribunal. Several weeks later, the President of the Council of Ministers (i.e. the other limb of the dualist executive)

8 I.e. *Polska Razem* [Poland Together] and *Solidarna Polska* [Poland characterized by Solidarity].

was to have her own part refusing to publish the judgment of the Constitutional Tribunal that undermined the amendment.

The Constitutional Tribunal considered the amendment of the Act on Constitutional Tribunal enacted on 25 June 2015, including the very statutory foundation of electing the 5 judges of the Constitutional Tribunal to places opening in 2015 by the Sejm of the previous term of Parliament.

Paying no heed to the Constitutional Tribunal and its judgment that could be expected on 3 December 2015, the Sejm took unprecedented legal steps using the extraordinary legal instrument of a resolution 'establishing the lack of legal effect of the Resolutions on Electing Judges of the Constitutional Tribunal' of 8 October 2015.[9] The resolutions sought to 'abrogate' the election of all judges of the constitutional court had been passed by the Sejm of the Previous term of Parliament.

Having declared the election of judges to the Constitutional Tribunal null and void on 25 November 2015, the Sejm took the decision to proceed with electing 5 judges to the places thus 'liberated'. Resolutions on electing 5 judges were under elaboration. It is worth underlining the fact that all this took place mere days – and then hours – before the Constitutional Tribunal would be in a position to make an official determination on the constitutional validity of the procedure for electing in the 5 judges to vacancies open as the term of office of judges expired in 2015.

Because the matter was under constitutional review, the Constitutional Tribunal requested that the *Sejm* withhold any actions that would amount to a *via facti*. This request was made upon the motion by the group of Members of Parliament who requested constitutional review of the legislation that underscored the election of 5 judges by the Sejm of the previous term of Parliament. Should the Sejm proceed with electing 5 new judges before the Constitutional Tribunal entered a judgment, the constitutional review of the legislation would be frustrated. The Constitutional Tribunal proceeded by the way of a resolution and issued an injunction, which is an extraordinary legal measure temporarily suspending actions and legal effect of actions taken by public authorities until the matter is duly considered by a court. The very substance of injunctive relief consists in preventing the advent of situations whereby consequences that cannot be undone are effected by a public authority. Injunctive relief in this case seems understandable enough. Far from providing any unconsidered substantial effects, the Constitutional Tribunal's resolution sought to temporarily protect the constitutional matter under review. Temporarily suspending action or legal effect of determinations made by other public authority until the constitutional controversy was resolved indeed seems a fitting measure where such constitutional controversy could be subject to action or implementation by one authority or another.

9 Resolutions published in the *Polish Monitor*, the official journal for acts other than those reserved for the Official Journal, *Monitor Polski* 2015, item 1131, item 1132, item 1133, item 1134 and item 1135.

The power of injunction is a special instrument of constitutional law enforcement protecting the constitutional order; the instrument was fittingly used by the Constitutional Tribunal in the extraordinary circumstances and at the very early stage of constitutional crisis. It is to be noted that the constitutional controversy was substantial and serious. The matter subject to constitutional review concerned the power of the Sejm of one term of Parliament to enjoin the resolution of the Sejm of the following term of parliament. In the meantime, the resolution proclaiming null and void the resolution of the Sejm of the previous term of Parliament, the Sejm apparently enjoined the powers of the Sejm of the previous term.

As the events would unfold, however, the constitutional stakes were much higher and the injunction was justified on the grounds of protecting the constitutional order. The crux of the matter concerned primarily the constitutional status of the 2 judges elected ahead of schedule. The matter, however, equally concerned the constitutional status of the 3 judges whose term of office was apparently 're-viewed' by the Sejm at the time. The constitutional controversy considered by the Constitutional Tribunal in substance concerned the possible violation of the Constitution and statutes by state authorities; the violation of the Constitution and statutes did not concern the powers of the Sejm as such but the power of the Sejm to terminate the term of office of the sitting judge of the Constitutional Tribunal. It is to be noted that the Constitution explicitly states that the assumption of office by a judge coincides with election by the Sejm and the nearest available day the office is vacated commences the term of office of he judge of the Constitutional Tribunal; the terms of the Constitution also suggest that assumption office by a judge coincides with election by the Sejm and therefore non-administration of the oath does not make the judge any less of a judge so as to be removed by the Sejm's at whim.[10] Constitutional review would in any effect assert the Constitutional Tribunal's authority over the commencement of the term of office of judges and thus the constitutional structure of parliamentary powers.

The Sejm paid no attention to the request by the Constitutional Tribunal that any measures concerning electing 5 new judges be stayed. 5 new judges were formally elected by the Sejm to places 'liberated' by the resolution establishing the lack of legal effect of the resolution electing the judges made in October by the Sejm of the previous term of Parliament. On 2 December 2015, late at night, the Sejm enacted 5 resolutions and thus elected 5 judges of the Constitutional Tribunal. According to the legislative body, the judges were elected to fill in vacancies made available by the resolutions proclaiming null and void the October 2015 resolutions electing 5 judges of the Constitutional Tribunal. On 3 December 2015, the resolutions were published immediately and – in the early hours of the day – the President administered oath to the three judges who were to fill spots vacated on 8 November 2015 following the expiry of the term of office and then 'evacuated'

10 Cfr. note 17 *infra*.

by the 25 November 2015 resolutions voiding resolutions on the election of judges made on 8 October 2015.

On 3 December 2015 and during regular business hours, the Constitutional Tribunal issued a judgment concerning the constitutionality of the legal basis upon which 5 judges of the Constitutional Tribunal were elected by the Sejm of the previous term of parliament. In its judgment,[11] the Constitutional Tribunal corroborated the constitutionality of the original 2015 Act on the Constitutional Tribunal to the extent that it enabled electing 3 judges of the Constitutional Tribunal who were to fill vacancies open upon the expiration of the term of office of three judges on 8 November 2015. The Constitutional Tribunal, however, declared the statute unconstitutional to the extent that it enabled electing judges to vacancies available only upon the expiration of the term of office of the judges on 2 December 2015 and 8 December 2015, respectively. It was stated that the statute thus violated the Constitution because the Sejm of the following term of parliament was to be – and was in fact – operational at that time.

Importantly enough, the Constitutional Tribunal confirmed the constitutionality of the election of 3 judges. The decision also confirmed implicitly the constitutional problem in the refusal – by omission – by the President of the Republic to administer oath. At the date of the judgment, however, the President already sided with the Parliament's view proclaiming their election null and void and participated in substituting new candidates just hours before the judgment of the Constitutional Tribunal.

The legal process thus produced a singular situation. On 8 November 2015, three judges of the Constitutional Tribunal were to be appointed as the term of office of three judges expired. The Sejm, however, elected 6 judges to fill three vacancies available on the Constitutional Tribunal. 3 judges were legally[12] and constitutionally[13] elected by the Sejm but were not administered oath by the President of the Republic. 3 judges were elected by the Sejm of the following term of parliament purporting that assumption of office by the judges elected by the previous parliament was ineffective, based on the premise that the declaration of voidness of previous election was effective. Even though the election to 'vacancies' created by evacuating judges who assumed office upon election by the Sejm on 8 October might well seem imaginary, it was rendered somewhat real by the President of the Republic who promptly administered oath as if there was no legal issue with the evacuation of judges from office. What this meant is that the Constitutional Tribunal's membership suddenly exceeded the constitutional number of judges by 3. The Constitution provides for 15 judges of the Constitutional Tribunal. Three

11 K 34/15.

12 To say that the judges were legally elected is to deny the allegation that the election was void and to insist that the resolution establishing voidness sought to invalidate election my invalidating the resolution on election, except that it could not.

13 To say that the judges were elected constitutionally means that the Constitution commands that their election must be respected; this is much more meaningful than to say that the legal basis for the election was conforming to the Constitution.

members of the highest constitutional court, however, had double human existence. Three judges were duly administered oath by the President but certainly lacked the quality of having been duly elected by the Sejm as judges of the Constitutional Tribunal because there were no vacancies to be filled (the vacancies were taken by judges who assumed office on the day of election by the Sejm on 8 October 2015); three judges, on the other hand, had the quality of having been duly elected by the Sejm and assumed office with the moment of election by the Sejm but were not granted the honour of having been administered oath by the President of the Republic.

Acting on the principle of constitutional legality, the President of the Constitutional Tribunal withheld the power of judicial authority of the three judges sworn in by the President. The Judgment of 3 December 2015 (K 34/15) confirmed the constitutionality of the legal basis for electing 3 judges who were therefore to be deemed effectively elected by the Sejm of the previous term of parliament on 8 October 2015 to vacancies available as the term of office of 3 judges expired on 8 November 2015. The President of the Constitutional Tribunal, however, complied with various statutory obligations in respect to persons administered oath in by the President of the Republic in as far as internal administrative and financial law were concerned. There is no doubt that the President of the Constitutional Tribunal was correct in seeking to secure the constitutional order because the Constitution itself and the judgment of the Constitutional Tribunal dictated that the President of the republic had administered oath to persons elected to vacancies that could not be filled by the Sejm of this term.

Whereas the institutional aspect of the Parliament's actions was taking its course, the Parliament's decisions were challenged before the Constitutional Tribunal. A group of deputies and the Commissioner for Citizens' Rights had formal standing to challenge the resolutions establishing voidness of resolutions electing the 3 judges of the Constitutional Tribunal of 8 October 2015 as well as the resolutions electing the 3 judges dated 2 December 2015. The National Barrister's Council, on the other hand, filed an *amicus curiae* brief with the Constitutional Tribunal supporting the gist of the argument of the applicants. The major problem of the legal argument concerned the nature of those resolutions. The resolutions did not obviously correspond to the legal system's definition of a 'normative act' whereas the Constitutional Tribunal's powers do not extend beyond constitutional review of 'normative acts'.

The Constitutional Tribunal discontinued[14] proceedings in respect of both categories of resolutions, i.e. (1) the 'Resolutions establishing voidness of *Resolutions electing Judges of the Constitutional Tribunal of 8 October 2015*' dated 25 November 2015 and (2) the 5 resolutions on electing judges of the Constitutional Tribunal dated 2 December 2015. The Constitutional Tribunal based its determination on the argument that neither the resolutions establishing voidness of reso-

14 Resolution of 7 January 2016, case call No. U 8/15.

lutions on electing judges nor resolutions on electing judges of the Constitutional Tribunal fell within the ambit of its jurisdiction for want of the quality of being a 'normative act'. It has to be noted that the constitutional notion of a 'normative act' under the Constitution of the Republic of Poland pertains to acts that create generally applicable legal norms.[15] Since both instruments failed to display the characteristics of a 'normative act', they fell outside of the ambit of constitutional review by the Constitutional Tribunal.

The Constitutional Tribunal, however, did affirm its authority over matters of constitutional interpretation. In *obiter dicta*, the resolution argued (or simply proclaimed) that there was nothing legally or constitutionally wrong in the resolutions on electing 3 judges of the Constitutional Tribunal of 8 October 2015 which would justify the actions of the *Sejm*. In particular, the resolution dismissed as irrelevant the argument that the candidates were nominated by unqualified agents as well as the argument that the resolutions were extinguished under the principle of discontinuation of parliamentary business alongside other parliamentary resolutions. In no ambiguous terms, the Constitutional Tribunal reiterated that the new resolutions on electing the 3 judges would have legal effect only if the previous resolutions on electing judges showed characteristics of illegality amounting to legal nullity; in this case the act would not be valid within the legal system and would not be subject to invalidation. The Constitutional Tribunal relied on its previous judgment to show that this was not the case:[16] the gist of the iterations is that the 3 judges were effectively elected and assumed office on 8 October 2015, and commenced their term of office on 9 November 2015 as their respective vacancies opened with the expiry of the term of office of judges on 8 November 2015.

The arguments made by the Constitutional Tribunal in respect of the parliamentary power of electing judges of the Constitutional Tribunal to vacancies that were

15 E.g. Article 88 regulates the publication of 'normative acts'; the constitutional complaint can be directed against a 'a statute or another normative act upon which basis a court or organ of public administration has made a final decision on his freedoms or rights or on his obligations specified in the Constitution' (Article 79).

16 This is the primary problem with the Constitutional Tribunal's reasoning that underscored the resolution that discontinued proceedings. Judge M. Zubik presented an excellent and compelling argument in his dissenting opinion. The Sejm's resolutions establishing voidness of resolutions electing 3 judges of the Constitutional Tribunal by the Sejm of the previous term had the character of a 'normative act' *ad casum*. Cf. The dissenting opinion by M. Zubik. The 'normative act' character of the resolutions is present in the fact that the resolutions purport to provide the legal basis for the termination of the term of office of a constitutional judge who assumed office on the day of election on 8 October with the term of office commencing upon the first day of available vacancy to which the election was made. (viz. based on the resolution on electing the judge taken by the Sejm of the previous term of Parliament). In other words, it is enough for any decision to potentially and *ad casum* interfere with the application of statutes to fall within the ambit of the notion of a 'normative act' – the legislator would have to pass a proper 'normative act' in order to achieve the effect for which other means are used; in this case any instrument is substantially a 'normative act' even though it cannot be formally abrogated by the Constitutional Tribunal except through abrogating the 'normative act' by which it was enabled. The resolution in the case U 1/06 indeed had previously recognized the competence of the Constitutional Tribunal extending over such scenarios arguing that the resolution of the Sejm contained legal norms and was not only the expression of political position (the resolution concerned the establishment of a parliamentary commission on transfer of property and capital in the banking sector).

not available because they had been filled by the Sejm of the previous parliamentary term are sound. The legal form of the Constitutional Tribunal's action, however, is lacking in effectiveness. The Resolution and the reasoning *obiter dictum* could not possibly constitute an unambiguous statement on the unconstitutionality of the Parliament's actions.

The parliament further took further legislative steps to override the Constitutional Tribunal by providing judicial authority to 3 persons sworn in as judges of the Constitutional Tribunal by the President of the Republic in the place of persons elected by the Sejm of the previous. As has been mentioned, the President of the Constitutional Tribunal could not but consider those persons unqualified to exercise judicial authority as judges of the Constitutional Tribunal; the new statute provided for this impediment to be overcome on the basis of a statutory command.[17] Enacting the statute, the Parliament enforced the actions it had taken by the way of resolutions. Although the statute had the appearances of overcoming the opposition of the Constitutional Tribunal acting in *forum internum*, there is no doubt that the statute was unconstitutional 'by the way of a cascade'. There is now no legal means to ascertain the unconstitutionality and invalidate the normative source of violation of the Constitution and thus to restore the supremacy of the Constitution. The source of the violation of the Constitution can be traced to the *Resolution on Establishing Voidness of the Resolutions on Electing the Judges of the Constitutional Tribunal of 8 October 2015* dated 25 November 2015.

It was only natural that one of the main elements for analysing European rule of law standards concerned the status of the judges of the Constitutional Tribunal elected under the resolutions of the Sejm of the previous term of Parliament on 8 October 2015 that were subject to 'invalidation' by the resolution of the Sejm of 25 November 2015. The Venice Commission of the Council of Europe and later the European Commission voiced critical remarks. The Venice Commission referred to the Judgment of the Constitutional Tribunal of 3 December 2015 that corroborated the constitutional basis of the 3 judges commencing tenure on 9 November 2015. The Venice Commission has stated that the solution to the conflict over the composition of the Constitutional Tribunal 'must be based on the obligation to respect and fully implement the judges of the Constitutional Tribunal'. The Venice Commission therefore called 'on all State [authorities] and notably Sejm to fully respect and implement the judgments'.[18] The European Commission cross-referred to the opinion adopted by the Venice Commission but also observed that the statute of 22 July 2016 amended the Act on the Constitutional Tribunal in ways that violate the principles governing the composition of the Constitutional Tribunal as specified by the Constitutional Tribunal. The European Commission highlighted the fact that 'Art. 90 and Art. 6(7) require the President of the Constitutional Tribunal to assign cases to all judges who have taken oath of

17 Cf. *infra*.

18 European Commission for Democracy through Law (Venice Commission), opinion 833/2015, CDL-AD (2016)001 adopted 11-12 March 2016, para. 136.

the President of the Republic but have not yet taken up their duties as judges. This provision seems targeted at the situation of the three judges which were unlawfully nominated by the new legislature of the Sejm in December 2015. It would enable these judges to take up their function while using the vacancies for which the previous legislature of the Sejm had already lawfully nominated three judges. These provisions are therefore contrary to the judgments of the Constitutional tribunal of 3 and 9 December 2015 and the opinion of the Venice Commission'.[19]
The Constitutional Tribunal declared Article 90 of the amendment passed on 22 July 2016 unconstitutional.[20] The Constitutional Tribunal never deviated from its position concerning the status of the 3 judges elected by the Sejm of the previous term of parliament (affirmation of legality) and the status of 3 persons elected by the Sejm of the consecutive term of parliament (affirmation of illegality). The reasoning of the Constitutional Tribunal fully corresponds to the opinion voiced by the European Commission. In the Commission Recommendation it was stated that the Commission 'in conclusion considers that the Polish authorities should respect and fully implement the judgments of the Constitutional Tribunal of 3 and 9 December 2015. These judgments require that the state institutions cooperate loyally in order to ensure, in accordance with the rule of law, that the three judges that were nominated by the previous legislature can take up their function of the judge of the Constitutional Tribunal, and that the three judges nominated by the new legislature without a valid legal basis do not take up the post of judge without being validly elected'. The European Commission further observed that 'the relevant provisions of the law adopted on 22 July 2016 on the Constitutional Tribunal are contrary to the judgments of the Constitutional Tribunal od 3 and 9 December 2015 and to the opinion of the Venice Commission and raise serious concerns in respect of the rule of law'[21].
Whereas there was no ambiguity in the position adopted by the Constitutional Tribunal and the authorities of the Council of Europe and European Union, the Polish legislator suffered no loss of direction. The Act of Parliament of 22 July 2016 entered into force as indirectly unconstitutional. The legislator wilfully adopted a law that was already substantially declared unconstitutional by the Constitutional Tribunal.
The Parliament repeated the same mechanism of 'legalization' of the election of the three judges that were not granted leave to exercise judicial authority by the President of the Constitutional Tribunal. The *Act on Entering into Force of the Act on Organization of the Constitutional Tribunal and on Proceedings before the Constitutional Tribunal as well as the Act on the Status of the Judge of the Consti-*

19 European Commission, Commission Recommendation of 27.7.2016 regarding the rule of law in Poland, C (2016) 5703 final, para 16.
20 Judgment of 11 September 2016, K 39/16.
21 Commission Recommendation, para. 17.

tutional Tribunal of 13 December 2016[22] provided a convoluted device for that purpose. The Act obligated 'the judge granted the powers and duty of *exercising the powers of the president of the Constitutional Tribunal* by the President of the Republic' to 'allocate cases to the judges who took an oath before the President of the Republic' and to 'create conditions necessary for the discharge of the duties of the a judge of the Constitutional Tribunal' (Article 18.2). This obligation apparently corresponds to a new regulation on the status of the judge of the Constitutional Tribunal provided by the Act on the Status of a Judge of the Constitutional Tribunal.[23] Article 5 of this Act provides for the judge of the Constitutional Tribunal to 'enter into relationship of service' after taking an oath; the non-apparent purpose of the regulation springs to mind upon considering the rather hot-headed wording of the Act: 'immediately after taking an oath, the judge shall report for duty at the Constitutional Tribunal and the President of the Constitutional Tribunal shall assign cases to the judge and create conditions necessary for the judge to discharge judicial duties'.[24] Despite resistance, the legislator had its way in overwhelming the Constitutional Tribunal in this respect.

2. The Rule of Law, Constitutional Review, and Reform of Constitutional

In what follows, I propose an analysis of the most fundamental aspects of the rule of law that are implicated in the reform of the fundamental tenets governing the operation of constitutional review.

Whilst the role of the President of the Republic of Poland might seem tangent to the constitutional crisis, the analysis would not do justice to the matter if it did not commence with the institution of the President of the Republic and its role in respect to constitutional review. To be more precise, the matter concerns the nature and the character of the oath that is taken by the judge of the Constitutional Tribunal and administered by the President of the Republic. It is to be noted that the

22 Act on Entering into Force of the Act on Organization of the Constitutional Tribunal and on Proceedings before the Constitutional Tribunal as well as the Act on the Status of the Judge of the Constitutional Tribunal (Official Journal 2016, item 2074).

23 Act on the Status of a Judge of the Constitutional Tribunal of 30 November 2016, Official Journal 2016, item 2073.

24 The sequence of events that would unfold was characteristic of the constitutional crisis. Just hours after the law came into force, the President of the Republic appointed the 'judge performing the office of the President of the Constitutional Tribunal'. This is characteristic in that the President of the Republic had to ignore the fact that the Constitution indicates the Alternate President of the Constitutional Tribunal as the authority competent to exercise the office of President. The judge 'performing the office of the President of the Constitutional Tribunal' called the General Assembly of Judges of the Constitutional Tribunal for the purpose of nominating candidates for the office of the President of the Constitutional Tribunal. This was done in violation of statute. The judge 'performing the office of the President of the Constitutional Tribunal' thereupon forwarded the names of 2 candidates to the President of the Republic. Within the next hours, the President of the Republic appointed the President of the Constitutional Tribunal. The judge 'performing the office of the President of the Constitutional Tribunal' for a couple of hours was thereupon appointed the President of the Constitutional Tribunal. One of the first decisions taken as President of the Constitutional Tribunal was to bestow the exercise of judicial authority on the judges whose judicial authority was withheld by the former President of the Constitutional Tribunal on the basis that they did not have the quality of 'having been elected to office by the Sejm' though having been administered oath of office by the President of the Republic.

constitutional crisis originated in the refusal of the President of the Republic to administer oath to the three judges legally elected to fill the vacancies available after the term of office of 3 judges expired on 8 November 2015. The President's failure to administer oath not only marks the beginning of the crisis but is one of its essential elements. Constitutional custom had it that the term of office of the judge of the Constitutional Tribunal commenced on the day of being elected by the Sejm or another day immediately following the day of expiry of the term of office of a sitting judge.[25] The oath (or affirmation) taken by the judge of the Constitutional Tribunal was to be administered the President of the Republic of Poland and was considered to be a public oath to abide by the norms implied by the credo (or wording) indicated by the oath. It was considered to be a legally-significant event because it was a condition for the execution on of the office and exercising the mandate of a judge. As has been noted, this means that the oath has as much ceremonial as legal significance, because it creates the effects indicated by the law'[26].

The power of the President of the Republic to administer the oath does not fall within the ambit of presidential prerogative. Ever since the Constitutional Tribunal was created, the matter of administering an oath was regulated by statute. Constitutional law scholarship and – importantly enough – the case-law of the Constitutional Tribunal both ascertain that the President of the Republic does not only enjoy the power but is also bound by the duty to administer the oath without delay. The duty is absolute; the President does not enjoy any discretion in respect to considering the substance or the procedure of the decision taken by the Sejm.[27] The oath should be administered without undue delay and the timely discharge of the duty is required by the principle of uninterrupted operation of constitutional authorities of the state. The Constitutional Tribunal is one of the constitutional authorities of the state regulated by the constitutional system of government and the President of the Republic is obligated and has a specific role in facilitating the uninterrupted operation of state authorities.

There is no way to see a discretionary power of the president to refuse to administer an oath taken by the judge of the Constitutional Tribunal assuming office based on election by the Sejm; such an idea is contrary to the very idea of the office of the President of the Republic within the system of government set up by the Constitution of the Republic. Should the power to administer the oath not be associated with the duty of administering the oath, it would mean that the President of the Republic would be implicated in the mechanism of nominating the judges of the Constitutional Tribunal. The President would be in a position to negatively influence the election of judges and would thus be an authority impli-

25 Judgment of the Constitutional Tribunal in the case K 35/15 p. 6.3.

26 '[O]ath (or affirmation) conforming to the wording provided and allows for exercising the office and mandate; this means that the oath (affirmation) is not ceremonial in nature or kind but produces legal effects', Judgment in the case K 34/15, para. 8.5.

27 K 43/15, para. 8.5.

cated in the creation of the composition of the Constitutional Tribunal alongside the Parliament. The Sejm, however, is the sole authority endowed with the power of electing the judge of the Constitutional Tribunal under Article 194.1 of the Constitution. It has been noted accordingly that the 'President is not obligated to consider an application made by the Sejm to nominate a candidate to the Constitutional Tribunal; to the contrary, the President is obligated to administer an oath taken by the Sejm's nominee. The President thus is obligated to represent the majesty of the State. Thus administering the oath consists in making a public representation of the meaning and significance of the oath to serve the Nation'[28].

As far as the Constitution is concerned, there is no other construction of the power of administering the oath but as a duty of performing an Official Act[29]. The official act is not enumerated in Article 144.3 of the Constitution consecrated to independent powers of the President. None the less the official act of administering an oath does not entail the obligation of seeking countersignature. This is precisely because the Constitution reserves all the power of electing judges of the Constitutional Tribunal to the Sejm.[30] The power of administering an oath is co-extensive with the duty to do just that; there can exist no presidential power beyond the duty to administer the oath in respect of the Constitutional Tribunal. To require the official act to be counter-signed by the Prime Minister would be to implicate the government in the mechanism of nomination of judges of the Constitutional Tribunal. On the other hand, it should be observed that there would be any grounds for considering any question of discretionary power of the President or discretionary power of the President and the President of the Council of Ministers only in the event the countersignature was explicitly ruled out or required.

In as far as the principle of the rule of law is concerned, it is essential to insist that there is no explicit disposition of positive law that could possibly imply that the President of the Republic enjoyed the power of refusing to administer the oath taken by the person who assumed the office of a constitutional judge upon election by the Sejm. Because there is no such enabling norm to be construed, there is legally nothing like refusing to administer the oath. The Constitution of the Republic of Poland explicitly forbids presuming powers of any state authority; the principle of legality provides for state authorities to act only in so far as a discrete, unambiguous and positive norm so commands or enables. The Constitutional Tribunal confirmed this principle in stating that 'in the absence of clear conferral of powers, no authority can imply such powers. In the absence of a clear conferral of the power to negatively participate in the election of the judges of the Constitu-

28 'Is not to consider an application made by the Sejm for the person to be appointed as judge of the Constitutional Tribunal; to the contrary, the President is to emphasise the meaning, profundity and importance of the act of taking an oath whereunder the person publically undertakes to serve the Nation', K 43/15, para. 8.5.

29 The term of an "Official Act", which pertains to the legal form of action of the President under Article 144. The term "official deed" might be better suited.

30 Article 194.1 stipulates 'The Constitutional Tribunal shall be composed of 15 judges chosen individually by the Sejm'.

tional Tribunal by refusing to administer the oath, no such power can be implied'[31].

The argument has been elaborated in the judgment of the Constitutional Tribunal concerning the Act of 19 November 2015.[32] The Act provided for the assumption of office by the judge made upon election by the Sejm to become ineffective when the judge-elect fails to take an oath before the President of the Republic. Article 21.1 of the Act read: 'the person elected to become a judge of the Constitutional Tribunal shall take an oath within 30 days of the day of such election [...]'. The Constitutional Tribunal invalidated this disposition because it violated the Constitution. The statutory device, it was stated, suggests that the effectiveness the Sejm's choice is conditional on assent by the President of the Republic. It was stated that assumption of office by the judge cannot be made conditional upon the administration of the oath by the President. Because the Constitution equates election by the Sejm and the assumption of office by the constitutional judge, the statutory device violated the Constitution. Any failure to administer the oath within the time limit would be susceptible to be interpreted as extinguishing the constitutional assumption of office under the terms of the statute. It was stated further that the Act's wording suggested that taking an oath before the President of the Republic was the obligation incumbent on the nominee and that the President's failure to administer the oath could be considered to extinguish the assumption of office because it could quite possibly be considered as an implied resignation.

No *vacatio legis*. One of the cardinal sins committed by the legislator in respect of the Constitutional Tribunal that offended the principle of the rule of law was the disposition of the *Act amending the 2015 Act on Constitutional Tribunal* of 22 December 2015[33] that provided for the Act to take effect on the day of promulgation. The Act thus provided for no period between its promulgation and the time it would take legal effect. *Vacatio legis*, however, is not the privilege the legislator can decide not to exercise. The principle of adequate *vacatio legis* has been inscribed in the theory of the rule of law because it implements a number of fundamental values, such as the effectivity of the aim of legislation, the value of harmonious functioning of the legal system developed by the legislator by new statutes, the value of proper implementation and administration in that the legal system needs time to prepare materially and organizationally not only to comply with the statute but – importantly – to implement the statue's aims, as well as the value of proper implementation and administration that lies with adjusting obligations, workloads and work-plans to the new normative situation. Adequate *vacatio legis*, however, is also required in as much as it secures the public interest. The

31 K 35/15, para. 5.3.3.

32 The *Act amending the Act on the Constitutional Tribunal* of 19 November 2015 (Journal of Laws 2015, item 1928) was considered by the Constitutional Tribunal in the case K 35/15.

33 *Act amending the 2015 Act on Constitutional Tribunal* of 22 December 2015, *Official Journal*, 28 December 2015, item 2217.

principle requires that that statutes not be enacted with the sole purpose of serving the political interests of the day or the interests of the parliamentary majority as dictated by the demands of the moment. The principle also requires that statutes not be enacted for the sole purpose of securing the outcomes of the model of political cooperation between the actors of the parliamentary majority of the day.

The case-law of the Constitutional Tribunal required adequate *vacatio legis* ever since the principle of the rule of law was part of constitutional law. The principle is not absolute but any deviation from the minimum 14-days period between promulgation and effect of legislation would normally require strong reasons. The reasons should be fundamentally strong whenever the shortening of *vacatio legis* pertains to legislation governing the basic tenets of the constitutional order of the State. The constitutional court no doubt belongs to the basic tenets of the constitutional order of the state. Fundamentally strong reasons, however, are not a matter of the strength of conviction. Shortening the *vacatio legis* in this case requires that it be shown that some constitutional principle justifies deviating from the principle.

The disposition that provided for the Act to take effect on the day of promulgation was invalidated by the Constitutional Tribunal. The disposition violated the Constitution because it failed to allow the Constitutional Tribunal the space to comply with the Act and effectively fulfil its constitutional functions, and it failed to allow the parties to proceedings to take notice of the amendments and take measures accordingly. Further, '[P]roviding for immediate and unconditional effect of the new law […] violated the constitutional principle of the democratic state ruled by law'[34]. The list of matters governed by the new law was so extensive as to remove any hint of exaggeration or drama from the pronouncement. The statute governed the making of resolutions by the General Assembly of judges of the Constitutional tribunal, the election of candidates for the position of President and Alternate President of the Constitutional Tribunal; election of judges of the Constitutional Tribunal by the Sejm; disciplinary proceedings against judges of the Constitutional Tribunal; dismissal of a judge from the Constitutional Tribunal; termination of judicial mandate before the expiration of the term of office of the judge of the Constitutional Tribunal; allocation of docket to sections of the Constitutional Tribunal; the establishment of majority and super-majority requirements for the decisions of the Constitutional Tribunal; the rules of procedure governing proceedings before the Constitutional Tribunal; the allocation of cases to open court and to chambers proceedings; the management of the calendar of open court and in camera determinations; the abrogation of the rules governing the determination of impediments and handicaps for the exercise of the duties of office by the President of the Republic; abrogation of the rules governing the rights of the lawyers and civil servants working at the Constitutional Tribunal.

34 K 47/15, para. 4.6.9.

Finally, there one practical consequence of any provision stipulating that there is no lapse of time between promulgation and the entry into force of a statute. This practical consequence is important because it translates the violation of the *vacatio legis* requirement into a violation of the fundamental principle of non-retroaction of laws. In the past, statues were published in official journals and there was a legal fiction at play that said that the statute was promulgated on a particular day; the exact time of publication had no legal meaning because it was invisible. Nowadays, however, every legal act is published with a time-stamp. When the law takes effect on the day of promulgation, it will effectively take effect before it is effectively promulgated. Polish law-books show that this marginal retroaction of immediate-effect statutes is common. The retroactive effect of statutes that provide no *vacatio legis* can be a matter of hours or seconds but none the less should be considered a serious normative concern. In and of itself, marginal violation of the principle of non-retroaction by the legislator does seem overly dramatic. It does not take much imagination to be convinced that what happens in a day can have dramatic consequences when the retroaction loophole is abused. The *Act amending the Act on the Constitutional Tribunal* of 22 December 2015 was promulgated on 28 December 2015 and bears the official time stamp 16:44:10.

The second element of the constitutional crisis concerns the publication of the judgments of the Constitutional Tribunal. According to Article 190, judgments of the Constitutional Tribunal have universally binding application, are final and are required to be published immediately in the official publication in which the original normative act was promulgated. The quality of finality and of universally binding application mean that there exists no procedure or other means to challenge the judgment of the Constitutional Tribunal within the legal system. No state authority can thus technically challenge its legal effect. The Constitution also requires that the judgments be published immediately. There therefore exists a direct constitutional obligation incumbent on state services to publish the judgments without any delay. The point of this regulation is to guarantee that the judgment of the Constitutional Tribunal be published in the proper official journal to preserve the integrity of the sources of law. This regulation therefore furthers the values of the rule of law and does not allow any discretion as to the moment or otherwise of publication. The publication of the judgments of the Constitutional Tribunal is immediate and unconditional. No state authority has the power to scrutinize any aspect of the judgment. There is strictly no scope for the state authorities to moderate the obligation to publish the judgment by considering any aspect of the form, procedure, or substance of the judgment. Until December 2015, so much was clear. The matter of publication of the judgments of the Constitutional Tribunal was not only uncontroversial but also uninteresting.

As it happens, however, the President of the Council of Ministers is responsible for the publication services; the obligation to perform the technical actions required for the publication thus concerns directly the services and the President of the Council of Ministers. The President of the Council of Ministers refused to publish the judgments of the Constitutional Tribunal dated 3 and 9 December 2015. The Prime Minister argued that the Constitutional Tribunal had failed to demonstrate that the Constitutional Tribunal had proceeded properly making the judgments. It was argued that the judgments transferred by the President of the Constitutional Tribunal did not meet all the relevant criteria to recognize them as judgements of the Constitutional Tribunal. Acting on application by concerned citizens, public prosecutors started proceedings concerning abuse of powers by the President of the Council of Ministers by abridging the publication service's obligation to publish the judgments of the Constitutional Tribunal. Under pressure, the President of the Council of Ministers reluctantly and unhurriedly allowed the judgments to be published. The disgrace was not an accidental incident of the Prime Minister. After the Constitutional Tribunal issued a judgment concerning the Act of 22 December 2015 amending the Act on the Constitutional Tribunal (K 47/15), the President of the Council of Ministers relapsed into recidivism.

It has to be noted that this time there could be some cognitive problems; those, however, would only justify a momentary lapse of judgment. Because the judgment concerned an Act of Parliament that purported to govern the Constitutional Tribunal, the Constitutional Tribunal felt compelled to adjust the reach of the Act on the Constitutional Tribunal as to make sure that the proceedings were not governed by the very dispositions that were subject to constitutional review. The proceedings were to be governed by the Constitution alone to extent that particular dispositions of the Act on the Constitutional Tribunal were the subject of constitutional review. The Constitutional Tribunal invalidated the Act and itemized a number of violations of the Constitution. The President of the Council of Ministers refused to publish the judgment and refused to recognize that the Constitutional Tribunal would not be governed by the dispositions it invalidated. Thereafter, dozens of judgments of the Constitutional Tribunal remained unpublished over the period of several months. This situation was not only a display of action without valid legal reasons but also a direct violation of the Constitution.

As has been noted, the obligation to immediately publish the judgments of the Constitutional Tribunal is directly applicable to any relevant publication service. When the President of the Council of Ministers refused to publish the judgements such a refusal was in fact an order directed at the services responsible to the President of the Council of Ministers. Such an order, however, cannot be traced to any legal basis. As to offending the Constitution itself, there are two aspects of the matter. First of all, the Constitution commands that the judgements be published immediately. Secondly, the Constitution structures the separation of powers; the President of the Council of Ministers encroached on the powers of the judicial branch, thus directly violating the Constitution. The executive has no powers or functions concerning the substance, form or procedure of the decisions of the judicial branch. The executive thus has no powers to consider the propriety of proceedings of the Constitutional Tribunal and no powers of refusing to publish the judgements of the Constitutional Tribunal.

The constitutional delict of the President of the Council of Ministers did not go unnoticed. It inspired controversy as well as legislative efforts to translate the constitutional delict into the law of the land. Two legislative ideas were drafted.

First of all, it was proposed that the publication of the judgment of the Constitutional Tribunal be made upon application by the President of the Constitutional Tribunal. This suggests that transferring the judgement to the publication services was not to trigger the obligation to publish the judgment; instead the Prime Minister would be in the position to consider the application and decide if and when the judgment could be published.[35] Under this statutory regulation, the Prime Minister seemed to enjoy the power of considering the form and substance as well as the procedural propriety of the judgment. In any case, the power of refusing to publish a judgment was implicit but clear. Furthermore, the Act does not provide for the Constitution alone to govern the publication. The Act provided a blanket referral to another law: the publication of judgments was to be made according to the 'procedure' [pol. – tryb] indicated in the Constitution and the act governing official journals. The Constitution, however, precludes any discretion of the publication authorities whatsoever.

Secondly, the legislator proceeded to distinguish two categories of judgements of the Constitutional Tribunal.[36] The criterion allowing the categories to be distinguished is both temporal and substantial. The temporal criterion governs the obligation to publish unpublished judgments; judgments made before 20 July 2016 are to be published within 30 days. The material criterion is much more interesting. Firstly, the statute recognizes the theory underpinning the constitutional delict of the executive in that the statutory regulation spells out the existence of 'judgments of the Constitutional Tribunal issued in violation the Act on the Constitutional Tribunal'. Secondly, the Act precludes the publication of the judgments that were the origin of the constitutional delict because judgments concerning Acts that have 'lost binding power' are not to be published (the 2016 Act on Constitutional Tribunal abrogates the previous Act on the Constitutional Tribunal).

The Constitutional Tribunal found the ideas underpinning the statute unconstitutional. The Sejm does not enjoy the power to make distinctions between judgments of the Constitutional Tribunal. Primarily, however, the Constitution of the

35 Article 80.4 of the Act on the Constitutional Tribunal of 22 July 2016: 'The President of the Constitutional Tribunal shall apply to the President of the Constitutional Council for the judgments and resolutions [...] to be published. The publication shall be made following the procedure indicated in the Constitution and the Act of 20 July 2000 on the Publication of Normative Acts and Some Other Legal Acts [...].

36 Article 89 of the Act on the Constitutional Tribunal of 22 July 2016: 'Within 30 days of the coming into force of the statute, the judgments of the Constitutional Tribunal issued before 20 July 2016 shall be published despite being made in violation of the Act of 25 June 2015 on the Constitutional Tribunal, except for judgments pertaining to normative acts that have since been subject to invalidation or abrogation or otherwise 'lost binding power'.

Republic does not allow for moderating the obligation to publish the judgments of the Constitutional Tribunal.[37]

The issue of withholding the publication of the judgments of the Constitutional Tribunal concerning statutes governing the Constitutional Tribunal was discussed by the Constitutional Tribunal, by the Venice Commission as well as by the European Commission. The subject matter indeed is the focal point of the idea of constitutionalism and the rule of law in Poland. It would seem that there were no options available except to proceed with unconditional and immediate publication of the judgments. It turned out, however, that the Parliament was prepared to play at hide-and-seek and to introduce legislation characterized by tributary unconstitutionality. In the Act introducing the Regulations on Organization and Procedures Applicable to the Constitutional Tribunal and on the Status of Judges of the Constitutional Tribunal, the legislator precluded the publication of the judgments of the Constitutional Tribunal concerning acts that lost 'binding power', i.e. acts abrogated by the Acts. Moreover, the legislator spells out a category of judgments and resolutions made by the Constitutional Tribunal in violation of the Act on the Constitutional Tribunal of 25 June 2015 that are none the less to be published, except – of course – for the judgments the Parliament chose to covertly withdraw from publication in the Act on the Constitutional Tribunal of 22 July 2016.

3. Concluding Remarks

In its Recommendation, the European Commission comprehensively enumerates the matters that are susceptible to undermine the rule of law in Poland. It stipulates that Polish authorities are obligated to 'ensure that the effectiveness of the Constitutional Tribunal as a guarantor of the Constitution is not undermined by requirements, whether separately or through their combined effect, such as [...] the attendance quorum, the handling of cases in chronological order, the possibility of the Public Prosecutor-General to prevent the examination of cases, the postponement of deliberations or transitional measures affecting pending cases and putting cases on hold.'

In the main, the legislation adopted by the Parliament might seem hot-headed but has indeed a common thread. The intention of the legislator is to 'maximally minimize' the effectiveness constitutional review in Poland. The legislative design, on the other hand, goes far outside of the bounds of the system of government set up by the Constitution. Under the Constitution of the Republic, the Constitutional Tribunal has a prominent place within the system of government. In other words,

37 K 39/16, The Constitutional Tribunal explicitly criticized the fact that 'the Parliament adopted a regulation that purported to attach a stigma to judgments of the Constitutional Tribunal. Any legislation that undertakes to qualify any judgment of the Constitutional Tribunal as 'made in violation of law' is 'beyond the limits of the powers of the legislative branch within the system of government'. The particular qualification, on the other hand, had no factual basis and no substance. The wording used by the legislation was characterized by vacuity and motivation that do not merit any protection' (para. 9.3.3). The behaviour of the Parliament is contrary 'to the standards of a democratic state ruled by law' and alien to the legal culture to which Republic of Poland belongs or has aspired' (para. 9.3.4).

the Parliament sought to fundamentally upturn the constitutional order of the State. This constitutional upheaval was attempted by the form of statutes. This project, however, cannot be legally undertaken without a constitutional amendment. Constitutional review is a pivotal element of the constitutional system of government. Summarily, the strategy could be characterized as a 'hostile takeover' of the constitutional order by the parliamentary majority of the day.[38]

II. Initial Attempts at Reforming and Deforming Constitutional Review in Poland

The evolution of the constitutional model of constitutional review in Poland was driven by successive amendments enacted by the Parliament on 18 November 2015[39] and 22 December 2015[40] that governed the status of the Constitutional Tribunal (1.) as well as the Act on the Constitutional Tribunal of 22 July 2016 (2.). The following paragraphs seek to showcase the methods and artifices used to 'extinguish' constitutional review by the Polish parliamentary majority. The verb 'to extinguish' was indeed one of the buzzwords used by the parliamentary majority.

1. Reforming Constitutional Review in Late 2015

The 2015 amendments to the Act on the Constitutional Tribunal adopted by the Sejm of the previous term of parliament were prepared with great haste in parallel to the sequence of events concerted in order to overrule the assumption of office by judges elected by the Sejm of the previous term of Parliament. The sheer number of the devices conceived, however, was impressive. The ideas for frustrating constitutional review, on the other hand, also do not fail to impress.

1. The possibility of renewing the term of office of the President of the Constitutional Tribunal.[41] This regulation was considered to violate the Constitution because it provides for the President of the Republic to evaluate the conduct of a judge of the Constitutional Tribunal. The President of Republic is part of the dualist executive and the institution's involvement in nominating the President of the Constitutional Tribunal is different in nature from the power of renewing the term of office of the President of the Constitutional tribunal. Such a regulation could create a certain scope of interference with the independence of the judge of the Constitutional Tribunal. Furthermore, such a

38 *M. Wyrzykowski*, 'Hostile Takeover of the constitutional order' [Wrogie przejęcie" porządku konstytucyjnego] (in print).

39 The *Act amending the Act on the Constitutional Tribunal* of 19 November 2015 (Journal of Laws 2015, item 1928).

40 *Act amending the 2015 Act on Constitutional Tribunal* of 22 December 2015, *Official Journal*, 28 December 2015, item 2217.

41 Article 12.1 of the 2015 Act on the Constitutional Tribunal (Article 1.1 of the Act of 19 November 2015).

regulation could implicate the Constitutional Tribunal in the workings of the political branch and thus undermine the image of the judicial branch.[42]

2. The obligation of taking oath before the President of the Republic within 30 days of election by the Sejm to become a judge of the Constitutional Tribunal.[43] The Constitutional Tribunal stated that the regulation was unconstitutional because the Sejm is the sole authority empowered by the Constitution to elect the judges of the Constitutional Tribunal. The legislator thus cannot empower the President of the Republic (or any other authority) to influence the membership of the Constitutional Tribunal by administering or not administering the oath. The Parliament cannot thus dilute the constitutional power of the Sejm. If the President of the Republic were to enjoy discretion as to administering the oath within the specified time-limit, the Sejm's choice would no longer correspond to what the Constitution stipulates because the statute would in effect implicate the President in choosing the membership of the Constitutional Tribunal.[44]
3. Dismissal of the President of the Constitutional Tribunal and Alternate President of the Constitutional Tribunal by a new statutory regulation of the office and a provision to the effect that the office of President and Alternate President be vacated after three months of the coming into effect of the statute.[45] This regulation was considered to violate the Constitution because the legislator chose to terminate the term of office of the President and Alternate President of the Constitutional Tribunal whilst both constitutional offices were already assumed under previous statute for a term corresponding to the term of office of the respective judges of the Constitutional Tribunal. 'Extinguishing the term of office' provided for by the statute could be confused with the term of office as a judge and thus to extend the termination clause on the holding of the judicial office by both judges. This very possibility made the provision overbroad and justified the provision to be struck down.[46]
4. The supermajority requirement of 2/3 of votes in the presence of at least 13 judges quorum requirement at the General Assembly of Judges.[47] The Constitutional Tribunal is composed of 15 judges. The supermajority requirement was considered to violate the Constitution because the double supermajority requirement made it difficult or impossible to make decisions. It was argued that the supermajority requirement had no rational justification and was thus arbitrary. As such it violated the requirement that the General Assembly of Judges be effective. It should be noted further that the regulation corresponded to the fact that the Constitutional Tribunal at the time did not command 13 judges. The Constitutional Tribunal has a membership of 15 judges and 3 va-

42 K 35/15, para. 4.3.
43 Article 21.1 of the Act of 19 November 2015.
44 K 35/15, para. 5.3.4.
45 Article 2 of the Act of 19 November 2015.
46 K 35/15, para. 9.1.
47 Article 1 (3) of the Act of 22 December 2015 (Article 10.1 of the 2015 Act on the Constitutional Tribunal).

cancies were not properly filled. 3 judges elected by the Sejm of the previous term of parliament were not administered oath by the President of the Republic whereas the 3 judges sworn in by the President were refused judicial authority by the President of the Constitutional Tribunal because the persons thus sworn in did not have the qualification of having been effectively elected by the Sejm. The Constitutional Tribunal does not mention this circumstantial evidence but it can show that the disposition was a blatant attempt to paralyze the General Assembly of Judges.

5. The supermajority quorum requirement of 13 judges for cases originating in applications for abstract constitutional review.[48] This regulation was considered to violate the Constitution because it negated the principle of judicial diligence (viz. independence and impartiality) as well as effectiveness (viz. promptness of judgment). It is a long-standing tradition for the Constitutional Tribunal to perform its duties sections of varying number of judges. It was considered that implicating all judges in cases originating in applications for abstract constitutional review would violate the possibility of conducting cases in parallel. It was thus stated that the legislator does not have full discretion in determining such internal and practical matters of the judicial branch as the matter of membership of sections delegated to pronounce judgements and resolutions. The legislator's discretion is allowed only to the extent that membership and criteria of allocating docket correspond to the requirements of the judicial branch and the interest of proper administration of justice.
6. The requirement to schedule open court hearings and in camera proceedings chronologically according to the date of respective filings (i.e. on the first-come-first-served basis)[49]. This regulation violates the principle of separation of powers, the right to a court and the principle of independence of the judicial branch. The regulation precluded the Constitutional Tribunal from considering cases until all prior cases were concluded. The regulation was considered to violate the right to a court in its promptness aspect because a number of cases would delay trials until the Constitutional Tribunal could respond to the application made by the court for a preliminary ruling in cases where the court entertained doubts as to constitutionality of the legislation applicable to the case. Furthermore, it was considered that the principle of effective operation of justice and public authorities was violated by the requirement that cases be considered according to principles that had no rational correspondence to the practicalities of administration of justice. It was also noted that the regulation violated other regulations that governed the proceedings of the Constitutional Tribunal (e.g. constitutional review of the bud-

48 Article 1 (9) of the Act of 22 December 2015 (Article 44.1 & 44.3 of the 2015 Act on the Constitutional Tribunal).

49 'The dates of hearings or the dates of sittings in camera, at which applications are considered, shall be set in the order in which cases are received by the Tribunal', Article 1 (10) of the Act of 22 December 2015 (Article 80.2 of the 2015 Act on the Constitutional Tribunal).

get and the provisory budget that are circumscribed temporarily where the judgment is required to be pronounced within 2 months. All observers of the constitutional crisis could see the true rationale of this idea: the parliamentary majority did not wish its legislation to be subjected to constitutional review anytime soon.

7. The prohibition of scheduling open court hearings within 3 months and within 6 months – for cases considered in full court – of delivery of the notification of hearing.[50] The Constitutional Tribunal considered this disposition to violate the principle of autonomy of the Constitutional Tribunal and the principle of independence of the judicial branch from other branches of government. The lapse-of-time requirements were considered to be important. Importantly, however, the conditions prohibited the Constitutional Tribunal from expediting cases that were ripe for a judgment on grounds that lacked any rational justification. The requirement also violated the right to a court without undue delay in cases where the Constitutional Tribunal would be required to postpone preliminary ruling proceedings initiated by the courts. The regulation was also considered to be dysfunctional and arbitrary. It violated the principle of autonomy of the Constitutional Tribunal and the principle of independence of the judicial branch from other branches of government.
8. The supermajority of 2/3 requirement in cases considered in full court.[51] The supermajority requirement for determining the outcome of voting on judgments was inconsistent with the Constitution in that the Constitution provides for decisions to be taken by simple majority (Article 190.5).[52] According to the Constitutional Tribunal, Article 190 precludes any modification of voting requirements either by requiring supermajorities or by requiring a supermajority in certain category of cases.
9. The requirement of re-allocating cases pending before the Constitutional Tribunal according to new requirements.[53] This requirement was recognized to require the Constitutional Tribunal to discontinue pending proceedings and start considering them anew. The regulation was considered to violate the principle of autonomy of the Constitutional tribunal and the principle of administering justice without undue delay.
10. The power of initiating disciplinary proceedings against a judge of the Constitutional Tribunal by the President of the Republic or the Minister of Justice.[54] The Constitutional Tribunal stated that the regulation was unconstitutional on the grounds that the authorities of the executive branch were at-

50 Article 1 (12) (a) and Article 2 of the Act of 22 December 2015 (Article 87.2 of the 2015 Act on the Constitutional Tribunal).

51 Article 1 (14) of the Act of 22 December 2015 (Article 99.1 of the 2015 Act on the Constitutional Tribunal).

52 'Judgments of the Constitutional Tribunal shall be made by a majority of votes'.

53 Article 2 of the Act of 22 December 2015.

54 Article 1 (5) of the Act of 22 December 2015 (new Article 28a of the 2015 Act on the Constitutional Tribunal).

tributed powers that are reserved to the judicial branch. The power of initiating proceedings by authorities of the executive branch in itself means that this very act emanates from outside of the judicial branch of government thus subjecting the judge to the vagaries of political pressure.

11. The transfer of the power of dismissing the judge of the Constitutional Tribunal from office from the Constitutional Tribunal to the Sejm.[55] The Constitutional Tribunal stated that the transfer of the disciplinary power of dismissing of the judge of the Constitutional Tribunal from office from the Constitutional Tribunal onto the Sejm constitutes an encroachment of the legislative branch on the sphere of autonomy of the Constitutional Tribunal. The Sejm is an authority of the legislative branch of government and as such can naturally interfere with the judicial branch only to the extent that the autonomy and independence of the judicial branch is preserved. The Constitution sets up a system of government whereby the Sejm's role in respect to the Constitutional Tribunal is limited to the power of electing judges of the Constitutional Tribunal. Under the Constitution, the Sejm has no power in relation to the judge once the judge has assumed office upon election. Moreover, the Constitutional Tribunal considered that the principle of autonomy requires that the Constitutional Tribunal retain the power of disciplinary removal from office of a judge who has offended the dignity of a judge, ethical standards or the law of the land. Moreover, the Constitutional Tribunal stated that disciplinary proceedings were regulated so as to allow the President of the Republic and the Minister of Justice to initiate disciplinary proceedings aimed at dismissing a judge of the Constitutional Tribunal form office and thus encroached beyond acceptable limits upon the principle of autonomy and independence of the Constitutional tribunal and the independence of the judge.
12. Transfer of the power of determination of vacation of office of a judge from the General Assembly of Judges onto the Sejm.[56] The transfer of the power to make the determination that the office of a judge is vacant from the General Assembly of Judges of the Constitutional Tribunal onto the Sejm was deemed to violate the Constitution. Such a power directly interferes with the status of the judge. The Constitution proscribes any recall or removal from office by the legislative or executive branch. Moreover, the powers of the Constitutional Tribunal consist primarily in constitutional review of legislation; the nature of its judicial function thus precludes any interference with the status of the judge of the Constitutional Tribunal by the Sejm.
13. Elimination of the exclusive powers of the Constitutional Tribunal to conduct disciplinary proceedings against the judge of the Constitutional Tribunal relating to conduct that took place before assumption of office.[57] The Constitu-

55 Article 1 (6), (7) & (8) of the Act of 22 December 2015 (Article 31 (3), 31a & 36.1 (4) of the 2015 Act on the Constitutional Tribunal).

56 Article 36.2 of the 2015 Act on the Constitutional Tribunal (Article 1.8 of the Act of 22 December 2015).

57 Article 16 of the Act of 22 December 2015 repealing Article 28.2 of the 2015 Act.

tional Tribunal considered this regulation to violate the Constitution. It was stated that the judge who is guilty of conduct that is contrary to the dignity of the office can be subject to external pressures; this is unacceptable considering the autonomy and independence of the Constitutional Tribunal and its judges. Disciplinary powers pertaining to facts dated before the assumption of office by the judge are the necessary instrument for the Constitutional Tribunal to be able to build up and command authority with the actors of the legal process as well as with the general public. The wide temporal reach of disciplinary powers of the Constitutional Tribunal is necessary for the safeguard of the dignity of the Constitutional Tribunal in cases where such facts are not known until the judge has assumed office.

14. Repeal of regulations governing proceedings to determine the existence of an impediment to the exercise of the office by the President of the Republic[58] Chapter 10 of the Act on the Constitutional Tribunal regulated emergency proceedings in which the President was not in a position to notify the Marshal of the Sejm on the President's impediment to exercising office. The repeal was considered unconstitutional on the grounds that the legislator is obligated to regulate such proceedings. Even though there is no such particular constitutional requirement of legislation, the Constitution indicates the Constitutional Tribunal as competent to make such a determination to the exclusion of other state authorities[59] and the legislator is therefore obligated to legislate on the instruments and the procedure to be followed in such an emergency.
15. Immediate entry into force of the Act upon the day of promulgation.[60] The lack of appropriate period between the promulgation and entry into force of the act was considered unconstitutional on a number of grounds. First of all, the Constitutional Tribunal was deprived of any scope for taking appropriate organizational and other preparatory measures to respond to the requirements of the new statute. Secondly, the lack of any appropriate period of *vacatio legis* of the new regulation negatively affected the rights and obligations of actors participating in proceedings. Thirdly, it was considered to violate the Constitution for the legislator to introduce legislation governing the Constitutional Tribunal without allowing the Constitutional Tribunal the time necessary to respond to constitutional review applications by actors directly entitled to make such requests by the Constitution before such new legislation takes effect.

All the matters analysed in paragraphs 4-15 above were discussed by the Constitutional Tribunal in its judgment of 9 March 2015, case call no. K

58 Article 1.15 of the Act of 22 December 2015.

59 Article 131. '[...]If the President [...] is not in a position to inform the Marshal of the Sejm of his incapacity to discharge the duties of the office, then the Constitutional Tribunal shall, on request of the Marshal of the Sejm, determine whether or not there exists an impediment to the exercise of the office by the President of the Republic [...]'.

60 Article 5 of the Act of 22 December 2015.

47/15. It is important to note again,[61] that the Act under review was unusual in that it was immediately applicable. It follows that the Constitutional Tribunal was confronted with the problem that the constitutional review was 'self-referential': The Act of 22 December 2015 was the object of constitutional review and the procedural basis of constitutional review at the same time. The Constitutional Tribunal considered this situation impossible and decided to exclude the dispositions that were the object of constitutional review from governing constitutional review itself. Interestingly enough, this allowed the Constitutional Tribunal to apply the Constitution directly for the first time.[62]

2. *Reforming of the Constitutional Review in Early 2016*

This was not the end of the constitutional marathon. The Parliament adopted yet another statute governing the organization and function of the Constitutional Tribunal of 22 June 2016.[63] Considering recent practice, the statute was only unusual to the extent that it allowed for a 14-days' *vacatio legis*. The Constitutional Tribunal was thus allowed some repose in considering the application for judicial review. The following items discuss particular issues relevant to the problem of the rule of law.

1. The obligation to consider cases in full court (15 judges) upon the request made by 3 judges made within 14 days of the receipt of copies of an application for constitutional review, a constitutional complaint, or a preliminary ruling request.[64] The Constitutional Tribunal deemed this regulation to violate the constitutional principle of effective operation of public authorities, the principle of diligent operation of public institutions, and the principle of effectivity of public authorities, respectively. Firstly, it was recognized that the power to request that a matter be considered by full court was structured as an arbitrary power because it was not made conditional on the judge being allocated the case in the first place, it was unrelated to anything specific about the case, and it did not require that the request be reasoned. Secondly, the regulation was the very contrary of the idea that full court would only consider exceptional cases. Finally, this regulation was not singular but was accompanied by other procedural anomalies, such as the obligation to consider cases on the first-come-first-served basis and the requirement that 13 judges participate in a full court case. There was, therefore, nothing to prevent the scenario whereby all cases would be required to be considered in full court which would upset the ability of the Constitutional Tribunal to de-

61 Cf. paragraph 1.2 *supra*.
62 Cf. *M. Wyrzykowski*, Antigone in Warsaw [Antygona w Warszawie] (in print).
63 The Act on the Constitutional Tribunal of 22 July 2016 (Journal of Laws 2016, item 1157).
64 Article 26.1 (1) (g) of the Act on the Constitutional Tribunal of 2016.

liver on its constitutional mission of effective and real constitutional review of legislation.

2. The obligation to consider abstract-review cases on a first-come-first-served basis.[65] Abstract constitutional review is the primary function of the Constitutional Tribunal. It involves a spectrum of public bodies and pertain to matters of fundamental value to the public interest. The spectrum of public bodies who enjoy standing to initiate abstract constitutional review include the Commissioner for Human Rights, the National Council of the Judiciary, the Prosecutor-General, as well as a group of Members of the Sejm who might well represent the majority or the minority in parliament. The legislative purpose of the new regulation was very simple indeed. The parliamentary majority sought to postpone for as long as possible the constitutional review of its legislation as such legislation was bound to be the object of constitutional review at the request made by the parliamentary minorities, or public authorities with a mandate to secure the observance of the Constitution. The Constitutional Tribunal concluded that the regulation violated the principle of a democratic state ruled by law, the principle of separation of powers, the principle of independence and autonomy of the judiciary as well as the constitutional status of the Constitutional Tribunal.
3. The power of the President of the Constitutional Tribunal to shorten by half the 30-day lapse-of-time requirement for holding a hearing in cases concerning preliminary ruling requests, constitutional complaints and resolution of questions of authority [*Kompetenzstreit*][66]. The problem concerned the fact that the disposition privileged cases that were not initiated by an application for abstract constitutional review by public actors. In this case, the Constitutional Tribunal found a violation of the Constitution on the grounds discussed above. It is interesting to note that the Constitutional Tribunal showed what is called judicial deference to the legislative branch: the invalidation removed only the differentiation of cases and thus left the power of shortening the lapse-of time requirement intact – it was henceforth to be applicable to all proceedings. The Constitutional Tribunal noted that 'the constitutional character of the power to apply for abstract constitutional review, its systematic importance for the protection of constitutional rights and freedoms and the fundamental tents of the system of government as well as the processual equivalence of applications, constitutional complaints and preliminary ruling requests all constitute an obstacle to a regulation that purports to give unconditional and automatic priority to cases originating in a constitutional complaint, preliminary ruling request and question of authority reference'.
4. The obligation to adjourn hearing when the Prosecutor-General is absent in cases where the Prosecutor-General has been duly-notified but the statute re-

65 Article 38.3-6 of the Act on the Constitutional Tribunal of 2016.
66 Article 61.3 of the Act on the Constitutional Tribunal of 2016.

quires that the Prosecutor-General participate in the hearing.[67] In cases the Prosecutor-General failed to attend, the Constitutional Tribunal would be unable to proceed but would be instead obligated to adjourn and schedule another date for the hearing. The statute thus conditioned the power of constitutional review on the behaviour of the Prosecutor-General. Since the Prosecutor-General is not a judicial officer but a politician (the office was merged with the office of Minister of Justice), the executive branch would be able to block constitutional review in cases considered by full court where attendance by the Prosecutor-General was obligatory. This situation obviously violates the principle of separation of powers, the principle of autonomy and independence of the judicial branch and the constitutional powers of the Constitutional Tribunal.

5. The right of a group of judges to require the deferment of proceedings by 3 months in opposition to apparent substance of the forthcoming judgment in cases considered by full court (The adjournment could be required twice)[68]. The unconstitutionality of the regulation is apparent in its violation of the constitutional powers of the Constitutional Tribunal, the right to court without undue delay and the principle of effective and diligent operation of public authorities. The regulation allowed for three judges who also enjoyed the right of requiring that a case be heard by full court to arbitrarily interfere with the autonomy of judges allocated the case and their power of decision to direct a case to be considered in full court when special nature of the case so required. The Constitutional Tribunal considered this device as institutionalizing judicial minorities by drawing inspiration from parliamentary institutions. As such, however, the regulation could not possibly be adapted to the Constitutional Tribunal in its role of an authority of the judicial branch as well as to the individual status of the judge of the Constitutional Tribunal.
6. The power of the President of the Constitutional Court to bestow full judicial authority to judges of the Constitutional Court who were administered oath of office by the President of the Republic but did not exercise office at the date of the statute coming to force.[69] The regulation was applicable to 3 judges elected by the Sejm to vacancies already filled by the Sejm of the previous term of parliament but who were administered an oath by the President of the Republic despite their lacking the quality of having been elected by the Sejm. The Constitutional referenced its judgment in the case K 34/15 that confirmed that the Sejm assigned the candidates to vacancies that were already filled by the Sejm of the previous term according to the law and the Constitution and that the office could not be considered assumed by persons administered oath by the President because the vacancies for which they were apparently elected had been already filled by judges who assumed of-

67 Article 66.6 of the Act on the Constitutional Tribunal of 2016.
68 Article 68.5-7 of the Act on the Constitutional Tribunal of 2016.
69 Article 90 of the Act on the Constitutional Tribunal of 2016.

fice on election by the Sejm but were unable to execute office for want of takin an oath due to be administered by the President of the Republic. The Constitutional Tribunal thus found against the disposition on the grounds of reiterated unconstitutionality [pol. – *wtórna niekonstytucyjność*].

3. *Concluding Remarks*

The European Commission and the Venice Commission are correct in noting that the strategy of corrupting constitutional review of legislation was characterized by the mechanism of factual rather than legal impairment of the Constitutional Tribunal in its capability to undertake constitutional review of legislation. The factual component transpires from two characteristics of the legal devices at work. First of all, a sequence of discrete unconstitutional regulations governing the Constitutional Tribunal (e.g. providing for the obligation to consider cases chronologically or to take decisions by super-majorities) frustrates the ability of the Constitutional Tribunal to respond adequately to the demands of the workload. Secondly, the Constitutional Tribunal's effectiveness suffers as it is burdened by the 'negative synergy' of particular regulations.
Particular pieces of statutory regulations, on the other hand, are the shining examples of the techniques and mechanisms of 'abusive parliamentarianism'. The Polish experiences can thus easily be a positive source of inspiration and study material for a textbook setting out the paradigm of 'anti-constitutionalism in action'. This would probably make an exciting read. As constitutionalism and the rule of law seem to wear away with every new day, constitutionalists and majoritarianists alike should make such a manual compulsory reading material. The textbook's structure should probably consists of the following subjects: the social and political context contributing to the erosion of constitutionalism and the rule of law; the idea of majoritarian democracy as the source and basis of legislative absolutism; constitutional authorities abusing the law by action and failing to act; gradual acclimation and generalization of the principle of indecent legislation;[70] conceptual abuse in respect to the meaning of institutions and notions received in the legal and constitutional culture; obstinate recidivism in violating the constitution by legislation reiterating regulations previously invalidated by a constitutional court, and – *last but not least* – the general disposition to legal nihilism, arrogance and populism in the mechanism of a 'hostile takeover' of the constitutional order.

III. Conclusion

In December 2016, the Polish Parliament enacted three statutes abrogating and substituting all statutes governing the Constitutional Tribunal that were enacted

70 Cf. *M. Wyrzykowski*, 'The Counter-Principle of Indecent legislation' [*Antyzasada nieprzyzwoitej legislacji*], (in print).

since 2015. As of March 2017, the *Law and Justice* Party commands a majority of 8 judges on the Constitutional Tribunal as well as the office of President of the Constitutional Tribunal. The verb 'to command' used in the last sentence unfortunately is no metaphor. The Party also commands a little more than a simple majority in Parliament. *Opinio communis* has established within the legal community and holds that the Constitutional Tribunal as we know it ceased to exist. This nostalgic conclusion might not be of import if not for the fact that the Constitutional Tribunal as it stands also no longer corresponds to the legal criteria set forth in the Constitution. The Constitutional Tribunal shows none of the basic constitutive elements required of it to be recognised as the corresponding institution entrenched in the Constitution. The Constitutional Tribunal under the Constitution is an independent, apolitical, and neutral constitutional legal authority mandated to enforce constitutional norms.

The Parliamentary majority does not command constitutional majority or anything by the way of an overwhelming popular support required by the Constitution for constitutional amendment concerning the rights and freedoms entrenched thereunder. Nonetheless, the parliamentary majority has opened hitherto unexplored avenues of informal constitutional change by statute. The crisis of constitutional review was not nurtured for the parliamentary majority to unexpectedly and suddenly turn to uphold the model of constitutional review that characterized the sovereign, free and democratic state. To the contrary, there are now no limits set for the effective operation of democratic rule by majority.

The parliamentary majority has operated under the political slogan 'Change for Good'; it has indeed delivered on its aim regarding constitutional review. What has been done cannot be undone. Unable to amend the constitution, the parliamentary majority has changed the constitutional order, leaving the Constitution an empty shell. Destroying the Constitutional Tribunal, however, also means that the empty shell of a Constitution can also serve no useful purpose as a political fig leaf. Even if the rule of law in Poland persists in some and important respects, no one can tell it does anymore.

The mechanism set forth in Article 7 TEU and in the *New EU Framework to Strengthen the Rule of Law*, turns out very difficult to implement. It seems that both instruments simply presuppose something that is missing. Indeed, they proceed on the assumption that the principle of mutual trust, loyalty, and cooperation between EU institutions and the Member State are observed. The Polish authorities, however, have proved unprecedented perseverance in rejecting those fundamental values of the EU. This is the real meaning of all representations and declarations made by the legislative and the executive that transpires from the blatant lack of coherence on the part of the Polish government. The Prime Minister said that the 'Polish government will never be subject to an ultimatum'[71] one day only

71 Communication of the President of the Council of Ministers concerning the Communication of European Commission concerning the Situation in Poland, 19th Sitting of the Sejm of 20 may 2016, shorthand, p. 283.

to state the opposite the next day. We are now told that the legislation enacted in December 2016 'constitutes the definitive and comprehensive resolution of the problem of organization and operation of the Constitutional Tribunal, taking account of a series of recommendations set out by the Venice Commission'[72].

Crisis therefore characterises both Polish constitutional system of government and the relationship between the Polish state and the EU. The ways and effects of this crisis' resolution shall be the litmus test of the EU's capability of acting on the principles and values of the Treaties it is based on.

72 Communiqué by the Minister for Foreign Affairs in response to the Recommendation of the European Commission of 21 December 2016, 20 February 2016, http://www.msz.gov.pl/pl/aktualnosci/wiadomosci/oswiadczenie_msz_dotyczace_odpowiedzi_strony_polskiej_na_uzupelniajace_zalecenie_komisji_europejskiej_z_dnia_21_grudnia_2016_roku.

Part III: Enforcement

Beyond Voting Rights Suspension. Tailored Sanctions as Democracy Catalyst under Article 7 TEU

*By Tomas Dumbrovsky, Prague**

Article 7 TEU empowers the Council to suspend certain rights derived from the application of the Treaties. The suspension of voting rights in the Council is one such example. This contribution examines which other rights can be suspended. It uses sanction theories and a textual and contextual analysis of the sanction provision contained in Article 7 TEU to assess the options the Council has, and develops guidelines and suggests *improvements* of *the institutional framework for devising sanctions. The contribution argues for targeted sanctions against individuals and entities that form the political and economic basis of regimes deviating from the fundamental liberal-democratic values. The sanctions must be tailored to the causes of the deviation in such a way that they can enhance democratic pluralism.*

Introduction

The suspension of voting rights of a Member State that seriously and persistently violates the fundamental values of our common enterprise is neither the only option nor a desirable one. The EU's discretion in devising sanctions is broad, and its institutions must use their sanctioning powers effectively and creatively to stop the proliferation of illiberal structures in its Eastern part. The EU has the necessary powers to do so, and it is under obligation to its citizens to do so. It should start with identifying the economic bases of the Law and Justice Party (PiS) and Fidesz and hit hard. Simultaneously, the EU should find ways to correct deformed plurality by supporting liberal institutions such as independent media, non-governmental organizations, and universities.
In this contribution, I analyze the EU's options under the sanction provision of Article 7 TEU, and suggest a method and guidelines for devising the sanctions. After setting my research within the context of the Article 7 debate, I proceed to a textual analysis of the sanction provision followed by a contextual dimension focusing on the purpose of Article 7 as such. Thereafter, I examine the major political theories of sanctions that will help us understand how to achieve that objective. In the next step, I review institutional architecture for sanctioning and suggest improvements. The final two sections outline the principles that should govern the process of devising the sanction regime and identify different areas of

* Assistant Professor, Centre for Comparative Law, Charles University. The article is a result of the project PRIMUS/HUM/20 "Constitutional Transformation in Europe in Post-Sovereignty Conditions".

rights that might be suspended. In the conclusion, I urge for sanctions tailored to the causes of deviation and political and societal structures in a target state.

I. The EU's Failure

In December 2017, the Commission backed by France and Germany launched Article 7 procedure against Poland.[1] At last. For several years, the politicians of a generation raised during the Cold War have been discarding Article 7 TEU as a nuclear option, that ought not to be used.[2] The EU policy-makers has repeatedly signaled that Article 7 does not provide them with a viable option to deal with the backsliding of some Member States from common European values.

The nuclear analogy is misleading. The concept of mutually assured destruction counsels against deploying such weapons. It is also the reason why misconduct on a lower scale might be tolerated. However, it applies only to those in possession of the weapon or those under a protection of the weapon holder. Hungary and Poland do not have a counter-weapon that would assure the EU's destruction at their disposal. The purpose of Article 7, within the nuclear paradigm, must then be to *deter* from wrongful conduct. If Article 7 were to create a deterrence effect, it *ought to* be used first.[3] The Commission has taken the first step.

The hesitance of the EU to deal decisively with Viktor Orbán's gradual illiberal reforms in Hungary after the 2010 parliamentary elections have relaxed, or even inspired, others with similar political agendas; such as Jaroslaw Kaczynski's Law and Justice Party (PiS) after winning the 2015 presidential and parliamentary elections with a majority vote.

Although critics point to the ineffectiveness of the Article 7 procedure resulting from its cumbersome voting requirements,[4] the high majorities required by Article 7 in each step of the procedure are not manifestly disproportional to the seriousness of the issue Article 7 aims to address. In the current EU-28, nine Member States, the European Parliament (acting by two-thirds majority of the votes cast, representing the majority of MEPs)[5] or the Commission may initiate the procedure. Twenty-two Member States may conclude that there is a risk of serious

1 European Commission – Press release, Rule of Law: European Commission acts to defend judicial independence in Poland, Dec. 20, 2017, at http://europa.eu/rapid/press-release_IP-17-5367_en.htm.

2 *J. M. Barroso*, State of the Union Speech, at http://europa.eu/rapid/press-release_SPEECH-12-596_en.htm, 2012.

3 The closing days of the WWII in the Pacific made it clear that only the use of atomic bomb would end Japan's determination to continue fighting; the existence of the weapon was not enough. For the posterity, the deterrence effect has been established through the actual use of the nuclear option. The reader might forgive me for using this example (which surely exceeds the scale of the problem we deal with here), given that it was not me who has resorted to nuclear weapon analogy, so tirelessly repeated in the discourse on Article 7 time and again.

4 For an elaborate critique see e.g. *U. Sedelmeier*, Political safeguards against democratic backsliding in the EU: the limits of material sanctions and the scope of social pressure, Journal of European Public Policy 2017, p. 337-351.

5 Art. 354 TFEU.

breach of common values by a Member State.[6] Again, a reasonable majority[7] is required to prevent abuse of the mechanism.[8] Thereafter, the European Council will decide unanimously, without counting the vote of the investigated Member State, on the existence of a serious and persistent breach of the common values. In the final stage, which is the object of this contribution, the Council, acting by a qualified majority, may suspend Member State's rights.

The requirement of unanimity in the European Council is considered the major hurdle in the process. The European Council must enlist support from regimes that interpret the common values of the Union differently than those that are shared by its majority members. Allow me a few remarks on the margins. Firstly we shall consider a possibility to initiate a joint Article 7 procedure against two or more states if the merits of the case are similar and offended values identical. This will disqualify the regimes that are worried to be the next in line from vetoing the European Council's decision. Such an interpretation would require a thorough contextual analysis to overcome the obvious problem that the Article 7 refers to a procedure against "a Member State".

Secondly, the European Council's vote takes place in the concluding stage of the procedure. Passing through the Rule of Law Framework procedure and the steps required by Article 7 (1), means that the EU must gain support from a vast majority of stakeholders including at least twenty-two of the Member States and the majority of the MEPs. It would place considerable pressure on the states opposing the measures, and consequently force them to reveal the reasons for their objections.

Thirdly, reaching the concluding stage of the Article 7 procedure may be beneficial even if the European Council's decision is eventually vetoed. It may afford additional legitimacy to the liberal opposition both in the deviating state and in the vetoing state(s), stimulate public debate, and increase support of the general public for regime change.

The potential of Article 7 has been undermined since its inception. In 2000, the Member States mishandled the situation when the Freedom party (FPÖ) joined the Austrian government.[9] They bypassed the new mechanism of Article 7 at the first possibility of its application. A decade thereafter, the EU, preoccupied with

6 The investigated Member State is not counted in the calculation of the required one-third and fourth-fifths majorities. See Art. 354 TFEU.

7 Whether the required majority shall be 19, 22 or 24 states is a political decision. A constitutional analysis may only assess the minimum that would be required to prevent an abuse of the mechanism and the maximum that would make the mechanism manifestly unattainable.

8 The requirement that the European Parliament acts by two-thirds majority of the votes cast, representing the majority of MEPs is reasonable in light of majorities required for comparable instruments devised to neutralize or sanction constitution-threatening conduct such as presidential impeachment in several EU countries.
The investigated Member State is ensured basic rights of defense – by the requirement of the initiator of the procedure to submit a *reasoned* proposal and by the obligation of the Council to hear the investigated Member State (Art. 7 para. 1 TEU).

9 *M. Merlingen/C. Mudde/U. Sedelmeier*, The Right and the Righteous? European Norms, Domestic Politics and the Sanctions Against Austria, Journal of Common Market Studies, 2001, p. 59-77; *C. Leconte*, The Fragility of the EU as a 'Community of Values': Lessons from the Haider Affair, West European Politics, 2005, p. 620-49.

the Euro crisis and increased immigration, reacted sluggishly to the developments in Hungary and Poland.[10] Finally, EU representatives raised the threshold for launching the Article 7 procedure when they declared it as a nuclear option.[11]

One of the reasons why Article 7 has achieved the aura of Rubicon is the notion that its ultimate result would be the suspension of voting rights. Once I deconstruct the sanction provisions of Article 7, it will become clear that the EU has an array of better options for remedying the conduct of a deviating Member State.

Before turning to the textual analysis of Article 7, several preliminary observations must be considered. Firstly, human rights protection within the Union is relatively high in comparison with examples of states that have been sanctioned for human rights violation by the international community. Sanctions will affect these rights. Furthermore, the EU, by using the Article 7 procedure, will impose sanctions on its own citizens. A higher degree of scrutiny of direct and collateral damages that might be caused by sanctions to the general public is therefore necessary.

Secondly, Article 7 is not a political provision that provides political sanctions, but creates a legal regime. The common values contained in Article 2 TEU form an equivalent to a constitutional core which signifies the constitutional identity of the European political community. The target state is guaranteed, albeit limited, judicial protection; the fulfilment of the procedural requirements is reviewable by the Court of Justice. The fact that the sanctions are not imposed by a judicial organ does not make Article 7 a political mechanism. This regime cannot be compared to other situations of pure political accountability, such as the failure to deliver on election promises. In the case of Article 7, the position of the European Council, the Council, the Commission, and the European Parliament as agents is much clearer. If there is a "serious and persistent breach" by a Member State of the values enshrined in Article 2, the agents must act on behalf of EU citizens. The citizens have, at least, the right to be protected from a decision-making on the EU level, that could compromise Article 2 values ('insulation' rationale). Under an expansive reading of Article 7, the EU is obligated to its citizens to ensure that no public authority (on any level of governance) is manifestly arbitrary ('political community' rational). The use of the word "may" in each of the stages of Article 7, does not give a cart blanch to Member States and EU institutions to ignore a breach of the values contained in Article 2. It provides them with flexibility as to the means for correcting the breach.

Finally, choosing an effective sanction presupposes that we have in-depth knowledge about the causes of a Member State's deviation from the common values.

10 See e.g. *L. Pech/K.L. Scheppele*, Illiberalism Within: Rule of Law Backsliding in the EU, Cambridge Yearbook of European Legal Studies, 2017, p. 3-47.

11 Cf. also the introduction to the New EU Framework to strengthen the Rule of Law, which justified the introduction of effectively another step in Article 7 procedure with a milder language: "current EU mechanisms and procedures have not always been [understand: never] appropriate in ensuring an effective and timely response to threats to the rule of law." Communication from the Commission to the European Parliament and the Council, A new EU Framework to strengthen the Rule of Law, COM (2014) 158 final, p. 2.

Illiberal trends, caused by unfinished democratic revolutions, failed market economy transformation or recent challenges – from the Euro crisis and expansion of Russian and Chinese economic and political influence to immigration influx and terrorist attacks – have proliferated in the EU. Some member states have openly started to reconstruct their constitutional system on national-conservative grounds,[12] others have silently adjusted their pre-liberal power structures to a new era,[13] some have done so with occasional EU outcry,[14] yet others have slid when attempting to co-opt the populist electorate[15] or have deformed the democratic plurality in order to gain political and economic advantage and consequently laid down a system of patronage.[16]

A proper response under Article 7, in the form of tailored sanctions that are likely to bring a change in the objectionable behavior of a target state, requires a deep understanding of the causes of these trends and of the societal structure in that state. Especially, the senders of sanctions must determine which intrastate forces underpins the illiberal-prone regimes and reasons for failure of liberal forces to counteract these developments.

12 The obvious examples are post-2010 Hungary and post-2015 Poland. *K. L. Scheppele*, Hungary's Constitutional Revolution, Conscience of a Liberal Blog (Dec. 19, 2011), at http://krugman.blogs.nytimes.com/2011/12/19/hungarys-constitutional-revolution; *B. Bugarič*, A crisis of constitutional democracy in post-Communist Europe: "Lands in-between" democracy and authoritarianism, ICON, 2015, p. 219-45; *M. Bánkuti/G. Halmai/K.L. Scheppele*, Disabling the Constitution, J. Democracy, 2012, p. 138-146.

13 See recent efforts to uncover the depth of the problem in Slovenia. *B. Bugarič* 2015, (fn. 1211), (comparing Slovenia and Hungary); *M. Avbelj*, Failed Democracy: The Slovenian Patria Case – (Non) Law in Context, SSRN at https://papers.ssrn.com/sol3/papers.cfm?abstract_id=2462613, translation from Slovenian original *M. Avbelj,/P. Zadeva* Patria – (ne)pravo v kontekstu, Pravna praksa, 2014; *P. Guasti/B. Dobovšek/B. Ažman*, Deficiencies in the Rule of Law in Slovenia in the Context of Central and Eastern Europe, J. Crim. Justice & Security, 2013, p. 175-190.

14 See the establishment of Cooperation and Verification Mechanism, an unprecedented rule of law monitoring mechanism, to assess rule of law deficiencies in Romania and Bulgaria that has become effective upon their accession to the EU. *D. Kochenov/L. Pech*, Monitoring and Enforcement of the Rule of Law in the EU: Rhetoric and Reality, European Constitutional Law Review, 2015, p. 512-40; *M. A. Vachudova/A. Spendzharova*, The EU's Cooperation and Verification Mechanism: Fighting Corruption in Bulgaria and Romania after EU Accession, SIEPS European Policy Analysis, 2012. Cf. also contributions in *A. von Bogdandy/P. Sonnevend (eds.)*, Constitutional Crisis in the European Constitutional Area: Theory, Law and Politics in Hungary and Romania, 2015.

15 Most notable example is the Haider case in Austria in 2000, but cf. also policy shifts in French mainstream parties in reaction to an electorate increase of Le Pen's National Front, France's response to 2005 ethnic riots, its 2012 policies concerning Roma minority, or borders' restrictions with Italy in response to immigration influx. For Austria, see contributions in *R. Wodak/A. Pelinka* (eds.), The Haider Phenomenon in Austria, 2009. For France see e.g. *B. J. Kelley/C. J. Edwards*, France's Roma Row: An Examination of the French Government's Violation of EU and International Law, Willamette J. Int'l L. & Dis. Res., 2017, p. 169-210; *M. des Neiges Léonard*, The Effects of Political Rhetoric on the Rise of Legitimized Racism in France: The Case of the 2005 French Riots, Critical Sociology, 2016, p. 1087-1107.

16 E.g. Italy in Berlusconi's era and constraints on media plurality. Cf. *P. Ginsborg*, Silvio Berlusconi: Television, Power and Patrimony, 2005. Also, the Czech Republic's experience has shown several instances in which Article 2 TEU values were compromised over the last five years or so. If put together, these incidences reveal cracks in a liberal democracy wall: midnight amnesty of President Klaus preventing prosecution of large-scale economic crimes of 1990s; his unilateral stalling of ratification of Lisbon Treaty and refusal to ratify the Article 136 TFEU Amendment resulting alongside the amnesty controversy into a high treason indictment against him; President Zeman's selective refusal to appoint university professors; his tampering with constitutional process of government formation in 2013, bypassing the Parliament; a dubious economic and political influence of China and Russia in the Czech Republic; the landslide victory of populist ANO party in 2017 parliamentary elections, likely to form a minority government supported by an odd coalition of the Communists and the far-right SPD.

II. Deconstructing the Sanction Provision of Article 7

The third paragraph of Article 7 states that “the Council, acting by a qualified majority, may decide to *suspend certain of the rights deriving from the application of the Treaties* to the Member State in question, *including the voting rights of the representative of the government of that Member State in the Council*. In doing so, the Council shall take into account *the possible consequences of such a suspension on the rights and obligations of natural and legal persons*. The obligations of the Member State in question under this Treaty shall in any case continue to be binding on that State.”

Only *certain* rights can be suspended. If all the rights of a deviating Member State are suspended, the result would equal to expulsion of the state from the EU. This scenario is not legally possible.

Rights can only be *suspended*. Therefore, the suspended rights must be restorable. The sanctions placed on a deviating state cannot deprive the state from exercising these rights after the sanctions are lifted.

Only rights “*deriving from the application of the Treaties* to the Member State” in question can be suspended, that is only the rights that EU membership has created are subject to the provision of Article 7. From the general definition of “application of the Treaties” (in connection to structural features of EU law, such as direct effect and supremacy) it can be assumed that Article 7 also includes the rights afforded by secondary EU law.

The requirement that “*the possible consequences of such suspension on the rights and obligations of natural and legal persons*” must be taken into account, limits the range and depth of sanctions. The words “take into account” direct the attention to proportionality, but only in respect to “rights and obligations of natural and legal persons.” From all the possible sanctions that satisfy the desired goal, those sanctions that have the least negative consequences for the rights and obligations of natural and legal persons will be preferred. Besides this special requirement of proportionality, the general principle of proportionality will apply (see part V).

Article 7 states that the obligations in the Treaty remain binding. A reciprocity recourse is not possible. For instance, withdrawing disbursement of EU funds to deviating state does not mean that the sanctioned state can stop paying its share into the EU budget.

Voting rights suspension is only one of the possible sanctions. The range of sanctions available are limited by the requirement that the object of sanctions must be suspendible rights derived from the application of the Treaty.

Whose rights may be suspended? The provision of Article 7 para. 3 TEU does not refer to “Member State’s rights”, but to rights deriving from the Treaty. Who the beneficiary of the rights is, does not matter. It could be either a Member State or individuals. Article 7 therefore allows for the suspension of individual rights. A corrective, I will introduce it in the next section, is that the suspension of rights must be able to alter the objectionable policy of target state. This imposes limits on the choice of rights that can be suspended.

A suspension of rights derived from the application of EU Treaties (that is afforded by the existence of the Treaties) is only possible on the basis of the Treaties, and the secondary law authorized by the Treaties. Of course, Article 7 TEU is only one of many instances where the Treaties permit sanctions or suspension of certain rights.[17] The point being that the Article 7 TEU procedure cannot be substituted by coordinated bilateral or multilateral actions that are not authorized by the Treaties and that have the effect of suspending rights derived from the Treaties. In such cases, the sanctioned state could bring an infringement action against the senders of sanctions.[18]

III. Purpose of Article 7

1. A Sanction Regime

Article 7 does not speak of 'sanctions.' The term in international relations theory, as well as in international law scholarship, has never been meant to serve as a punishment. It refers to a policy of the sender state to alter, through a negative incentive, the behavior of the target state.[19] The general understanding of the scholarship on Article 7 and rule of law seems to be the same. The aim of the mechanism is to alter the behavior of a deviating Member State. In this context, the use of the term 'sanction' in connection to Article 7 is warranted. The term 'suspension of rights' simply suggests a limitation as to what kind of sanctions can be imposed.

2. Limited Reading of Article 7: Insulation of Deviating State from EU Decision-Making

The comprehension of Article 7, including its legislative history and Copenhagen criteria origins,[20] is not straightforward. The only example of possible sanctions mentioned by para. 3 of Article 7 is a suspension of voting rights. We may rea-

17 Most importantly Art. 260 TFEU. Cf. also sanctions within the EMU – Art. 126/11 TFEU concerning excessive government deficit authorizes sanctions ranging from "inviting" the EIB to reconsider its lending policy to imposing fines; the Excessive Imbalance Procedure may lead to gradual sanctions, ranging from an interest-bearing deposit to annual fines; etc.

18 Several commentators urged Austria to turn to the CJEU against concerted sanctions imposed by fourteen Member States, either dissimulating that their decision was in fact a decision of the Council or pleading breach of loyalty clause by the fourteen Member States towards Austria. The Austrian government decided to wait for an early end of the sanctions rather than to escalate the issue through a legal battle. See *G. Winkler*, Europa quo vadis. Die Anatomie eines europäischen Willküraktes, Zeitschrift für öffentliches Recht, 2000, p. 231-68, 259; *E. Regan*, Are EU Sanctions Against Austria Legal?, Zeitschrift für öffentliches Recht, 2000, p. 323-36, 331.

19 *G. C. Hufbauer/J. J. Schott/K. A. Elliot/B. Oegg*, Economic Sanctions reconsidered, 3rd ed., 2007, 65 ff.

20 *W. Sadurski*, Adding Bite to a Bark: The Story of Article 7, E.U. Enlargement, and JorgJörg Haider, Colum. J. Eur. L., 2010, p. 385-426.

sonably construe a limited understanding of Article 7 as a mechanism to insulate the EU from the impact of a Member State that deviates from the common values.[21] The objective is that the EU functioning, mainly its decision-making, is not compromised by the participation of the deviating state, given that the Member State governments are EU co-legislators and sometime sole legislators. Such comprehension of Article 7 would have a profound impact on the range of possible sanctions. The principle of proportionality would require only such sanctions that are necessary to insulate EU decision-making from the influence of a deviating state that attempts to expand its different values on the EU as a whole. The relative decision-making power of such state would have to be taken into account alongside, perhaps, its policy preferences at the EU level and coalition potential.

3. Expansive reading of Article 7: Protection of EU Citizens

Three structural arguments can be made in favor of an expansive reading of Article 7. Firstly, the EU relies, in a vast majority of cases, on Member State institutions for implementation, application, and enforcement of EU law. In order for these institutions to fulfil their European mandates, they must act in accordance with the values contained in Article 2 TEU. State institutions apply and enforce EU law in situations that often involve other Member States' natural and legal persons. Both in Hungary and Poland, the objectionable policy has included an attack on the independency of courts. In Hungary, several instances were recorded of pressure on the judiciary to alter its decisions involving interpretation and application of EU law.

Secondly, the original aim of the Article 7 mechanism must have been to eventually resolve the deadlock. The suspension of rights is not intended to insulate the EU indefinitely from a deviating Member State, but to pressure the state to alter its objectionable policy. The term 'suspension of rights' itself suggests temporality.

Thirdly and most importantly, the EU has a constitutional quality. Not because the Court of Justice said so, but because it has been practiced as such by the vast majority of officials for a considerable time. Scholars differ in assessing the depth of such constitutional quality, but nevertheless, the majority would agree that the values of Article 2 TEU create normative expectations for EU citizens, including those with Hungarian or Polish citizenship. Hence, Article 7 protects, to a certain degree depending on our understanding of how deep the EU constitutional quality goes, these citizens against a Member State's parliamentary majority that encroaches on the values of Article 2 TEU.

21 Cf. *J.-W. Müller*, Should the EU Protect Democracy and the Rule of Law inside Member States?, European Law Journal 2015, p. 141-160, 144.

IV. Political Theory of Sanctions and Article 7

1. Mechanisms Through Which Sanctions Operate

The expansive reading of Article 7 suggests that the sanctions are meant to achieve the same aim as international sanctions; that is to eventually change the objectionable behavior of target state. Crawford and Klotz divide the tools through which sanctions aim to influence the target state's actions into four categories: normative communication, compellance, resource denial, and political fracture.[22] By imposing sanctions, the sender states morally disapprove the target state's policy and hope that the domestic pressure would force the state authorities to change the objectionable policy (normative communication).[23] The logic behind the compellance is that by imposing costs on the state's objectionable policy, the cost-benefit analysis would prompt the rational state elite to change their policy. The resource denial mechanism operates by targeting resources that are needed to sustain a state's objectionable behavior. Finally, political fracture is the most intrusive mechanism. Here, the objective of the sanctions is to function as a catalyst of a legitimacy crisis. The crisis should stimulate political opposition, create ruptures in the regime base and eventually bring a switch of a part of regime supporters to an opposition, resulting in a change of regime.

2. From State as a Black Box to in-depth Analysis of its Political, Economic, and Social Structures

The move to targeted (or smart) sanctions in the 1990s was not originally driven by the desire to increase the effectiveness of sanctions, but to minimize their impact on the population of target state.[24] The United Nations shifted their focus towards individuals and entities whose actions threatened international peace and security, and towards the economic sectors that made these actions possible. Early data indicated that targeted sanctions were, in fact, less effective than comprehensive sanctions. The demand for more creative sanctioning mechanisms that would work against non-state transnationally-operating actors prompted by the 9/11 terrorist attacks on the United States has brought new impetus to sanctions research. Traditionally IR theories failed in explaining how sanctions do (not) work, and offered limited counsel to the decision-makers that devised targeted sanctions. Their focus on aggregated state interests (simplified in fact into leader's preferences)

22 *N. C. Crawford/A. Klotz*, How Sanctions Work: A Framework for Analysis, in: N.C. Crawford/A. Klotz (eds.), How Sanctions Work: Lessons from South Africa, 1999, p. 25 ff.

23 Cf. *F. Giumelli*, The Success of Sanctions: Lesson Learned from the EU Experience, 2014, p. 12 and 135 ff.

24 The international public outcry over humanitarian consequences of comprehensive sanctions imposed on Iraq following its invasion to Kuwait in 1990 made the United Nations to rethink its approach. Since 1994 no new sanctions imposed by the UN have included comprehensive economic sanctions. See *A. Pellet/A. Miron*, Sanctions, in: R. Wolfrum (ed.), The Max Planck Encyclopedia of Public International Law, 2012, Vol. IX, 1, 6-7, para 29 ff.

has been inadequate for projecting sanctions' impact in the internal affairs of target states.

The liberal theory's most promising contribution to sanction research is coalitional liberalism, according to which a state's international behavior is a result of interactions among domestic interest groups.[25] It relies predominantly on the compellance rationale following the assumption of the liberal theory that rational utility-maximizing actors would change (or would be forced to change by a domestic alliance that underpins the regime) an objectionable state's policy if the costs of keeping the policy imposed by the sanctions outweigh its benefits.[26]

A rational utility-maximizing actor is also at the center of public choice theory of sanctions. According to the public choice theory, the public interest is a result of the aggregated individual interests and must therefore be Pareto improving. It is unlikely that a new policy will be favorable to all, therefore concessions to opposing individuals are made.[27] For sanctions research, it implies that the objectionable policy has a definable structure of support set in the marketplace. The theory shifts the focus from the government elite to various kinds of domestic groups (whose preferences are, again, defined as aggregated individual preferences) and their capacity to influence government policy. Major intrastate actors are defined as rent-seeking groupings of individuals (various producers' and consumers' groups, state employees, etc.).[28] These social groups compete to influence state policies. "Because they derive differential utility from any given policy, they have different 'demand curves'."[29] When an equilibrium is reached, a policy is supplied. Sanctions must be designed in such a way that their effect shift the demand curves of the competing social groups and set a new equilibrium in which the objectionable policy is replaced by a new one.[30]

One of the major flaws of the public choice theory of sanctions is its perception of state as neutral broker between interest groups. In fact, these groups do not have an equal access to state. Also, the public choice theorists underestimate ideological drivers of policy formation since their intellectual framework treats ideology simply as goods exchangeable in the marketplace.

Although policies depending on shifting demand curves shall be inherently unstable, empirical research has shown that institutions were able to produce stable policies. Shepsle calls it a 'structure-induced equilibrium': what public choice

25 *A. Moravcsik*, Taking Preferences Seriously: A Liberal Theory of International Politics, International Organizations, 1997, p. 513-53.

26 *E. Solingen*, Introduction: The domestic Distributional Effects of Sanctions and Positive Inducements, in: E. Solingen (ed.), Sanctions, Statecraft, and Nuclear Proliferation, 2012.

27 *J. M. Buchanan/G. Tullock*, The Calculus of Consent: Logical Foundations of Constitutional Democracy, 1962. Cf. also *R. Nozick*, R., Anarchy, State, and Utopia, 2001 (on incorporating the independents).

28 *W. H. Kaempfner/A. D. Lowenberg*, International Economic Sanctions: A Public Choice Approach, 1992. *T. C. Morgan*, Clinton's Chinese Puzzle: Domestic Politics and the Effectiveness of Economic Sanctions, Issues and Studies, 1995, p. 19-45.

29 *E. Jones*, Societies Under Siege: Exploring How International Economic Sanctions (Do Not) Work, 2015, p. 26.

30 *W. H. Kaempfner/A. D. Lowenberg*, The Theory of International Economic Sanctions: A Public Choice Approach, American Economic Review, 1988, p. 786-93, 790-2.

theorists consider free competition of social groups is in fact largely defined by an overall structure of decision-making process.[31] Consequently, attention must be drawn to how actors design "institutions to secure mutual gains, and how those institutions change or persist over time."[32] For sanctions theory, it means to define structure-induced equilibria in different institutional settings and arrive at reasonable amount of regime types. The regime types differ according to how broad coalition they need for sustaining themselves. For instance, democracies shall be more vulnerable to sanctions than autocracies because they involve broader coalitions.[33] According to the institutionalists, leaders pursue minimum-winning coalitions, and a country's politics will define how broad such coalition must be. Autocracies' lack of representative institutions narrows down the minimum-winning coalition because most people are prevented from influencing the government's decisions. Therefore, autocratic regimes can withstand sanctions by diverting scarce resources from the general public to their narrow supporting coalition.[34]

Institutionalist's' attempts to refine their crude democracy-autocracy dichotomy into a more nuance categorization have largely failed on empirical grounds.[35] For example, emerging illiberal democracies within the EU can sustain considerable outside pressure due to broad popular support, while some traditional democracies rely on increasingly narrower political coalitions due to the fact that a considerable part of the political space is 'blocked' by protest parties. An evaluation of institutional structure cannot predict how sanctions will affect a regime without taking into account societal, religious, and economic structures, resources availability, foreign partnerships, etc.

The insights of coalitional liberalism, public choice theory of sanctions, and regime-oriented institutionalism has been synthesized by Blanchard and Ripsman[36] in an approach reviving Max Weber's assumptions on state-society relationships.[37] For neo-Weberians, the state is not a neutral broker that mediates between the interests of different social groups. There is a substantial capacity of states to "implement official goals, especially over the actual or potential opposition of powerful social groups or in the face of recalcitrant socioeconomic cir-

31 *K. A. Shepsle*, Institutional Equilibrium and Equilibrium Institutions, in: H. Weisberg (ed.), Political Science; The Science of Politics, 1986, p. 51-81.

32 *M. A. Pollack*, The New Institutionalisms and European Integration, in: A. Wiener/T. Diez, (eds.), European Integration Theory, 2nd ed., 2009, p. 125-43, 126.

33 *S. Allen*, The Determinants of Economic Sanctions Success and Failure, International Interactions, 2005, p. 117-38.

34 *D. Lektzian/M. Souva*, An Institutional Theory of Sanctions Onset and Success, Journal of Conflict Resolution, 2007, p. 848-71, 852-3.

35 As Jones points out, the U.S. president can be elected by just one quarter of the population, while Cuba's Castro regime have survived US sanctions only by mobilizing enormous popular support. *E. Jones* 2015, (fn. 29,28), p. 31.

36 *J.-M. Blanchard/N. M. Ripsman*, Asking the Right Question: When Do Economic Sanctions Work Best?, Security Studies, 1999, p. 219-53; *J.-M. Blanchard/N. M. Ripsman*, A Political Theory of Economic Statecraft, Foreign Policy Analysis, 2008, p. 371-98.

37 *M. Weber*, Wirtschaft und Gesellschaft, 1922. For English translation of Part I see *M. Weber*, The theory of social and economic organisation, 1947.

cumstances."[38] Applied to sanctions design, senders of sanctions must analyze domestic political institutions and structures of the target state to realize which groups have access to state and which groups' interests the state can ignore.[39] Three institutional attributes determine the robustness of state autonomy or 'stateness': decision-making autonomy ("structural ability of the foreign policy executive to select and implement policies" despite domestic opposition), state capacity ("policy resources available […] to co-opt or coerce key societal groups"), and legitimacy (degree to which domestic groups defer to the leader's right to rule, i.e. his/her authority).[40] The higher the stateness, the more the state is able to diffuse, divert, or overcome the impact of sanctions.

Neo-Weberians have been criticized for approaching the state autonomy in isolation from state-society dynamics. What they understand as capacity or resources of the state *per se* are in fact the results of a lengthy power struggle among various social forces within the state. For the state is a "complex and constituted set of relationships between frameworks of political authority and the international political economy, domestic social forces, and the broader ideational notions of authority[...]".[41] The social power relations are dynamic, allowing for new patterns to emerge. This approach builds on Gramscian state theory.[42] "[S]tate power is fundamentally a social relation. That is, rather than existing as a 'thing' independent of society, state institutions and capacities are condensations of historically specific, dynamically evolving relationships between social forces."[43] The ruling elites must forge relatively broad coalitions of socio-political forces to capture state power. Subsequently, dominant coalitions reconfigure state institutions and the allocation of resources to maintain the power. Each coalition is composed of a number of groups, which may form new coalitions or shift their allegiance to opposition coalitions if their interests are harmed by sanctions.

Jones illustrates how sanctions work within the Gramscian framework in an example of South Africa during the apartheid regime. Sanctions at first helped the ruling elite to hold their power. The reason was that arms and oil embargoes pushed the state-controlled economy to develop new industrial capacities, through which the ruling coalition could co-opt rising social forces. Only the economic downturn in the 1980s forced the state to let the business outgrow state patronage, who, as sanctions bit, realized that it was in their best interest to end the racial-social conflict.[44]

38 *T. Skocpol*, Bringing the State Back In: Strategies of Analysis in Current Research, in: P. Evans/D. Rueschemeyer/T. Skocpol (eds.), Bringing the State Back In, 1985, p. 3-37, 9.

39 *J.-M. Blanchard/N.M. Ripsman* 1999, (fn. 36.35).

40 Id. at 378-9.

41 *K. Jayasuriya*, Beyond Institutional Fetishism: From the Developmental to the Regulatory State, New Political Economy, 2005, p. 381-7, 383.

42 *A. Gramsci*, Prison Notebooks (transl. by J. Buttigieg/A. Callari), Vol. 1-3, 2007; *N. Poulantzas*, State, Power, Socialism, 1976; *B. Jessop*, State Power: A Strategic-Relational Approach, 2008.

43 *E. Jones* 2015, (fn. 29, 28), p. 39.

44 Id. at 10 and 52 ff.

The overview of major sanctions theories developed from international relations, economic, and political science theories indicates the specificity of sanction research. Devising successful sanctions requires a complex understanding of the material, institutional, and ideational bases of power. Bare knowledge about intrastate decision-making processes is insufficient. The challenge is to locate the weakest link in a coalition supporting the state's objectionable policy, with the potential to change the balance of power, and devise incentives that would direct the behavior of the selected group in a desired way. Jones proposes to proceed in three steps: first, to identify socio-political coalitions contesting state power and the political economy context that structures them; second, to assess the economic impacts of sanctions and their distribution across societal groups; and third, to examine the strategic response of key societal forces and their political consequences.[45]

V. Sanctioning Principles

The EU institutional framework aims at promoting human dignity, freedom, democracy, equality, the rule of law and respect for human rights (values).[46] According to the Treaty, these values are best attained in a "society in which pluralism, non-discrimination, tolerance, justice, solidarity and equality between women and men prevail" (structural conditions).[47] When these values are seriously and persistently breached over a period of several domestic elections, it indicates that the safeguards built into a liberal-democratic system failed, and that the structural conditions have been deformed. Sanctions imposed under Article 7 must therefore aim at reforming the structural conditions that allow the society to realize the full potential of the values.

1. Democracy-inbound

The weakening of the fundamental structures of a liberal-democratic state, such as independent and values-oriented constitutional review of executive and legislative actions, objective reporting by media independent of the government, and critical scientific research, impedes the voters' ability to form an informed opinion within the boundaries of a liberal-philosophy framework. The example of Hungary and Poland reveals a pattern for dismantling a pluralist system. After a landslide victory in general elections, the winning party elite controls both the executive and the legislative bodies. The constitutional court becomes the first target; then comes a subjugation of news media; and finally, a containment of NGOs and universities, control of foreign capital flow into political activities and the establish-

45 Id. at 42-46.
46 Art. 3 (1) TEU and Art. 13 TEU in connection with Art. 2 TEU.
47 Art. 2 TEU.

ment of political patronage over major domestic economic actors. This process disrupts 'democratic equality' understood as an equal opportunity of political actors for influencing the electorate. The first sanctioning principle, which I call 'democracy-inbound', requires the sanctions to aim at restoring democratic equality. The focal point, when devising sanctions, must be on democracy, not on the rule of law. The rule-of-law approach to the problem, for instance in Poland, blinds us to see the roots of the deviation.[48] We shall not ask how the assault on constitutional court have occurred, but why.[49]

2. *Effectiveness*

The principle of the effectiveness of law is one of the cornerstones of the CJEU's jurisprudence.[50] The Treaty further emphasizes the efficient functioning of EU institutions and the effectiveness of their policies and actions.[51] An effective sanction design must fulfil two goals: first, the EU must opt for such sanctions that are able, through a chain of actions, to alter the objectionable policy of target state. To achieve that, the EU must employ a state of the art sanction theory and apply it on the target state's power structures. Second, the principle of effectiveness requires a thorough examination of all the options available to the target state that may neutralize the sanctions' impact. Sanctioned states have proved to be creative in busting its sanctions. Third states and individuals line up, immediately after the introduction of sanctions, to benefit from a premium the sanctioned state must pay (either in economic or political terms) to bypass the sanctions.[52] For instance, cutting EU funds to Hungary may create opportunities for Russia to increase its financial and political presence. Russia has been gradually filling the void created by the rupture between Hungary and the EU, using the far-right Jobbik party, or an expansion of Paks nuclear plant,[53] eventually overcoming Orbán's initial reluctance to engage in closer relations.[54]

48 Despite the Article 7 debate being understood as a 'great rule of law debate', a good number of scholars perceive the rule of law in material, not formal sense, with democracy being one of the yardsticks.

49 Then we see a very different story, a remake of 'midnight judges' story during the transition of power from Federalists to Jeffersonian Democrats. This, however, does not legitimize in any way the response of Kaczynski's regime.

50 See e.g. *A. von Bogdandy*, Founding Principles, in: A. von Bogdandy/J. Bast (eds.), Principles of European Constitutional Law, 2nd ed., 2009, p. 11-54, 29 ff.; *L.* Tichý/*M.* Potacs/*T.* Dumbrovský (eds.), Effet Utile, 2014.

51 TEU Preamble; Art. 13 TEU.

52 Bryan Early gives an example of sanctions against Iran. When the United States seemed to finally succeed in isolating Iran from the global financial system helped by the EU cutting Iran's access to SWIFT, Iran started selling its natural gas to Turkey in return for Turkish lira, for which gold was bought in Turkey and shipped to Dubai. In order to comply with UAE's customs rules, gold bricks were brought into Dubai by individuals. For instance, "$1.45 bn of Turkey's August [2012] gold exports were shipped through the customs office at Ataturk airport's passenger lounge." In Dubai, the gold vanished in over 8.000 Iranian-owned business and 'clandestinely' (over 200 ships leaving daily) shipped into Iran. *B. R. Early*, Busted Sanctions: Explaining Why Economic Sanctions Fail, 2015, 1-2.

53 In March 2017, Russia announced it would finance in credit 100% of the costs (around €14bn). *A. Byrne/N. Buckley*, EU approves Hungary's Russian-financed nuclear station, Financial Times, March 6, 2017, at https://www.ft.com/content/0478d38a-028a-11e7-ace0-1ce02ef0def9.

54 Orbán, alongside Czech President Zeman, emerged as the most vocal critics of EU sanctions against Russia.

3. Proportionality

Sanctions under Article 7 are subject to the general and special obligations of proportionality. The general three-part proportionality test guides the intellectual process of devising sanctions: the measure is suitable to change the objectionable policy of the target state; the objectionable policy cannot be changed by a less intrusive measure (the measure is necessary); and even if there is no less intrusive mean of achieving the aim, the measure does not have an excessive effect on the target state's rights.[55]

Senders of sanctions also have a special obligation of proportionality. Article 7 requires the Council to "take into account the possible consequences of such a suspension on the rights and obligations of natural and legal persons." The special obligation qualifies the third part of general proportionality test. Also, since the provision does not oblige the Council to do everything possible to avoid negative consequences for natural and legal persons, but only to take them into account, the construction of the provision suggests that the senders of sanctions *may*, on the one hand, target individuals (natural and legal persons)[56] and, on the other hand must limit possible *collateral* damage that the sanctions will inevitably cause to persons that are not the direct object of sanctions.

4. Beneficiary-focus

From the extensive reading of Article 7, which I mentioned in part III, it follows that the purpose of Article 7 is to ensure that exercise of public power within the territory of the EU respects the fundamental values listed in Article 2 TEU. Many decisions of national authorities have effect in other EU Member States without further conditions, from judicial decisions in civil and criminal matters, including issuance of a European Arrest Warrant, to administrative decisions, certifications of quality and qualification, etc. Natural and legal persons residing in the EU, who are not citizens or entities incorporated in the deviating state, might be subject to the decisions of public authorities of such state on a regular basis and to an extent incomparable with other regions. The application of both EU law and national law, their effects, and their subjects are intertwined. It is almost impossible to quarantine a deviating Member State and leave it to 'its' citizens to deal with the problem.

The ultimate beneficiaries of Article 7 are therefore natural and legal persons, in particular EU citizens and EU incorporated firms, regardless of their Member State citizenship or residence. They legitimately expect that fundamental stan-

55 *AG Van Gerven*, Opinion of 11 June 1991 in Case C-159/90 (SPUC/ Grogan). Cf. also *G. de Búrca*, The Principle of Proportionality and its Application in EC Law, Yearbook of European Law, 1993, p. 105-50, 113; *P. Craig*, EU Administrative Law, 2012, 2nd ed., ch. 19-20.

56 Cf. *W. M. Reisman/D. L. Stevick*, The Applicability of International Law Standards to United Nations Economic Sanctions Programmes, European journal of international law, 1998, p. 86-141, 129 ff. (functioning of principles of necessity and proportionality in international law).

dards in the exercise of public power anywhere in the EU are adhered to. The beneficiary-focus principle requires, first, to realize who is the beneficiary of the sanction provision of Article 7, and, second, to devise sanctions in the way in which they are capable to better the position of beneficiary. It is misleading to ask whether Article 7 should protect democracy inside a Member State and whether it shall protect, for instance, Polish citizens against its government. As long as a Member State does not leave the EU by way of Article 50 TEU procedure, it is a *federal* matter (due to structural reasons mentioned above) to ensure that the exercise of public authority anywhere in the Union, and on any level of government (subject to subsidiarity)[57] is in compliance with the basic standards that follow from the values listed in Article 2 TEU.

VI. EU Institutional Architecture for Sanctioning

Since the introduction of CFSP in the Maastricht Treaty, the European Union has accumulated considerable experience with sanctioning third states, non-state groups, and individuals. Currently, the EU consolidated sanction list contains some 40 states and a number of terrorist organizations and individuals using various tools from arms embargoes, embargoes on nuclear and oil-extracting technologies, trade restrictions, freezing of funds and economic resources, travel bans, to embargoes on goods that can be used for human trafficking or illegal exports.[58] A dedicated body of the Commission, the Service for Foreign Policy Instruments (FPI), is responsible for preparing a proposal for regulation imposing sanctions for the Council, discussing the proposal with Member States' experts,[59] and facilitating sanctions' implementation within the EU, including issues of interpretation raised by economic operators, and reviewing of listings on the sanction lists.[60]
The FPI's know-how in sanctioning must be combined with the expertise of the European Union Agency for Fundamental Rights (FRA) and to some extent, its predecessors, the European Monitoring Centre for Racism and Xenophobia and the EU Network of Independent Experts on Fundamental Rights.[61] In any stage of the Article 7 process, the Agency is empowered to provide the EU institutions

57 All Member States institutions are bound by Article 2 TEU, which must form a part of constitutional courts' review standard. Only when a Member State's highest judiciary fails to correct a structural deviation from Article 2 values, the federal organ will step in. Subsidiarity is embedded in Article 7 by way of the threshold (serious and persistent breach) which must be surpassed before sanctions are imposed. Once the threshold is surpassed, subsidiarity does not apply anymore. Therefore, subsidiarity is not one of the sanctioning principles.

58 EU Restrictive measures (sanctions) in force (Regulations based on Art. 215 TFEU and Decisions adopted in the framework of the Common Foreign and Security Policy) as of August, 4, 2017, at https://eeas.europa.eu/sites/eeas/files/restrictive_measures-2017-08-04.pdf.

59 RELEX Working Party. In 2004, a special formation of RELEX working party for sanctions was created to share best practice and to revise and implement common guidelines for EU sanction regimes.

60 Council Regulation (EC) No 881/2002 of 27 May 2002 imposing certain specific restrictive measures directed against certain persons and entities associated with Usama bin Laden, the Al-Qaida network and the Taliban.

61 The Network existed between 2002-2006. However, it has been criticized for ideological biases, its modus operandi, and lack of genuine legal expertise.

and the Member States with assistance and expertise. The question of the FRA's competence in regards to Article 7 has been contentious.[62] The Agency's jurisdiction is limited to assistance and expertise relating to fundamental rights when EU institutions or Member States implement the EU law "in order to support them when they take measures or formulate courses of action [...] to fully respect fundamental rights."[63] Article 7 gives the EU the competence to initiate an Article 7 procedure by a *reasoned* opinion, to *determine* that there is a risk of serious breach of Article 2 TEU values, to *determine* that there has been breach of the values, and consequently *sanction* a Member State that breaches these values. These steps are an implementation of EU law involving fundamental rights (the ones that are at risk of breach or being breached, and the fundamental rights that might be affected by sanctions). The Agency is therefore empowered to assist the EU institutions with collecting and analyzing data on fundamental rights protection in the Member State in question and supply evidence on fundamental rights violations that might indicate a clear risk of a serious breach of fundamental rights and, subsequently, a serious and persistent breach of fundamental rights corresponding to Article 2 TEU values (access to justice, gender and minority discrimination, right to vote, etc.).[64] In the sanctioning phase of Article 7 procedure, the Agency can assist the Council with conducting research on structural problems that have made the breach of fundamental rights possible and indicate possible ways to correct the situation, as well as pointing out consequences of sanctions for the fundamental rights of natural and legal persons.[65]

The EU may also build on its experience with evaluating state compliance with Article 2 TEU values during the accession process with Central and Eastern European states,[66] and in particular the experience with the Mechanism for Cooperation and Verification for Bulgaria and Romania that provides for post-accession reviews of progress of intrastate reforms of judicial and law enforcement institutions and processes.[67] The European Parliament has repeatedly called for the introduction of regular assessments of all Member States' compliance with EU fun-

62 *W. Sadurski* 2010, (fn. 20,19), p. 419 ff.

63 Art. 2 of the Council Regulation (EC) No 168/2007 of 15 February 2007 establishing a European Union Agency for Fundamental Rights.

64 Art. 2 TEU lists "human rights" as one of the values. All the other values such as democracy, rule of law, equality, etc. are also translatable into fundamental rights.

65 The FRA specific objectives are set every five years by the Council on a proposal from the Commission and after consulting the EP. For the current framework see the Council Decision (EU) 2017/2269 of 7 December 2017 establishing a Multiannual Framework for the European Union Agency for Fundamental Rights for 2018-2022, OJ L 326, 1. The Council missed the opportunity to involve the FRA explicitly into the Article 7 process.

66 Art. 49 TEU. *C. Hillion*, The Copenhagen Criteria and their Progeny, in: C. Hillion (ed.), EU Enlargement: A Legal Approach, 2004, p. 1-22.

67 Arts. 37-38 of the Act of Accession of Bulgaria and Romania. *M. A. Vachudova/A. Spendzharova*, The EU's Cooperation and Verification Mechanism: Fighting Corruption in Bulgaria and Romania after EU Accession, European Policy Analysis, SIEPS, 2012.

damental values.[68] The introduction of the EU Framework to strengthen the Rule of Law has brought some flexibility into the Article 7 process (although it is not its formal part).[69] In the case of Hungary and Poland, the introduction of the Framework might have been self-defeating since it has signaled certain quandary on the side of EU institutions concerning the use of Article 7, regardless the fact that the latter procedure was eventually initiated.[70] It may prove useful for the future. By putting the Commission in charge, the Framework may help with gathering evidence in cooperation with the FRA, the European Parliament, and the Venice Commission,[71] identifying the causes of systemic problems in deviating state(s), and increasing European public awareness[72] that could place pressure on Member States reluctant to support the Article 7 process. The Commission, as one of the initiators of Article 7, may serve as a prosecutor that submits a well build case against a Member State to the Council.

EU institutional architecture for sanctioning must improve its review process for the purposes of Article 7 sanctions. In the area of external sanctioning, targeted individuals and entities are notified by letter or by means of a notice in the EU Official Journal. They may submit a request, supported by evidence, to the Council to reconsider their listing, and eventually file an annulment action against the listing decision before the General Court. The Court of Justice repeatedly criti-

68 European Parliament resolution of 3 July 2013 on the situation of fundamental rights: standards and practices in Hungary (based on the Tavares Report); European Parliament resolution of 27 February 2014 on the situation of fundamental rights in the European Union (based on Louis Michel Report); European Parliament resolution of 12 March 2014 on evaluation of justice in relation to criminal justice and the rule of law (based on Kinga Göncz Report); European Parliament resolution of 10 June 2015 on the situation in Hungary; European Parliament resolution of 8 September 2015 on the situation of fundamental rights in the European Union.

69 Communication from the Commission to the European Parliament and the Council, A new EU Framework to strengthen the Rule of Law, COM (2014) 158 final.

70 The first Commission Recommendation (EU) 2016/1374 of 27 July 2016 regarding the rule of law in Poland, OJ L 217, 53 and the second Commission Recommendation (EU) 2017/146 of 21 December 2016, OJ L 22, 65 have not made Poland to rectify the structural problems. The Commission concluded that "there is a situation of a systemic threat to the rule of law in Poland" (Rec. 2016/1374, par. 72). In July 2017, the Commission sent already a third set of recommendations to Poland (Commission Recommendation (EU) 2017/1520 of 26 July 2017, OJ L 228, 19) and threatened it with initiating the Article 7 procedure if the situation were not to improve within a month." Cf. also European Parliament resolution condemning the "serious violations" of the rule of law in Poland and calling for initiation of the Article 7 procedure (European Parliament resolution of 15 November 2017 on the situation of the rule of law and democracy in Poland). The Commission finally started the procedure in December 2017.
In case of Hungary, the Commission has not even initiated a dialogue under its Rule of Law Framework, despite being called to do so repeatedly by the European Parliament (e.g. EP resolutions of 10 June 2015 and 16 December 2015 on the situation in Hungary).

71 The Opinion of the Venice Commission no. 833/2015 on Amendments to the Act of 25 June 2015 on the Constitutional Tribunal of Poland, March 11, 2016 has supplied an independent (understand outside-EU) legal in-depth analysis of the rule of law shortcomings in Poland that aligned with the conclusions of the European Commission. Cf. also Opinion of the Venice Commission no. 889/2017 on the Draft Law on the Transparency of Organizations Receiving Support from Abroad, Hungary, June 20 2017. "For a cooperation between the FRA and the Council of Europe in general see the 2008 Agreement between the European Community and the Council of Europe on cooperation between the European Union Agency for Fundamental Rights and the Council of Europe (OJ L 186, 7)".

72 That presupposes access of the public to the outcomes of the dialogue between the Commission and a state under review. In the first employment of the new Framework, the Commission, however, kept its Rule of Law Opinion on the situation in Poland of June 1, 2016, a result of an "intensive dialogue" with Polish authorities initiated in January 2016, confidential. Press Release, Commission adopts Rule of Law Opinion on the situation in Poland, June 1, 2016, at http://europa.eu/rapid/press-release_IP-16-2015_en.htm.

cized EU institutions for their failure to develop sufficient due process standards in the instances where individuals are targeted. In the 2014 decision in *Yusef v Commission*, the General Court held that the Commission failed to follow the procedures set down in the *Kadi* cases.[73] In particular, the Commission bound itself to the findings of the U.N. Sanctions Committee, instead of reviewing the findings independently.[74] Albeit in sanctioning under Article 7, the issue of UN-EU jurisdiction overlap is obsolete, the anti-terrorism sanctions listing cases set the standard for targeted sanctions against individuals as far as the scope of evidence, its publicity, burden of proof, and right of rebuttal are concerned.

1. What Rights Can Be Suspended?

Sanctions can take myriads of forms. The Union may, for instance, blacklist individuals and entities that form economic bases of deviating regimes and ban them from participating in EU co-funded projects, submit exports of selected entities to common tariff for third countries, ban candidates of government parties from participating in elections to the European Parliament, refuse individuals nominated by the deviating states to EU posts, require visas for selected individuals to enter other Member States, cease to recognize judicial decisions in civil matters originating in these countries, etc.

The challenge is to find such sanction mix that would be able to correct a deformation of political pluralism (the structural conditions) in a deviating Member State that allows the regime to stay in power and dismantle independent control of its power step by step. Such positive sanctions ideally include options to increase the influence of independent media, the freedom of scientific research, and the voice of liberal opposition parties.

In the last part of my contribution, I can only sketch major areas of possible sanctions. 'Rights deriving from the application of the Treaties' include rights afforded by both primary law and secondary law. After this initial research on the Council's options in selecting the appropriate sanctions, experts in different areas of EU law will have to step in and analyze concrete examples, their impact on rights of others, and their international law limits.

2. Targeting Individuals

The decision of the European Council on the existence of a breach of EU values is directed against a concrete Member State. Consequently, targeted individuals and entities must have legal or substantive relations to that Member State (citizenship, long-term residency, incorporation in the deviating Member State, conduct-

73 ECJ, Joined Cases C-402/05 P and C-415/05 (Kadi I), ECLI:EU:C:2008:461, ECR 2008, I-06351; ECJ, Joined Cases C-584/10 P, C-593/10 P and C-595/10 P (Kadi II), ECLI:EU:C:2013:518 (holding that none of the reasons given by the UN Sanctions Committee in its summary of reasons was substantiated and since no other evidence has been produced to the Court, the listing of Mr. Kadi could not be justified).

74 ECJ, Case T-306/10 (Yusef/Commission), ECLI:EU:T:2014:141.

ing majority of their business in the Member State). EU citizenship is not a condition as long as targeted individuals benefit from the rights derived from the application of the Treaties. The principle of proportionality further requires that it must be established that a targeted individual's conduct contributes to the state authorities' breach of the Article 2 TEU values. The test is not burdensome, because here the principle of proportionality must be balanced against the principle of effectiveness.[75]

3. Political Rights

Suspension of political rights involves, first of all, the suspension of participation in the functioning of EU institutions, especially the right to vote. This is primarily based on the insulation rationale. Representatives of a regime that does not respect the same set of fundamental values as the rest of the EU should not co-create laws and policies for EU citizens. From this point of view, a suspension of voting rights in the Council would be insufficient. A deviating Member State participates in EU decision-making through the European Council and its representatives in the European Parliament. Moreover, despite a requirement of independence, the Member State is likely to use its nomination and appointment powers to insert its like-minded candidates into the European Commission, the CJEU, and other EU institutions and its agencies.

Insulating rationale that supports a suspension of voting rights in the Council as a preferable sanction is further undermined by the fact that a single Member State, however big, does not have enough power to meaningfully effect EU decision-making, given that the areas requiring unanimity have been significantly narrowed down and the coalition potential of a deviating state is low.[76] In the European Parliament, on the other hand, a Member State's influence might be amplified. Despite Fidesz having only eleven seats in the 8th Parliament (fourteen seats in the previous Parliament), its good standing within the EPP[77] has been an important factor in moderating the EU's response to Hungary's assault on liberal statehood.[78] The EPP's public record includes voting against the 2013 Tavares re-

75 Moreover, Article 7 explicitly allows a sanction that limit rights of persons irrespective of their contribution to the breach of EU values: a suspension of voting rights affects the right to vote of all citizens of a deviating state.

76 Coalition potential of a deviating state shall be in theory low as other states try to avoid to be tainted by cooperating with a state having serious issues respecting fundamental values. If there are states willing to cooperate with such state on a permanent basis (so that we can even think of the possibility of uploading illiberal values on EU level through its law making), it is very unlikely that the Article 7 procedure will reach the sanction phase (due to the requirement of unanimity for the European Council's assessment of existence of values' breach).

77 In the 7th European Parliament (2009-14), the balance of power between two major ideological groups was 274 seats for the EPP and 183 for Social Democrats. In the 8th Parliament (2014-19), the EPP has 221 seats and Social Democrats 191 seats.

78 See *P. Müller/R. Neukirch/C. Schröder/C. Schult*, Booming Silence: Europe's Conservatives Fail to Criticize Hungary, Spiegel Online, January 24, 2012, at http://www.spiegel.de/international/europe/booming-silence-europe-s-conservatives-fail-to-criticize-hungary-a-810863.html. Silvio Berlusconi also benefitted from the EPP's tolerance to its politically valued members. Id.

port,[79] and the EPP president Daul's endorsement of Orbán during the 2014 Hungarian parliamentary election campaign. Fidesz's position might have weakened since.[80] Yet, the balance of power between the EPP and the Social Democrats, which has narrowed down to thirty votes in the 8th Parliament, is favorable to outcasts within the major blocks.[81] The PiS has been less successful. Its EP group, the Alliance of Conservatives and Reformists in Europe (ACRE), is on the fringes of EP decision-making. Still, being in control together with British Conservatives of ACRE parliamentary group amplifies PiS's influence.[82]

A further problem is that a suspension of voting rights will not apply to Treaty revisions.[83]

For any meaningful attempt at insulating the EU from the influence of a deviating state, sanctions will have to target the EU institutions in a complex way. Besides suspending voting rights, as well as the right to participate in the functioning of the Council, the Council may suspend the right of a Member State in the meetings of the European Council, suspend the right to stand in the European elections and suspend voting rights of the MEPs from Fisdesz and PiS, suspend the right to suggest a candidate for a member of the Commission[84] and suspend the right to participate in appointing members of the Court of Justice (Judges and Advocates General), General Court, and specialized courts.[85]

A suspension of political rights is not limited to the right to stand for office, but also includes citizens' rights to vote in the European elections and the right of resident non-nationals to vote and stand as candidates in municipal elections (although a purpose of suspending the latter right is dubious).

Use of these sanctions may be prevented by the principle of separation of powers. Critics may argue that the Council cannot impose sanctions that encroach on the functioning of other EU institutions. This argument is strengthened by lower procedural requirements for imposing sanctions once the existence of a serious and persistent breach by a Member State of Article 2 TEU values has been determined. In the sanction stage of the Article 7 mechanism, the Council acts alone (neither the European Council, nor the Parliament, nor the Commission are involved) and the qualified majority suffices for suspension of rights.

79 European Parliament, Report on the situation of fundamental rights: standards and practices in Hungary, 25 June 2013 (the Tavares Report).

80 In a recent resolution of the European Parliament calling upon the Civil Liberties Committee to draw up a report on the situation in Poland, the votes from EPP members secured the majority (European Parliament resolution of 17 May 2017 on the situation in Hungary). One of the reasons for declining support within the EPP for Viktor Orbán was Fidesz's opposition to Jean-Claude Juncker, the official candidate of the EPP, for the Presidency of the Commission.

81 Consider the scenario that Forza Italia and Fidesz are removed from the EPP caucus. Consequently, the EPP would lose the majority to Social Democrats.

82 ACRE has 50 seats.

83 Cf. Art. 48 (4) TEU.

84 Art. 17 (7) TEU. Cf. also Art. 17 (3) TEU (requiring that members of the Commission shall be chosen on the grounds of their "European commitment").

85 Art. 253 and 254 TFEU.

Such an argument is not warranted. The European Parliament must consent to both determining the risk of breach of Article 2 values, and subsequently the existence of the breach. The Commission should assume a role of prosecutor initiating both of these procedures and be responsible for the submission of a well-build case against a Member State. Its proposal initiating the procedure leading to the determination of existence of breach of the values must include an in-depth analysis of the causes of the breach and identification of persons and institutions responsible for the breach. Since, under such an approach, the European Council will assume a role of an independent evaluator of the evidence submitted by the Commission and the defense of the investigated Member State, the Commission will be also responsible, due to its institutional capacities (namely the FPI) and available assistance from the FRA, for devising sanctions. In such a case, the consent of the European Parliament required in key stages of the procedure will include proposed sanctions as well.[86] When deciding on sanction mix, the Council will be bound by the decision of the European Council regarding the determination of the existence of value breach, in which the European Council will specify whether and how it differs from the Commission's proposal. The Council will then simply implement the decision of the European Council by opting for such sanction mix for such period as will be appropriate regarding the evidence the European Council considers proven after examining the Commission's proposal and hearing the investigated Member State.

Furthermore, the Court of Justice will most likely have its say in the procedure. Firstly, Article 269 TFEU empowers the Court to examine, upon a petition of the Member State, against which the procedure is held, whether the 'procedural stipulations' of Article 7 were respected in the decisions of the European Council and the Council. The meaning and extent of 'procedural stipulations' must be examined by the Court itself. And secondly, targeted individuals may bring the decisions adopted within the Article 7 procedure to the Court under the annulment procedure. The Member State in question would not sustain the standing since the Article 269 TFEU procedure is special to the annulment procedure.[87]

The Council, subject to the principles outlined in Part V of this contribution, seems to be authorized by Article 7 to suspend a right to participate in EU institutions for nationals of a target Member State *en bloc*. Such a general ban would prevent nationals of a deviating state to be involved in the functioning of the European Central Bank, European System of Central Banks, the Court of Auditors, the Economic and Social Committee, the Committee of the Regions and EU agencies. The ban may also include bureaucracies of the Commission and other institutions' apparatus. The general ban to participate in EU institutions does not fall within political rights suspension anymore. It is rather a suspension of the

86 The EP can use its 'power of consent' in order to negotiate with the Commission its proposal for sanctions. The EP has a considerable experience with using this strategy.

87 Cf. ECJ, Case C-247/87 (Star Fruit/Commission), ECLI:EU:C:1989:58, ECR 1989, 291 (holding that the petitioner cannot use the annulment procedure to bypass its lack of standing in the infringement procedure).

right not to be discriminated based on nationality. Its rationale, if combined with comprehensive suspension of economic rights, is to cause a collapse of deviating regime (political fracture).[88] The general ban will, however, hardly pass a proportionality test and will be in conflict with most of the other principles.

4. Economic Rights

Insulating sanctions (suspension of various rights to participate in the EU decision-making) are highly unlikely to change the objectionable behavior of a target state and would, if not combined with other sanctions, fail the effectiveness and the democracy-inbound principles. Suspension of economic rights, especially if targeting the economic base of the regime, can be more effective.

The EU has two major options regarding economic sanctions that fulfil the definition of suspension of rights derived from the Treaties – suspension of free movement rights and suspension of EU funds.[89] Both options can be used in a targeted way.

Several scholars suggested to apply economic sanctions outside the Article 7 framework. Jan-Werner Müller's recommends to create a Copenhagen Commission empowered to investigate the situation of fundamental values breach. Based on the findings of the Copenhagen Commission, the European Commission will be required, for instance, to cut EU funds or impose significant fines.[90] In theory, there is no reason to consider an investigation conducted by the European Commission to be biased, so that a new institution would be required. As I argued above, the Commission may use the expertise of the Fundamental Rights Agency to gather and analyze evidence of the values breach. Article 7 does not allow imposing outright fines, since the sanction must be a suspension of a certain right and for such an option, a new mechanism would have to be created as Müller suggests.

The experience with fines imposed by Court of Justice for non-compliance with its judgment regarding the infringement of Treaties shows that Member States are able to stall the payments for decades. If one considers that it takes about nine years from the infringement action to the Court's decision imposing fines, then the ineffectiveness of the procedure is alarming.[91] It can be assumed that if fines are imposed, through whatever procedure, for a fundamental values breach

88 Sanctions under Article 7 are not restricted by the scope of the European Convention of Human Rights, since the EU is not a party to the Convention. The incorporation of Convention rights as general principles, as well as the rights guaranteed by the EU Charter of Fundamental Rights do not limit the scope of sanctions, since Article 7 explicitly allows suspension of rights. Both, the Charter and the general principles in the meaning of Art. 6 (3) TEU, will play a role in general and special proportionality tests of imposed sanctions only.

89 Cf. the possibility to cut Cohesion Funds in case of excessive government deficit according to Art. 4 of the Council Regulation (EC) No 1084/2006 of 11 July 2006 establishing a Cohesion Fund (repealed by Regulation (EU) No 1300/2013 of the European Parliament and of the Council of 17 December 2013 on the Cohesion Fund).

90 *J.-W. Müller* 2015, (fn. 2120), at 150-1.

91 *B. Jack*, Article 260 (2) TFEU: An Effective Judicial Procedure for the Enforcement of Judgements?, Eur. L.J., 2013, p. 404-21.

(meaning there is a deep structural problem in the Member State in question), it will be self-defeating for the EU as the target state will just ignore it. The solution might be to deduct the fines from EU funds allocated to that Member State.

The infringement proceeding, supposing the fines for non-compliance with the judgment will be imposed immediately after a reasonable deadline for correction of the infringement expires, does not prove to be a good venue. The reasons are a limitation of the Court as to what its judgment can achieve, but more importantly there has been a hesitation of the Court to be dragged into internal politics of a Member State and forced to evaluate the constitutional framework of such Member State.[92] The court can be forced to deal with the problem directly (and not through proxy issues) if infringement of Article 2 TEU is pled. Kim Lane Scheppele argued for rephrasing the infringement procedure to provide for an option of systemic infringement actions that would bundle several violations and use Article 2 TEU or Article 4 TEU (sincere cooperation) in connection with the Charter of Fundamental Rights as their basis.[93] However, as unfortunate as it might be that Article 7 TEU is cumbersome due to the unanimity requirement in its key stage, the constitutional legislator opted for this option. It cannot be bypassed without good reason.

Suspending payments from EU funds to a Member State found in breach of fundamental values under Article 7 is the preferred way.[94] In order to increase the effectiveness of this sanction and subsequently pass the proportionality test, I suggest targeted sanctions. Firstly, the Commission as preferred initiator of Article 7 procedure will deconstruct a target regime's political and economic structure and identify key individuals and entities. Then, the EU will, instead of paying the funds to the state and the state redistributing the funds based on calls for concrete projects within announced funding programs, temporarily fund concrete programs directly based on applications from individuals and entities and will not approve any funding for blacklisted individuals and entities.[95]

A suspension of free movement rights can assume various forms. It shall be again targeted. For instance, export of blacklisted entities can be subjected to the common tariff set for third countries. Free movement of services provided by blacklisted entities can be limited by the condition that the service provider must be in-

92 Cf. ECJ, Case C-286/12 (Commission/Hungary), ECLI:EU:C:2012:687 (the Court found Hungary's laws on compulsory retirement of judges discriminatory by age, but the judgment could not restore the judges into their positions). See *G. Halmai*, Much Ado About Nothing? Legal and Political Schooling for the Hungarian Government, Verfassungsblog, April 29, 2017, at http://verfassungsblog.de/much-ado-about-nothing-legal-and-political-schooling-for-the-hungarian-government-on/.

93 *K. L. Scheppele*, Enforcing the Basic Principles of EU Law through Systemic Infringement Actions, in: C. Closa/D. Kochenov (eds.), Reinforcing Rule of Law Oversight in the European Union, 2016, p. 105-132.

94 See Letter by the foreign ministers of Germany, the Netherlands, Finland and Denmark to the European Commission, March 6, 2013; at https://www.rijksoverheid.nl/binaries/rijksoverheid/documenten/brieven/2013/03/13/brief-aan-europese-commissie-over-opzetten-rechtsstatelijkheidsmechanisme/brief-aan-europese-commissie-over-opzetten-rechtsstatelijkheidsmechanisme.pdf.

95 The requirement that a Member State must co-finance a funded project would be suspended as well. This solution will allow the EU to channel the funds into projects that are able to reform the structural conditions necessary for Article 2 TEU values to function.

corporated in a Member State that is not subject to Article 7 sanctions. Certifications of quality may be required to fulfil requirements of a Member State in which it is marketed. Workers from a sanctioned Member State can be required to apply for a working permit. The EU rights of posted workers can be suspended. Free movement of finances may be restricted.
The EU can also refuse guarantees for European Investment Bank's loans to a sanctioned state. It may deny a right of targeted individuals to buy property in another Member State, etc.

5. *Other Rights*

Suspension of other than political and economic rights may include a suspension of automatic recognition of judicial decisions in other Member States. This option falls within the insulating category of sanctions. A Member States' tempering with the domestic judiciary raises the question of legitimacy of all judicial outcomes and their possible effect on nationals in other Member States. The Council may also suspend the recognition of qualifications if education institutions, their curriculum, research, and staff is corrupted by ideological views of a Member State found in breach of fundamental values.
The Council can further suspend the rights deriving from the Schengen acquis. Targeted individuals may be banned from traveling to other EU states or be subject to an administrative procedure of a type of granting a visa. However, effective enforcement of such sanctions would require reinstating border controls, which may be disproportionate.
Further research shall focus on possibilities of direct financial assistance to independent media, non-government-controlled universities, opposition parties, and civil society advocates, which would fall within the 'suspension of rights' condition of Article 7. Direct distribution of EU funds (constructed as selective suspension of a right to EU funds) might be an option for some of the institutions mentioned.

Conclusion: From Voting Rights Suspension to Tailored Sanctions

The Union failed and it is failing again. Creeping deviation of an entire region from liberal-democratic, common values is not a coincidence. The two most visible proponents, PiS and Fidesz, have stopped pretending to cherish these values, and declared that they want to restructure their political, economic, and social structures on a different political philosophy. Both parties command electoral majorities. If they continue winning future elections, they will secure a loyal constitutional court, presidency, central bank, media, and universities through their appointment and funding powers in a less contestable way. The case of Hungary has already proven that to some extent. But in the shadows of the excesses of Hungary's and Poland's legislatures stands the rest of Eastern Enlargement states with few exceptions. We should ask why Viktor Orbán has turned from a liberal to his current self and why so many others in the region follow the suit. But first the trend must be stopped and the EU must prove to its citizens that the fundamental values are indeed fundamental, warranting the imposition of Article 7 sanctions.

The Commission, assuming the role of prosecutor in the Article 7 procedure, should in cooperation with the Council and the European Parliament focus on devising such sanction mix, which effects enhance the possibility of public to realize the danger of an illiberal turn and liberal forces to take over. Insulating sanctions, such as the suspension of voting rights, are unable to fulfil this aim. Sanctions should not target an entire Member State, but focus on selected individuals and entities. They should be like a surgical intervention, carefully cutting away those parts of political and economic structures that underpin the regime. Simultaneously, the EU must be careful not to create a space for other illiberal states to step in to fill the commercial gap caused by sanctions and the political vacuum that might result from a backlash of sanctioned state against the EU and its Member States.[96]

The first step requires a proper diagnosis of deviation. In the second step, the EU must ask what measures can remedy the roots of the deviation. In the third step, it must find concrete options in the EU legal order (rights to be suspended) that can fulfil this goal. In the next step, it must combine the rights selected for suspension into a complex sanction regime, tailored to the causes of deviation and political and economic structure of the Member State in breach. Finally, the EU must test the devised sanction regime against the democracy-inbound, effectiveness, proportionality (general and special), and beneficiary-focus principles and correct the sanction regime accordingly.

A use of proper theory for the diagnosis is, from a legal point of view, required by not only the effectiveness principle, but also the other three principles. Gramscian analysis of state-society relationship offers a valuable assistance to senders of sanctions in isolating the forces that are vital for the state elite to stay in power in the long term. Its ideological charge shall not be deterring since it serves for diagnosis, not solution.

96 Russian and Chinese economic and political influence in the CEE and the Balkans has been steadily on the rise. Cf. Russian involvement in nuclear plants extension project like Paks, gas pipelines projects like Tesla Stream and TurkStream or China-led 16+1 cooperation with 16 CEE countries launched in 2012 that includes e.g. a construction of 350 km long high-speed rail line from Belgrade to Budapest. *E. Zalan*, Hungary-Serbia railway launched at China summit, EUobserver, Nov. 29, 2017.

Constitutional remedies of persons facing consequences of the Council decision on suspension of certain Member State´s rights

By Jiří Zemánek, Prague[*]

If the Council decides to suspend certain of the rights deriving from the application of the Treaties to a Member State, „the Council shall take into account the possible consequences of such a suspension on the rights and obligations of natural and legal persons" (Article 7 para 3 first subpara in fine TEU). Several questions remain in this respect open and require examination:

- *which „rights of a Member State" can be suspended by the Council ?*
- *which „rights and obligations of natural and legal persons" can be affected by the suspension ?*
- *what are the limits of justiciability of the Council decision?*
- *how can the injuries, harms, damages or other losses occurred to persons be remedied?*

I. The scope and the limits of discretion of the Council when suspending the rights of a Member State

There is no exhaustive list of sanctions against a Member State in Article 7 para 3 TEU. This provision puts on the stage expressly only („including") the voting rights of the representatives of the government of that Member State in the Council, cancellation of its participation and operation rights in any EU decision-making bodies and procedures,[1] of its access to drawing rights of the structural and cohesion funds (European Agricultural Guidance and Guarantee Fund, European Social Fund, European Regional Development Fund, facilities of the European Investment Bank and other financial instruments), as well as of other rights deriving from the application of the Treaties is admissible, too.[2] However, the Council shall avoid to deprive the Member State of all membership rights, otherwise its vital functions could become tied up, incl. its ability to recover the serious and persistent breach of the values referred to in Article 2 TEU and to meet its obligations towards the other Member States and individuals under the Treaties, which continue to be binding (Article 7 para 3 second subpara TEU).

* Jean Monnet Professor of European Law at the Charles University Faculty of Law, Judge of the Constitutional Court of the Czech Republic.

1 The rights of the members of the European Parliament and of the European Commission – the citizens of the respective Member State – cannot be restricted, as they do not represent their homeland; *F. Schorkopf*, Homogenität in der Europäischen Union – Ausgestaltung und Gewährleistung durch Art. 6 Abs. 1 und Art. 7 EUV, 2010, S. 180 f.

2 The suspension of the rights to start proceedings at the Court of Justice is from the perspective of the guarantees of lawful judge in EU law questionable: the right to submit an action for annulment and for failure to act can be limited only so far as the access of the Member State to judicial protection of its legal position would be preserved, see: *M. Pechstein*, in: Streinz (eds.), EUV/AEUV. Kommentar, 2. Aufl. 2012, Art. 7 EUV, Rn. 19.

Although the scope of discretion of the Council is very broad, the exercise of its competence – like, in general, the exercise of all powers conferred by the Treaties on the EU institutions and permitting interferences in the sphere of Member States or other parties – is not unlimited. When considering the suspension of certain rights of a Member State, the Council shall respect the principle of proportionality. In order to be effective, the sanctions must stand the test of adequacy towards the legitimate aim of removing obstacles, which caused the breach of values;[3] the means should prefer intervention in the rights of the State; any encroachments upon the rights of individuals, if unavoidable, should be undertaken in the most moderate way.[4]

II. Affected rights and obligations of persons

Suspension of voting and participatory rights of the Member State should not affect the sphere of natural and legal persons directly. On the other hand, hardly any sanction against a Member State resulting in cuttings of financial support for public policies could remain without a negative impact on private persons, especially investors, who relied on State guarantees of their projects.

The contractual foundations of investments co-financed by the European Union have been based, as a rule, on projects of public procurement or public-private-partnership. The venture, first, is to be guaranteed (as a rule pre-paid) – besides the own share of private investor – by the State budget. After all terms of the deal would have been met and guarantees or payments already provided certified, the costs will be refunded to the State and the investment may continue through co-financing taken over by an EU fund. However, if the Council would suspend the access of a Member State to the EU structural or cohesion funds, the refunding of the costs will not take place, co-financing of the project by the EU will be jeopardized and cannot continue. The following withdrawal of the State from its contractual obligations, which might occur, could frustrate the private investor´s legitimate expectations or vested rights.

The Council decision about a suspension of Member State rights, taking into account possible consequences for the rights and obligations of private persons, should aim at avoiding, so far as possible, a. o., such an impact of the sanction, even if it will be uneasy for the Council to assume, that the State´s action implementing the sanction could lead at the end of the day to a deprivation of the persons in question of their fundamental rights (right to property, freedom to conduct a business). When such consequences would be unavoidable, the decision of the Council will produce legal effects *vis-à-vis* third parties and have a direct concern

3 *P. Voet van Vormizeele*, in: von der Groeben/Schwarze/Hatje (eds.), Europäisches Unionsrecht, 7. Aufl. 2015, Bd. I, Art. 7 EUV, Rn. 14.

4 *F. Schorkopf*, in: Grabitz/Hilf/Nettesheim (eds.), Das Recht der Euroäischen Union, EL 41 Juli 2010, Art. 7 EUV, S. 13.

to them. For a private investor, the breakdown of the State guarantees of the project as a consequence of the Council sanction will be out of any reasonable risk management considerations and hardly can be covered by a contractual clause or by an insurance policy. The question arises, whether consequences of the intervention, imposed by the Council under Article 7 para 3 TEU on the State and implemented by its measure, for the position of the person as a party of a contract can be remedied under the provisions of Union law and/or national law on tort liability.

III. Justiciability of the Council decision

The legality of an act adopted by the Council pursuant under Article 7 para 3 TEU may be adjudicated by the Court of Justice *„solely at the request of the Member State concerned [...] and in respect solely of the procedural stipulations contained in that article“* (Article 269 first subpara TEU). This is *lex specialis* towards the general determination of the Court of Justice´s jurisdiction to review the legality of acts of the Council under Article 63 TEU. Therefore, natural or legal person cannot institute proceedings against the Council decision in question under subpara four of that provision, even if such a „regulatory act“ would produce direct concern to it and regardless of whether this would entail adoption of implementing measures by the State or not. The judicial review of compliance of the Council decision with material provisions of Union law, incl. the limits of Council discretion when taking into account the possible consequences of suspension on private persons, is denied to them, too. The discharge of the Council´s obligation duly justify its decision on type and scope of sanctions as a part of its procedural duties can be reviewed on the request of the Member State by the Court of Justice.
However, the natural or legal person can under Article 268 claim compensation of damage provided for in Article 340 TFEU, if induced by the Council decision, even when the material legality of this act of Union law could not be tested by the Court of Justice; its case-law (stare decisis) does not require the prior declaration of illegality of the act of Union law before claiming damages.

IV. Remedies against the Member State

A serious and persistent breach by a Member State of the values referred to in Article 2 TEU that will be the material reason for the Council decision on sanctions under Article 7 para 3 is to be assessed as an infringement of the Treaties of a specific nature. If the implications of suspension of State´s rights of access to structural and cohesion funds of the EU, adopted by the Council in reaction on this infringement, result in a State action cutting, for instance, drawing entitle-

ments of investors, their legitimate expectations and property rights will be injured or damaged. When causation between the State´s action and emergence of the damage would be evidenced, its compensation can be claimed by the private person on the basis of the doctrine on State liability developed by the *Francovich* jurisprudence[5] of the Court of Justice. Since the limits of discretion of the Council, when taking into account the possible consequences of the suspension of rights of persons, cannot be reviewed, no co-liability of the European Union with the Member State for the damage resulting from that suspension can be claimed.
Under the doctrine of the Court of Justice shared by the constitutional courts of Member States, the review of legality and proportionality of an act of a Union institution, which encroached upon constitutionally guaranteed fundamental rights of an individual, is at national level not permissible. Constitutional review should have to be, however, possible towards the State´s measure adopted for the implementation of the act of Union law, which has the causal link to a damage of a private person. Such a review must be limited to „unnecessitated measures" adopted outside of the scope of implementation duty resulting from the act of Union law. Procedural instrument of the review can, as a rule, be an additional motion attached to the constitutional complaint, which has been submitted by the person – if existing under the applicable national law, or motion submitted by the ordinary court within the procedure on payment of damages.

5 ECJ, C-479/93 (Francovich/Italy), ECLI:EU:C:1995:372, ECR 1995, I-3843.

Right and duty to pursue the "wrongdoer" and a possible abuse of Art. 7 TEU

By Matthias Niedobitek, Chemnitz[*]

A "wrongdoer" is a Member State of the Union stigmatized by the Union and with no effective legal remedy. The determination of a "wrongdoer" rests with the political institutions of the Union. The institutions involved in the procedure enjoy a virtually unlimited discretion. The European Court of Justice's role is restricted to the review of procedural stipulations. The possible legal consequences are grave. Thus, it is doubtful whether the Art. 7 TEU-procedure is in conformity with the requirements of the rule of law. In many respects, Art. 126 TFEU is an analogue to Art. 7 TEU and may help its interpretation.

I. Introduction

On December 20, 2017 the European Commission issued a reasoned proposal pursuant to Art. 7 para. 1 TEU regarding the rule of law in Poland.[1] Thus, after several preliminary stages, the first step to formally apply the Art. 7 TEU-procedure has been taken and the questions dealt with in this paper are no longer academic.

This paper, as it may seem, is devoted rather to formal and punctual aspects of Art. 7 TEU than to its very substance. However, such an understanding would underestimate the relevance of each element of the topic – "right", "duty", "abuse", wrongdoer" – for a comprehensive interpretation of Art. 7 TEU. An examination of the four concepts mentioned will exhibit the very nature of Art. 7 TEU as a *legal shell with political substance.*

All facets of the topic of this paper are connected by a number of overall aspects which are relevant to the interpretation of Art. 7 TEU and which shall thus be mentioned in advance. The first aspect concerns the purpose of Art. 7 TEU: Is it only aimed at safeguarding the values of the Union or also at protecting the rights of individuals? The answer to this question may, e.g., influence the answer to the question whether or not a duty to pursue the wrongdoer exists. The second aspect concerns the relationship between Art. 7 TEU and international law instruments such as Art. 60 para 2 lit. a) VCLT.[2] The third aspect concerns the question of justiciability of Article 7 TEU which is limited pursuant to Article 269 TFEU. The fourth and final aspect concerns the term "wrongdoer". Is it possible to call a Member State a "wrongdoer" before the Council or the European Council made determinations pursuant to Art. 7 TEU?

* Jean Monnet Professor of European Integration at Chemnitz University of Technology.

1 COM (2017) 835.

2 Vienna Convention on the Law of Treaties.

Rights and a possible duty to pursue the wrongdoer are enshrined in Art. 7 TEU, but such rights can also be derived from the infringement procedures of the TFEU. Thus, the relationship between the Article 7-procedure and Articles 258 and 259 TFEU must be dealt with.
A striking analogue to the Art. 7 TEU-procedure is the Art. 126 TFEU-procedure concerning excessive deficits of the Member States. Pursuant to that procedure, it is the Council alone who decides whether an excessive deficit exists. The Commission's right pursuant to Art. 258 TFEU to bring an action against a Member State whose budget is regarded as having an excessive deficit is ruled out (Art. 126 para 10 TFEU).[3] This analogue will prove to be helpful for the interpretation of Art 7 TEU.

II. Balancing the legal side and the political side of Art. 7 TEU

The concepts of "right", "duty" and "abuse" are primarily legal concepts. Not surprisingly, with a view to making Art. 7 TEU operable it suggests itself to draw on established legal categories including the pertinent jurisprudence of the European Court of Justice in order to determine, e.g., the concept of a "serious breach" which is an important concept in the ECJ's case-law on non-contractual liability of the Union.[4] At first glance such an approach seems to be perfectly justified given the overall *legal* character of Art. 7 TEU. At second glance this appraisal must be qualified in the light of the essentially *political* substance of Art. 7 TEU.[5] The political quality of Art. 7 TEU requires a qualified interpretation of its concepts. For example, its political quality influences the margin of discretion which the institutions involved in the Art. 7 TEU-procedure have. As the Commission rightly stated,[6] "the Council's hands are not tied either in determining that there is a clear risk or in determining that that there is a serious and persistent breach".

III. The "wrongdoer"

A "wrongdoer" (intentionally written in quotation marks) is a Member State of the Union who is the addressee of a determination (or decision) pursuant to Art. 7

3 Cf. *R. Bandilla*, in: Grabitz/Hilf/Nettesheim (eds.), Das Recht der Europäischen Union, looseleaf edition, Art. 126 TFEU, mn. 57, 58.

4 Cf. *G. Wilms*, Protecting Fundamental Values in the European Union through the Rule of Law, EUI 2017, accessible under http://cadmus.eui.eu/handle/1814/44987, p. 58 et seq., who refers to the case-law of the ECJ regarding, *inter alia*, non-contractual liability of the Union in order to clarify the meaning of Art. 7 TEU.

5 Cf. *D. Kochenov*, The Acquis and Its Principles – The Enforcement of the 'Law' versus the Enforcement of 'Values' in the EU, in: Jakab/Kochenov (eds.), The Enforcement of EU Law and Values, Oxford 2017, p. 9 et seq., characterises Art. 7 TEU as a "purely political procedure", p. 10, and emphasises its "purely political nature", p. 17; for a concurring view cf. *S. Mangiameli/G. Saputelli*, in: Blanke/Mangiameli (eds.), The Treaty on European Union – A Commentary, 2013, Art. 7 TEU, mn. 22. On the other hand, *G. Wilms* (fn. 4) contends that the criteria used in Art. 7 TEU "are essentially legal" while acknowledging that "the sanctions are political".

6 Communication on Article 7 of the Treaty on European Union, COM (2003) 606, p. 5.

paras 2, 3 TEU. Such a determination expresses the conviction of the Council/ European Council that this state's conduct causes a clear risk of a breach resp. a serious and persistent breach of the values referred to in Art. 2 TEU. The competence to make such determinations rests with the Council/European Council alone. The ECJ has no jurisdiction in that regard but "in respect solely on the procedural stipulations contained in [Art. 7 TEU]" as Art. 269 TFEU puts it. In other words, the "political" institutions of the Union have the right to apply the Art. 7-procedure while the ECJ is restricted to its legal instruments, in particular to the infringement procedure of Art. 258 TFEU.

A "wrongdoer" only becomes a wrongdoer (in a legal sense) by a determination pursuant to Art. 7 paras 2, 3 TEU. Prior to such a determination the Member State in question can at best be called an "alleged wrongdoer".[7] This means that a determination pursuant to Art. 7 paras 2, 3 TEU is *constitutive* and not merely, like the interpretation of the law of the Union by the ECJ,[8] *declarative*, in other words, the determination pursuant to Art. 7 paras 2, 3 TEU *constitutes a "wrongdoer"*.

In that respect, there is no difference to the Art. 126 TFEU-procedure. The Council's decision according to which an excessive deficit exists in a particular Member State[9] is also *constitutive*,[10] and the determination of an excessive deficit is exempt from the jurisdiction of the ECJ pursuant to Art. 126 para 10 TFEU. The existence of an excessive deficit decision prevents a Member State from introducing the Euro as the single currency.[11]

Given the vagueness of all terms involved in Art. 7 TEU (including the term "breach") as well as of the values referred to in Art. 2 TEU[12] it is puzzling to see how scholars feel themselves able to detect a (clear risk of a) serious (and persistent) breach of the values of the Union by a particular Member State without, however, revealing the applied standard.[13] Admittedly, the relevant standards are hard, if not impossible, to define. As a substitute scholars refer to statements of

7 For a concurring view cf. *G. Wilms* (fn. 4), p. 72, who correctly speaks of "alleged or presumed violations of the Rule of Law".

8 Cf., e.g., ECJ, C-110/15 (Nokia Italia and others), ECLI:EU:C:2016:717, mn. 50: "[A]ccording to settled case-law of the Court, the interpretation which, in the exercise of the jurisdiction conferred on it by Article 267 TFEU, the Court gives to a rule of EU law clarifies and defines the meaning and scope of that rule as it must be or ought to have been understood and applied from the time of its entry into force.".

9 Cf., e.g., Council Decision 2014/56/EU of 28 April 2014 on the existence of an excessive deficit in Croatia, O.J. EU 2014 L 36/13.

10 For a concurring view cf. *U. Häde*, in: Calliess/Ruffert (eds.), EUV/AEUV – Das Verfassungsrecht der Europäischen Union mit Europäischer Grundrechtecharta, 5th ed., 2016, Art. 126 AEUV, mn. 41; *D. Hattenberger*, in: Schwarze (ed.), EU-Kommentar, 3rd ed., 2012, Art. 126 AEUV, mn. 37.

11 Cf. Art. 2 of Protocol (No 13) on the Convergence Criteria, O.J. EU 2016 C 202/281.

12 Cf. *K. Serini*, Sanktionen der Europäischen Union bei Verstoß eines Mitgliedstaats gegen das Demokratie- oder Rechtsstaatsprinzip, 2009, p. 21 et seq.; *G. Wilms* (fn. 4), p. 58.

13 Cf., e.g., *R. Yamato/J. Stephan*, Eine Politik der Nichteinmischung – Die Folgen des zahnlosen Art. 7 EUV für das Wertefundament der EU am Beispiel Ungarn, DÖV 2014, p. 58 et seq.: It seems difficult, the authors say, not to speak of a threat to the Rule of Law of a systemic character in Hungary (at p. 61), the principles as referred to in Art. 2 TEU were ignored, p. 65; *W. Hummer*, Ungarn erneut am Prüfstand der Rechtsstaatlichkeit und Demokratie, EuR 2015, p. 625 et seq., contends that a number of values were flagrantly infringed which in sum amounted "*without doubt*" (*ohne Zweifel*) to a systemic breach of the Rule of Law, p. 626.

other institutions such as the Council of Europe's Venice Commission[14] although its aims and legal standards differ from Art. 7 TEU.[15] In the wake of the enlargements of 2004, 2007 and 2011 which brought states into the Union that have a different history, different traditions and a different understanding of the Union's values, the vagueness/broadness of the principles/values of the Union still increased. Being original co-founders of the Lisbon-Union[16] all then 27 Member States or (more precisely) "Contracting Parties" were on an equal footing having an equal influence on shaping the Union's values. The common values' basis of the Union justifies and requires "to consider all the other Member States to be complying with EU law and particularly with the fundamental rights recognised by EU law".[17]

The "values" of the Union (democracy, rule of law etc.) are, as regards their normative nature, "principles" (and not "rules").[18] Principles allow for a very broad spectrum of possible designs and standards, starting from minimum requirements which must not be gone below to a (probably undefinable) maximum, in other words "principles" cannot (like rules) be *observed* but *optimised* or *deteriorated.* Only when the minimum requirements fail to be met meaning that, e.g., a democracy or the rule of law *no longer exists*, a principle turns into a rule. In that case a "breach" of the principle (or value) is established. This view is in line with the approach taken by the ECJ who, when concerned with an alleged infringement of the principle of democracy by the Commission (the Commission withdrew a proposal), restricted itself to refer to Art. 17 TEU and to state that "there can be no question, in this instance, of an infringement of that principle".[19] Thus, the Court acknowledged that the principle of democracy has a broad scope and that its (lower) limits are hardly ever touched.

IV. The right to pursue the "wrongdoer"

1. Basic Observations

Art. 7 TEU entitles the European Union – not the Member States or the ECJ – to pursue a "wrongdoer". Within the procedure outlined in Art. 7 TEU the right to

14 As *R. Yamato/J. Stephan* (fn. 13), p. 62, do.

15 Cf. Opinion 720/2013, CDL-AD(2013)012, p. 3: The Venice Commission was requested to give an opinion "on the compatibility of the Fourth Amendment to the Fundamental Law of Hungary with the Council of Europe Standards.".

16 The Treaty of Lisbon founded a new Union, distinct from the Maastricht-Union. Cf. *M. Niedobitek*, Vertragliche Grundlagen, rechtliche Gestalt, Institutionen der Union, in: Niedobitek (ed.), Europarecht – Grundlagen der Union, 2014, mn. 121, 202.

17 ECJ, Opinion 2/13 (Accession to the ECHR), ECLI:EU:C:2014:2454, mn. 191.

18 Cf. *M. Niedobitek*, Die Europäische Union als Wertegemeinschaft, Hamburg 2012, p. 205, 212 et seq.; *D. Kochenov* (fn. 5), p. 10, who considers it a mistake to call those principles „values". Concerning the relationship between values and law cf. *T. Würtenberger*, Die Werte des Art. 2 EUV: Normativ verbindlich oder politisches Programm?, in: Bruns et al. (eds.), Festschrift für Rolf Stürner zum 70. Geburtstag, Part 2, 2013, p. 1975 et seq.

19 ECJ, Case C-409/13 (Council/Commission), ECLI:EU:C:2015:217, mn. 96.

trigger Art. 7 TEU is conferred upon different actors among which the Member States are mentioned in the first place. More correctly, depending on the particular paragraph or stage of Art. 7 TEU, it is one third or four fifth of the Member States who have the right to initiative. According to Art. 354 TFEU the Member State in question shall not be counted in the calculation of the one third or four fifths of Member States. The Member States share the right to initiative with the European Parliament (in paragraph 1) and the Commission (in paragraphs 1 and 2).

Even though the Commission is mentioned only in the third place, some authors argue that the Commission, as guardian of the Treaties, has a vital role and is superior to the Member States given that it can choose between an ordinary infringement procedure (Art. 258 TFEU) and the penalty mechanism of Art. 7 TEU.[20] This view seems to be confirmed by the Rule of Law Framework[21] which was lately elaborated by the Commission, encouraged, however, by the Foreign Ministers of several Member States,[22] and which demonstrates the Commission's particular sense of responsibility in that field. This, however, justifies no priority of the Commission in a legal sense although admittedly the Commission's access may be prior in a political sense.

The Council's and the European Council's action depends on an initiative taken by one of the actors mentioned. Both institutions have no right to trigger Art. 7 TEU. The Council, however, may, pursuant to Art. 241 TFEU request the Commission to submit a proposal. Once a proposal to trigger Art. 7 TEU was made the Council or the European Council have the right pursue a "wrongdoing" state.

The case of "Austria" which was dealt with outside the scope of the Art. 7 TEU-procedure[23] and the new Rule of Law Framework pose the question whether informal instruments designed to prevent an application of Art. 7 TEU are permitted. Admittedly, the mere existence of Article 7 TEU which establishes a sophisticated and graded procedure and which was continuously adapted to the supposed needs of state practice argues in favour of a conclusive interpretation of Art. 7 TEU. But a conclusive interpretation of Art. 7 TEU must not be construed as excluding any preliminary action by the Commission designed to clear the ground of a possible violation of the Union's values.[24] Rather, it seems plausible to conceive the Rule-of-Law-Framework of the Commission as a form of "EU Pilot Procedure" already accepted in other contexts.[25]

20 Cf. *S. Mangiameli/G. Saputelli* (fn. 5), Art. 7 TEU mn. 43.

21 COM (2014) 158.

22 Cf. the *Editorial Comments* „Safeguarding EU values in the Member States – Is something finally happening?, CMLRev. 52, 2015, p. 619 et seq.

23 Cf. *T. Schönborn*, Die Causa Austria, Frankfurt a. M. 2005, p. 148-155; *W. Hummer/W. Obwexer*, Die Verhängung der „EU-Sanktionen" und der mögliche Ausstieg aus ihnen, ZÖR 55, 2000, p. 269 et seq., 276; *H. Schäffer*, Europa – Raum des Rechts und „Werte-Gemeinschaft": Der Fall Österreich am Beispiel der rechtswidrigen sogenannten „Sanktionen" der EU-14 gegen Österreich, in: Alivizatos u.a. (eds.), Essays in Honour of Georgios I. Kassimatis, 2004, p. 827, 840 et seq.

24 Not convincing the Opinion of the Council's Legal Service, Doc. 10296/14 of 27 May 2014, which concludes that "there is no legal basis in the Treaties empowering the institutions to create a new supervision mechanism as regards the rule of law by the Member States […]" (mn. 24).

25 Cf. *G. Wilms* (fn. 4), p. 76 et seq.

In the absence of a provision like Art. 7 TEU, the Member States could possibly rely on international law instruments such as enshrined in Art. 60 para 2 lit. a) VCLT but according to Art. 60 para 4 VCLT the sanction mechanisms of Art. 7 TEU represent a special and conclusive procedure, in other words, the legal system of the Union is a self-contained regime in that respect.[26]

Finally, the infringement procedures of Art. 258 and 259 TFEU may confer rights to pursue the "wrongdoer". The relationship between Art. 7 TEU on the one side and Art. 258, 259 TFEU on the other is disputed. Both mechanisms should be distinguished as follows: When a breach of the Union's values is not associated with the "scope of application of the Treaties" in the meaning of Article 18 TFEU, when, in other words, the breach is purely national, Art. 7 TEU should be regarded as exhaustive – although admittedly Art. 258, 259 TFEU when referring to Member States who "failed to fulfil an obligation under the Treaties" are broad enough to include any violation of the Union's values. But when a breach of the Union's values touches upon the scope of application of the Treaties, the infringement procedures of Art. 258, 259 TFEU and the Art. 7 TEU-procedure should be regarded as being applicable simultaneously. In this case, the Commission or the Member States can choose between bringing an action pursuant to Art. 258, 259 TFEU for a breach of primary or secondary law of the Union that concretises the values of the Union (this happened in the case of Hungary[27]), or they can opt to bring an action pursuant to Art. 258, 259 TFEU for a breach of the values mentioned in Art. 2 TEU. The Commission or the Member States can also combine both options mentioned.

2. Limits to the right to pursue the "wrongdoer"

The right to pursue the "wrongdoer" has to face several limits which can only be summed up here. First, the national identity of the Member State in question must be respected pursuant to Art. 4 para. 2 TEU. Second, the principle of subsidiarity (if applicable)[28] must be respected. This principle "speaks in favour of leaving the solution of a threat to the rule of law to the national system [including the media; M.N.] as long as it is still functioning".[29] Third, the Union must respect the principle of proportionality according to which the Union "should not be biting, if barking does the job".[30] And fourth, the Union must act on the assumption that all Member States including the Member State in question comply with EU law[31]

26 Cf. *T. Giegerich*, in: Dörr/Schmalenbach (eds.), Vienna Convention on the Law of Treaties, 2012, Art. 60 VCLT, para 70.

27 Cf., e.g., ECJ, C-288/12 (Commission/Hungary), ECLI:EU:C: 2014:237, concerning the independence of the national data protection supervisor.

28 The principle of subsidiarity only applies to areas which do not fall within the exclusive competence of the Union. It is doubtful whether the competence categories outlined in Art. 2 et seq. TFEU are at all applicable to Art. 7 TEU.

29 Cf. *G. Wilms* (fn. 4), p. 73.

30 Ibid.

31 ECJ, Opinion 2/13 (Accession to the ECHR), ECLI:EU:C:2014:2454, mn. 191.

(including its values). These limits to the right to pursue the "wrongdoer" pursuant to Art. 7 TEU impose grave obstacles to a use of Art. 7 TEU which should not be disregarded nor disesteemed by the responsible institutions.

V. A duty to pursue the wrongdoer?

The question whether there exists a (legal) duty to pursue the wrongdoer is much more difficult to answer than the question concerning a corresponding right. The wording of Art. 7 TEU clearly runs contrary to a possible duty: Neither a duty to trigger Art. 7 TEU nor a duty to make determinations according to Art. 7 TEU can be derived from the provision. With regard to the latter duty, Art. 7 TEU even stresses the Council's/European Council's discretion in that it says that the two institutions "may" make the determinations in question.

Despite this, it is argued that at least with regard to the second stage of the Art. 7 TEU-procedure, the Commission and the Member States are obliged to trigger Art. 7 para. 2 TEU once they assured themselves that a serious and persistent breach of the Union's values exists.[32] Only a duty to act, it is argued, can safeguard the existence and functioning of the Union. Another possible argument in favour of a duty to trigger Art. 7 TEU could be derived from its purpose: The Member States (and the other actors entitled to trigger Art. 7 TEU) might be regarded as "agents of the victims" (as it was suggested in the Outline to this Conference). This, however, seems to be a misconception of the purpose of Art. 7 TEU. Art. 7's purpose is not to protect individuals rights rather it is aimed at safeguarding the values of the Union. Only by reflection individual rights may be affected, an interpretation which is confirmed in para 3 of Art. 7 TEU which obliges the Council to take into account the possible consequences of a suspension of Member States rights on the rights and obligations of natural and legal persons. Consequently, it is confusing to contend that every decision formally addressed to the Member States is addressed to the citizens too.[33]

To summarize, an interpretation of Art. 7 TEU which results in a duty to trigger or implement Art. 7 TEU runs contrary to its clear wording and its *political* character. Furthermore, it would deprive the institutions of their discretion which may prove necessary to deal with breaches of the Union's values. A reduction of the institutions' discretion to zero is hardly conceivable unless in situations when the Unions democratic existence is at stake.

With regard to the Commission, the ECJ has recently held, though in a different context, that "it is for the Commission to decide whether or not to submit a proposal for a legislative act, except in the situation [...] where it would be obliged

32 Cf. *F. Schorkopf*, in: Grabitz/Hilf/Nettesheim (eds.), Das Recht der Europäischen Union, looseleaf edition, Art. 7 TEU, mn. 29.

33 *S. Mangiameli/G. Saputelli* (fn. 5), Art. 7 TEU para 38.

under EU law to submit such a proposal".[34] Given that not only the Commission is entitled to trigger Art. 7 TEU, there are no compelling arguments in favour of a duty to trigger Art. 7 TEU whatever stage of procedure is in question.

With regard to the Council, the ECJ always has emphasized its legislative discretion,[35] and it is most probable that the Court would *a fortiori* stress the Council's discretion in the framework of Art. 7 TEU.

A duty of the Commission to trigger Art. 7 TEU could, however, be derived from Art. 225, 241 TFEU or 11 para 4 TEU. These provisions entitle the European Parliament, the Council or a Citizen's initiative to request or invite the Commission to submit a proposal. But while Art. 225 und 241 TFEU make sufficiently clear that in the end the Commission is not obliged to submit a proposal, this is different concerning Art. 11 para 4 TEU. The *effet utile* of this provision requires an obligation of the Commission to make an appropriate proposal should the citizen's initiative be successful.[36]

The citizen's initiative "*Wake up Europe! Taking action to safeguard the European democratic project*" may serve as an example. This initiative was registered on 30 November 2015 and withdrawn on 23 June 2016.[37] The subject-matter of this initiative was to request the Commission to refer the situation in Hungary to the Council, in accordance with Art. 7 TEU, in order to safeguard European values as defined in Art. 2 TEU. An action against the Commission's decision to register the initiative was brought by Hungary before the General Court on 3. February 2016.[38] Hungary mainly submitted that it was inadmissible to register the initiative because the legal act requested from the Commission was not "required for purpose of implementing the Treaties". In fact, it is *not obvious* that to trigger Art. 7 TEU is an act required for the purpose of "implementing the Treaties" since that depends on whether to interpret the term "implementing the Treaties" in a broad or in a narrow, more technical sense. However, the term "implementation of the Treaties" should definitively be construed in a broad way as including the observance of the Union's values. Regrettably (but necessarily), due to the withdrawal of the citizen's initiative, Hungary withdrew its action.[39]

VI. A possible abuse of Art. 7 TEU

Art. 7 TEU is particularly susceptible to an abuse. As a general rule, according to the settled case-law of the ECJ, EU law cannot be relied on for abusive ends.[40]

34 Cf. ECJ, C-409/13 (Council/Commission), ECLI:EU:C:2015:217, mn. 70.
35 ECJ, C-176/09 (Luxembourg/European Parliament, Council), ECLI:EU:C:2011:290, ECR 2011, I-3727, mn. 47, 50.
36 Cf. *M. Ruffert*, in: Calliess/Ruffert (fn. 10), Art. 11 TEU Rn. 21.
37 Cf. http://ec.europa.eu/citizens-initiative/public/initiatives/obsolete/details/2015/000005/de.
38 O.J. EU 2016 C 145/29.
39 Consequently, the case was removed from the register; cf. GC, Order of 21 October 2016.
40 Cf. ECJ, C-54/16 (Venyls Italia), ECLI:EU:C:2017:433, mn. 51 et seq.

The term "*abuse*" can be replaced by terms like "*arbitrariness*", "*disproportionality*" or others.

First, it is important to have a definition of an abuse of Art. 7 TEU. In that regard the jurisdiction of the ECJ concerning the abuse of EU law by individuals can be relied on, even though with some qualification: Abusive, the Court says, is a conduct which is formally in conformity with a provision of the law of the Union but which actually runs contrary to its purpose. Furthermore "the essential aim of the transactions concerned [must be] to obtain an undue advantage".[41] Due to the political character of Article 7 TEU all the elements are difficult to be balanced. Possible starting points for an abuse of Art. 7 TEU can be found in the elements of Art. 7 TEU:

- An abuse of para 1 would be to determine that there is a clear risk of a serious breach by a Member State of the values of the Union while it is *obvious* that no such risk exists and that the procedure is used for improper purposes.
- According to para 1 2nd subpara TEU "the Council shall regularly verify that the grounds on which such a determination was made continue to apply". An abuse of this provision would for example be to apply *overlong* verification periods.
- According to para 3 the Council may decide to suspend certain of the rights deriving from the application of the Treaties to the Member State in question. In that regard, literature contends that it would be admissible to suspend the rights of the Member State in question to an extent virtually amounting to an elimination of its legal position as a member state i.e. amounting to an expulsion from the Union. However, it seems that such a behaviour would be an abuse of para 3. The wording "certain of the rights" requires that the bulk of the Member States' right remain with the "wrongdoer".

But in more general terms, the question arises whether – save obvious cases (e.g. establishment of a dictatorship by coup) – the *use* of Art. 7 TEU *as such* should be regarded as *abusive*. The vagueness of the terms involved (see III.) and the purely political standards to be applied in the Art. 7 TEU-procedure militate in favour of a virtually unlimited discretion of the institutions involved which is not subject to the ECJ's control (see Art. 269 TFEU). As a matter of fact, it would be a "paradox to leave ECJ out of the equation of the Rule of Law".[42]

VII. Conclusion

Given that the ECJ's role within the Art. 7 TEU-procedure is strongly limited and that the institutions involved in the procedure *prima facie* enjoy a virtually *unlimited discretion*, it can be argued that Art. 7 TEU as such is in contradiction with

41 Ibid., mn. 52.

42 *G. Wilms* (fn. 4), p. 67.

the rule of law which is one of the values the Union is founded on. The Commission was well advised to do its best to avoid a use of Art. 7 TEU and to introduce (what it was entitled to do) a "soft" mechanism, the EU Rule of Law Framework. Recently, however, the Commission made a U-turn and formally triggered the Art. 7 TEU-procedure.[43] Some experts welcomed that step.[44] But that option is and remains "nuclear", as former Commission President Barroso warned in his "State of the Union 2012 Address",[45] even though its repercussions are not yet noticeable.

43 COM (2017) 835.

44 Cf. *D. Kochenov/L. Pech/K. L. Scheppele*, The European Commission's Activation of Article 7: Better Late than Never?, Verfassungsblog (https://verfassungsblog.de/), December 23, 2017.

45 Cf. http://europa.eu/rapid/press-release_SPEECH-12-596_en.htm.